T&P BOOKS

ALBANIAN
VOCABULARY

FOR ENGLISH SPEAKERS

ENGLISH-
ALBANIAN

The most useful words
To expand your lexicon and sharpen
your language skills

7000 words

Albanian vocabulary for English speakers - 7000 words

By Andrey Taranov

T&P Books vocabularies are intended for helping you learn, memorize and review foreign words. The dictionary is divided into themes, covering all major spheres of everyday activities, business, science, culture, etc.

The process of learning words using T&P Books' theme-based dictionaries gives you the following advantages:

- Correctly grouped source information predetermines success at subsequent stages of word memorization
- Availability of words derived from the same root allowing memorization of word units (rather than separate words)
- Small units of words facilitate the process of establishing associative links needed for consolidation of vocabulary
- Level of language knowledge can be estimated by the number of learned words

T&P Books Publishing
www.tpbooks.com

ISBN: 978-1-78767-009-9

This book is also available in E-book formats.
Please visit www.tpbooks.com or the major online bookstores.

ALBANIAN VOCABULARY
for English speakers

T&P Books vocabularies are intended to help you learn, memorize, and review foreign words. The vocabulary contains over 7000 commonly used words arranged thematically.

- Vocabulary contains the most commonly used words
- Recommended as an addition to any language course
- Meets the needs of beginners and advanced learners of foreign languages
- Convenient for daily use, revision sessions, and self-testing activities
- Allows you to assess your vocabulary

Special features of the vocabulary

- Words are organized according to their meaning, not alphabetically
- Words are presented in three columns to facilitate the reviewing and self-testing processes
- Words in groups are divided into small blocks to facilitate the learning process
- The vocabulary offers a convenient and simple transcription of each foreign word

The vocabulary has 198 topics including:

Basic Concepts, Numbers, Colors, Months, Seasons, Units of Measurement, Clothing & Accessories, Food & Nutrition, Restaurant, Family Members, Relatives, Character, Feelings, Emotions, Diseases, City, Town, Sightseeing, Shopping, Money, House, Home, Office, Working in the Office, Import & Export, Marketing, Job Search, Sports, Education, Computer, Internet, Tools, Nature, Countries, Nationalities and more ...

T&P BOOKS' THEME-BASED DICTIONARIES

The Correct System for Memorizing Foreign Words

Acquiring vocabulary is one of the most important elements of learning a foreign language, because words allow us to express our thoughts, ask questions, and provide answers. An inadequate vocabulary can impede communication with a foreigner and make it difficult to understand a book or movie well.

The pace of activity in all spheres of modern life, including the learning of modern languages, has increased. Today, we need to memorize large amounts of information (grammar rules, foreign words, etc.) within a short period. However, this does not need to be difficult. All you need to do is to choose the right training materials, learn a few special techniques, and develop your individual training system.

Having a system is critical to the process of language learning. Many people fail to succeed in this regard; they cannot master a foreign language because they fail to follow a system comprised of selecting materials, organizing lessons, arranging new words to be learned, and so on. The lack of a system causes confusion and eventually, lowers self-confidence.

T&P Books' theme-based dictionaries can be included in the list of elements needed for creating an effective system for learning foreign words. These dictionaries were specially developed for learning purposes and are meant to help students effectively memorize words and expand their vocabulary.

Generally speaking, the process of learning words consists of three main elements:

- Reception (creation or acquisition) of a training material, such as a word list
- Work aimed at memorizing new words
- Work aimed at reviewing the learned words, such as self-testing

All three elements are equally important since they determine the quality of work and the final result. All three processes require certain skills and a well-thought-out approach.

New words are often encountered quite randomly when learning a foreign language and it may be difficult to include them all in a unified list. As a result, these words remain written on scraps of paper, in book margins, textbooks, and so on. In order to systematize such words, we have to create and continually update a "book of new words." A paper notebook, a netbook, or a tablet PC can be used for these purposes.

This "book of new words" will be your personal, unique list of words. However, it will only contain the words that you came across during the learning process. For example, you might have written down the words "Sunday," "Tuesday," and "Friday." However, there are additional words for days of the week, for example, "Saturday," that are missing, and your list of words would be incomplete. Using a theme dictionary, in addition to the "book of new words," is a reasonable solution to this problem.

The theme-based dictionary may serve as the basis for expanding your vocabulary.

It will be your big "book of new words" containing the most frequently used words of a foreign language already included. There are quite a few theme-based dictionaries available, and you should ensure that you make the right choice in order to get the maximum benefit from your purchase.

Therefore, we suggest using theme-based dictionaries from T&P Books Publishing as an aid to learning foreign words. Our books are specially developed for effective use in the sphere of vocabulary systematization, expansion and review.

Theme-based dictionaries are not a magical solution to learning new words. However, they can serve as your main database to aid foreign-language acquisition. Apart from theme dictionaries, you can have copybooks for writing down new words, flash cards, glossaries for various texts, as well as other resources; however, a good theme dictionary will always remain your primary collection of words.

T&P Books' theme-based dictionaries are specialty books that contain the most frequently used words in a language.

The main characteristic of such dictionaries is the division of words into themes. For example, the *City* theme contains the words "street," "crossroads," "square," "fountain," and so on. The *Talking* theme might contain words like "to talk," "to ask," "question," and "answer".

All the words in a theme are divided into smaller units, each comprising 3–5 words. Such an arrangement improves the perception of words and makes the learning process less tiresome. Each unit contains a selection of words with similar meanings or identical roots. This allows you to learn words in small groups and establish other associative links that have a positive effect on memorization.

The words on each page are placed in three columns: a word in your native language, its translation, and its transcription. Such positioning allows for the use of techniques for effective memorization. After closing the translation column, you can flip through and review foreign words, and vice versa. "This is an easy and convenient method of review – one that we recommend you do often."

Our theme-based dictionaries contain transcriptions for all the foreign words. Unfortunately, none of the existing transcriptions are able to convey the exact nuances of foreign pronunciation. That is why we recommend using the transcriptions only as a supplementary learning aid. Correct pronunciation can only be acquired with the help of sound. Therefore our collection includes audio theme-based dictionaries.

The process of learning words using T&P Books' theme-based dictionaries gives you the following advantages:

- You have correctly grouped source information, which predetermines your success at subsequent stages of word memorization
- Availability of words derived from the same root (lazy, lazily, lazybones), allowing you to memorize word units instead of separate words
- Small units of words facilitate the process of establishing associative links needed for consolidation of vocabulary
- You can estimate the number of learned words and hence your level of language knowledge
- The dictionary allows for the creation of an effective and high-quality revision process
- You can revise certain themes several times, modifying the revision methods and techniques
- Audio versions of the dictionaries help you to work out the pronunciation of words and develop your skills of auditory word perception

The T&P Books' theme-based dictionaries are offered in several variants differing in the number of words: 1.500, 3.000, 5.000, 7.000, and 9.000 words. There are also dictionaries containing 15,000 words for some language combinations. Your choice of dictionary will depend on your knowledge level and goals.

We sincerely believe that our dictionaries will become your trusty assistant in learning foreign languages and will allow you to easily acquire the necessary vocabulary.

TABLE OF CONTENTS

PRONUNCIATION GUIDE

T&P phonetic alphabet	Albanian example	English example
[a]	flas [flas]	shorter than in ask
[e], [ɛ]	melodi [mɛlodí]	absent, pet
[ə]	kërkoj [kərkój]	driver, teacher
[i]	pikë [píkə]	shorter than in feet
[o]	motor [motór]	pod, John
[u]	fuqi [fucí]	book
[y]	myshk [myʃk]	fuel, tuna
[b]	brakë [brákə]	baby, book
[c]	oqean [ocɛán]	Irish - ceist
[d]	adoptoj [adoptój]	day, doctor
[dz]	lexoj [lɛdzój]	beads, kids
[ʤ]	xham [ʤam]	joke, general
[ð]	dhomë [ðómə]	weather, together
[f]	i fortë [i fórtə]	face, food
[g]	bullgari [buɫgarí]	game, gold
[h]	jaht [jáht]	home, have
[j]	hyrje [hýrjɛ]	yes, New York
[ʝ]	zgjedh [zʝɛð]	geese
[k]	korik [korík]	clock, kiss
[l]	lëviz [ləvíz]	lace, people
[ɫ]	shkallë [ʃkáɫə]	feel
[m]	medalje [mɛdáljɛ]	magic, milk
[n]	klan [klan]	name, normal
[ɲ]	spanjoll [spaɲóɫ]	canyon, new
[ŋ]	trung [truŋ]	ring
[p]	polici [politsí]	pencil, private
[r]	i erët [i érət]	rice, radio
[ɾ]	groshë [gróʃə]	Spanish - pero
[s]	spital [spitál]	city, boss
[ʃ]	shes [ʃɛs]	machine, shark
[t]	tapet [tapét]	tourist, trip
[ts]	batica [batítsa]	cats, tsetse fly
[tʃ]	kaçube [katʃúbɛ]	church, French
[v]	javor [javór]	very, river
[z]	horizont [horizónt]	zebra, please
[ʒ]	kuzhinë [kuʒínə]	forge, pleasure
[θ]	përkthej [pərkθéj]	month, tooth

ABBREVIATIONS
used in the vocabulary

English abbreviations

ab.	-	about
adj	-	adjective
adv	-	adverb
anim.	-	animate
as adj	-	attributive noun used as adjective
e.g.	-	for example
etc.	-	et cetera
fam.	-	familiar
fem.	-	feminine
form.	-	formal
inanim.	-	inanimate
masc.	-	masculine
math	-	mathematics
mil.	-	military
n	-	noun
pl	-	plural
pron.	-	pronoun
sb	-	somebody
sing.	-	singular
sth	-	something
v aux	-	auxiliary verb
vi	-	intransitive verb
vi, vt	-	intransitive, transitive verb
vt	-	transitive verb

Albanian abbreviations

f	-	feminine noun
m	-	masculine noun
pl	-	plural

BASIC CONCEPTS

Basic concepts. Part 1

1. Pronouns

I, me	Unë, mua	[unə], [múa]
you	ti, ty	[ti], [ty]
he	ai	[aí]
she	ajo	[ajó]
it	ai	[aí]
we	ne	[nɛ]
you (to a group)	ju	[ju]
they (masc.)	ata	[atá]
they (fem.)	ato	[ató]

2. Greetings. Salutations. Farewells

Hello! (fam.)	Përshëndetje!	[pərʃəndétjɛ!]
Hello! (form.)	Përshëndetje!	[pərʃəndétjɛ!]
Good morning!	Mirëmëngjes!	[mirəmənɟés!]
Good afternoon!	Mirëdita!	[mirədíta!]
Good evening!	Mirëmbrëma!	[mirəmbrə́ma!]
to say hello	përshëndes	[pərʃəndés]
Hi! (hello)	Ç'kemi!	[tʃ'kémi!]
greeting (n)	përshëndetje (f)	[pərʃəndétjɛ]
to greet (vt)	përshëndes	[pərʃəndés]
How are you? (form.)	Si jeni?	[si jéni?]
How are you? (fam.)	Si je?	[si jɛ?]
What's new?	Çfarë ka të re?	[tʃfárə ká tə ré?]
Goodbye!	Mirupafshim!	[mirupáfʃim!]
Bye!	U pafshim!	[u páfʃim!]
See you soon!	Shihemi së shpejti!	[ʃíhɛmi sə ʃpéjti!]
Farewell!	Lamtumirë!	[lamtumírə!]
to say goodbye	përshëndetem	[pərʃəndétɛm]
So long!	Tungjatjeta!	[tunɲatjéta!]
Thank you!	Faleminderit!	[falɛmindérit!]
Thank you very much!	Faleminderit shumë!	[falɛmindérit ʃúmə!]

You're welcome	Të lutem	[tə lútɛm]
Don't mention it!	Asgjë!	[asɟé!]
It was nothing	Asgjë	[asɟé]

Excuse me! (fam.)	Më fal!	[mə fal!]
Excuse me! (form.)	Më falni!	[mə fálni!]
to excuse (forgive)	fal	[fal]

to apologize (vi)	kërkoj falje	[kərkój fáljɛ]
My apologies	Kërkoj ndjesë	[kərkój ndjésə]
I'm sorry!	Më vjen keq!	[mə vjɛn kɛc!]
to forgive (vt)	fal	[fal]
It's okay! (that's all right)	S'ka gjë!	[s'ka ɟə!]
please (adv)	të lutem	[tə lútɛm]

Don't forget!	Mos harro!	[mos haró!]
Certainly!	Sigurisht!	[siguríʃt!]
Of course not!	Sigurisht që jo!	[siguríʃt cə jo!]
Okay! (I agree)	Në rregull!	[nə réguɫ!]
That's enough!	Mjafton!	[mjaftón!]

3. Cardinal numbers. Part 1

0 zero	zero	[zéro]
1 one	një	[ɲə]
2 two	dy	[dy]
3 three	tre	[trɛ]
4 four	katër	[kátər]

5 five	pesë	[pésə]
6 six	gjashtë	[ɟáʃtə]
7 seven	shtatë	[ʃtátə]
8 eight	tetë	[tétə]
9 nine	nëntë	[nəntə]

10 ten	dhjetë	[ðjétə]
11 eleven	njëmbëdhjetë	[ɲəmbəðjétə]
12 twelve	dymbëdhjetë	[dymbəðjétə]
13 thirteen	trembëdhjetë	[trɛmbəðjétə]
14 fourteen	katërmbëdhjetë	[katərmbəðjétə]

15 fifteen	pesëmbëdhjetë	[pɛsəmbəðjétə]
16 sixteen	gjashtëmbëdhjetë	[ɟaʃtəmbəðjétə]
17 seventeen	shtatëmbëdhjetë	[ʃtatəmbəðjétə]
18 eighteen	tetëmbëdhjetë	[tɛtəmbəðjétə]
19 nineteen	nëntëmbëdhjetë	[nəntəmbəðjétə]

20 twenty	njëzet	[ɲəzét]
21 twenty-one	njëzet e një	[ɲəzét ɛ ɲe]
22 twenty-two	njëzet e dy	[ɲəzét ɛ dy]

23 twenty-three	njëzet e tre	[ɲəzét ɛ trɛ]
30 thirty	tridhjetë	[triðjétə]
31 thirty-one	tridhjetë e një	[triðjétə ɛ ɲə]
32 thirty-two	tridhjetë e dy	[triðjétə ɛ dy]
33 thirty-three	tridhjetë e tre	[triðjétə ɛ trɛ]

40 forty	dyzet	[dyzét]
41 forty-one	dyzet e një	[dyzét ɛ ɲə]
42 forty-two	dyzet e dy	[dyzét ɛ dy]
43 forty-three	dyzet e tre	[dyzét ɛ trɛ]

50 fifty	pesëdhjetë	[pɛsəðjétə]
51 fifty-one	pesëdhjetë e një	[pɛsəðjétə ɛ ɲə]
52 fifty-two	pesëdhjetë e dy	[pɛsəðjétə ɛ dy]
53 fifty-three	pesëdhjetë e tre	[pɛsəðjétə ɛ trɛ]

60 sixty	gjashtëdhjetë	[ɟaʃtəðjétə]
61 sixty-one	gjashtëdhjetë e një	[ɟaʃtəðjétə ɛ ɲə]
62 sixty-two	gjashtëdhjetë e dy	[ɟaʃtəðjétə ɛ dý]
63 sixty-three	gjashtëdhjetë e tre	[ɟaʃtəðjétə ɛ tré]

70 seventy	shtatëdhjetë	[ʃtatəðjétə]
71 seventy-one	shtatëdhjetë e një	[ʃtatəðjétə ɛ ɲə]
72 seventy-two	shtatëdhjetë e dy	[ʃtatəðjétə ɛ dy]
73 seventy-three	shtatëdhjetë e tre	[ʃtatəðjétə ɛ trɛ]

80 eighty	tetëdhjetë	[tɛtəðjétə]
81 eighty-one	tetëdhjetë e një	[tɛtəðjétə ɛ ɲə]
82 eighty-two	tetëdhjetë e dy	[tɛtəðjétə ɛ dy]
83 eighty-three	tetëdhjetë e tre	[tɛtəðjétə ɛ trɛ]

90 ninety	nëntëdhjetë	[nəntəðjétə]
91 ninety-one	nëntëdhjetë e një	[nəntəðjétə ɛ ɲə]
92 ninety-two	nëntëdhjetë e dy	[nəntəðjétə ɛ dy]
93 ninety-three	nëntëdhjetë e tre	[nəntəðjétə ɛ trɛ]

4. Cardinal numbers. Part 2

100 one hundred	njëqind	[ɲəcínd]
200 two hundred	dyqind	[dycínd]
300 three hundred	treqind	[trɛcínd]
400 four hundred	katërqind	[katərcínd]
500 five hundred	pesëqind	[pɛsəcínd]

600 six hundred	gjashtëqind	[ɟaʃtəcínd]
700 seven hundred	shtatëqind	[ʃtatəcínd]
800 eight hundred	tetëqind	[tɛtəcínd]
900 nine hundred	nëntëqind	[nəntəcínd]
1000 one thousand	një mijë	[ɲə míjə]
2000 two thousand	dy mijë	[dy míjə]

3000 three thousand	tre mijë	[trɛ míjə]
10000 ten thousand	dhjetë mijë	[ðjétə míjə]
one hundred thousand	njëqind mijë	[ɲəcínd míjə]
million	milion (m)	[milión]
billion	miliardë (f)	[miliárdə]

5. Numbers. Fractions

fraction	thyesë (f)	[θýɛsə]
one half	gjysma	[ɟýsma]
one third	një e treta	[ɲə ɛ tréta]
one quarter	një e katërta	[ɲə ɛ kátərta]

one eighth	një e teta	[ɲə ɛ téta]
one tenth	një e dhjeta	[ɲə ɛ ðjéta]
two thirds	dy të tretat	[dy tə trétat]
three quarters	tre të katërtat	[trɛ tə kátərtat]

6. Numbers. Basic operations

subtraction	zbritje (f)	[zbrítjɛ]
to subtract (vi, vt)	zbres	[zbrɛs]
division	pjesëtim (m)	[pjɛsətím]
to divide (vt)	pjesëtoj	[pjɛsətój]

addition	mbledhje (f)	[mbléðjɛ]
to add up (vt)	shtoj	[ʃtoj]
to add (vi, vt)	mbledh	[mbléð]
multiplication	shumëzim (m)	[ʃuməzím]
to multiply (vt)	shumëzoj	[ʃuməzój]

7. Numbers. Miscellaneous

digit, figure	shifër (f)	[ʃífər]
number	numër (m)	[númər]
numeral	numerik (m)	[numɛrík]
minus sign	minus (m)	[minús]
plus sign	plus (m)	[plus]
formula	formulë (f)	[formúlə]

calculation	llogaritje (f)	[ɫogarítjɛ]
to count (vi, vt)	numëroj	[numərój]
to count up	llogaris	[ɫogarís]
to compare (vt)	krahasoj	[krahasój]
How much?	Sa?	[sa?]
sum, total	shuma (f)	[ʃúma]

result	rezultat (m)	[rɛzultát]
remainder	mbetje (f)	[mbétjɛ]
a few (e.g., ~ years ago)	disa	[disá]
little (I had ~ time)	pak	[pak]
few (I have ~ friends)	disa	[disá]
a little (~ water)	pak	[pak]
the rest	mbetje (f)	[mbétjɛ]
one and a half	një e gjysmë (f)	[ɲə ɛ ɟýsmə]
dozen	dyzinë (f)	[dyzínə]
in half (adv)	përgjysmë	[pəɾɟýsmə]
equally (evenly)	gjysmë për gjysmë	[ɟýsmə pəɾ ɟýsmə]
half	gjysmë (f)	[ɟýsmə]
time (three ~s)	herë (f)	[hérə]

8. The most important verbs. Part 1

to advise (vt)	këshilloj	[kəʃiɫój]
to agree (say yes)	bie dakord	[bíɛ dakórd]
to answer (vi, vt)	përgjigjem	[pəɾɟíɟɛm]
to apologize (vi)	kërkoj falje	[kərkój fáljɛ]
to arrive (vi)	arrij	[aríj]
to ask (~ oneself)	pyes	[pýɛs]
to ask (~ sb to do sth)	pyes	[pýɛs]
to be (vi)	jam	[jam]
to be afraid	kam frikë	[kam fríkə]
to be hungry	kam uri	[kam urí]
to be interested in …	interesohem …	[intɛrɛsóhɛm …]
to be needed	nevojitet	[nɛvojítɛt]
to be surprised	çuditem	[tʃudítɛm]
to be thirsty	kam etje	[kam étjɛ]
to begin (vt)	filloj	[fiɫój]
to belong to …	përkas …	[pərkás …]
to boast (vi)	mburrem	[mbúrɛm]
to break (split into pieces)	ndahem	[ndáhɛm]
to call (~ for help)	thërras	[θərás]
can (v aux)	mund	[mund]
to catch (vt)	kap	[kap]
to change (vt)	ndryshoj	[ndryʃój]
to choose (select)	zgjedh	[zɟɛð]
to come down (the stairs)	zbres	[zbrɛs]
to compare (vt)	krahasoj	[krahasój]
to complain (vi, vt)	ankohem	[ankóhɛm]
to confuse (mix up)	ngatërroj	[ŋatərój]

| to continue (vt) | vazhdoj | [vaʒdój] |
| to control (vt) | kontrolloj | [kontroɫój] |

to cook (dinner)	gatuaj	[gatúaj]
to cost (vt)	kushton	[kuʃtón]
to count (add up)	numëroj	[numərój]
to count on ...	mbështetem ...	[mbəʃtétɛm ...]
to create (vt)	krijoj	[krijój]
to cry (weep)	qaj	[caj]

9. The most important verbs. Part 2

to deceive (vi, vt)	mashtroj	[maʃtrój]
to decorate (tree, street)	zbukuroj	[zbukurój]
to defend (a country, etc.)	mbroj	[mbrój]
to demand (request firmly)	kërkoj	[kərkój]
to dig (vt)	gërmoj	[gərmój]

to discuss (vt)	diskutoj	[diskutój]
to do (vt)	bëj	[bəj]
to doubt (have doubts)	dyshoj	[dyʃój]
to drop (let fall)	lëshoj	[lɛʃój]
to enter (room, house, etc.)	hyj	[hyj]

to excuse (forgive)	fal	[fal]
to exist (vi)	ekzistoj	[ɛkzistój]
to expect (foresee)	parashikoj	[paraʃikój]
to explain (vt)	shpjegoj	[ʃpjɛgój]
to fall (vi)	bie	[bíɛ]

to find (vt)	gjej	[ɟéj]
to finish (vt)	përfundoj	[pərfundój]
to fly (vi)	fluturoj	[fluturój]
to follow ... (come after)	ndjek ...	[ndjék ...]
to forget (vi, vt)	harroj	[harój]

to forgive (vt)	fal	[fal]
to give (vt)	jap	[jap]
to give a hint	aludoj	[aludój]
to go (on foot)	ec në këmbë	[ɛts nə kémbə]

to go for a swim	notoj	[notój]
to go out (for dinner, etc.)	dal	[dal]
to guess (the answer)	hamendësoj	[hamɛndəsój]

to have (vt)	kam	[kam]
to have breakfast	ha mëngjes	[ha mənɟés]
to have dinner	ha darkë	[ha dárkə]
to have lunch	ha drekë	[ha drékə]

to hear (vt)	dëgjoj	[dəɟój]
to help (vt)	ndihmoj	[ndihmój]
to hide (vt)	fsheh	[fʃéh]
to hope (vi, vt)	shpresoj	[ʃprɛsój]
to hunt (vi, vt)	dal për gjah	[dál pər ɟáh]
to hurry (vi)	nxitoj	[ndzitój]

10. The most important verbs. Part 3

to inform (vt)	informoj	[informój]
to insist (vi, vt)	këmbëngul	[kəmbəŋúl]
to insult (vt)	fyej	[fýɛj]
to invite (vt)	ftoj	[ftoj]
to joke (vi)	bëj shaka	[bəj ʃaká]

to keep (vt)	mbaj	[mbáj]
to keep silent, to hush	hesht	[hɛʃt]
to kill (vt)	vras	[vras]
to know (sb)	njoh	[ɲóh]
to know (sth)	di	[di]
to laugh (vi)	qesh	[cɛʃ]

to liberate (city, etc.)	çliroj	[tʃlirój]
to like (I like ...)	pëlqej	[pəlcéj]
to look for ... (search)	kërkoj ...	[kərkój ...]
to love (sb)	dashuroj	[daʃurój]
to make a mistake	gaboj	[gabój]

to manage, to run	drejtoj	[drɛjtój]
to mean (signify)	nënkuptoj	[nənkuptój]
to mention (talk about)	përmend	[pərménd]
to miss (school, etc.)	humbas	[humbás]
to notice (see)	vërej	[vəréj]

to object (vi, vt)	kundërshtoj	[kundərʃtój]
to observe (see)	vëzhgoj	[vəʒgój]
to open (vt)	hap	[hap]
to order (meal, etc.)	porosis	[porosís]
to order (mil.)	urdhëroj	[urðərój]
to own (possess)	zotëroj	[zotərój]

to participate (vi)	marr pjesë	[mar pjésə]
to pay (vi, vt)	paguaj	[pagúaj]
to permit (vt)	lejoj	[lɛjój]
to plan (vt)	planifikoj	[planifikój]
to play (children)	luaj	[lúaj]

to pray (vi, vt)	lutem	[lútɛm]
to prefer (vt)	preferoj	[prɛfɛrój]
to promise (vt)	premtoj	[prɛmtój]

to pronounce (vt)	shqiptoj	[ʃciptój]
to propose (vt)	propozoj	[propozój]
to punish (vt)	ndëshkoj	[ndəʃkój]

11. The most important verbs. Part 4

to read (vi, vt)	lexoj	[lɛdzój]
to recommend (vt)	rekomandoj	[rɛkomandój]
to refuse (vi, vt)	refuzoj	[rɛfuzój]
to regret (be sorry)	pendohem	[pɛndóhɛm]
to rent (sth from sb)	marr me qira	[mar mɛ cirá]

to repeat (say again)	përsëris	[pərserís]
to reserve, to book	rezervoj	[rɛzɛrvój]
to run (vi)	vrapoj	[vrapój]
to save (rescue)	shpëtoj	[ʃpətój]
to say (~ thank you)	them	[θɛm]

to scold (vt)	qortoj	[cortój]
to see (vt)	shikoj	[ʃikój]
to sell (vt)	shes	[ʃɛs]
to send (vt)	dërgoj	[dərgój]
to shoot (vi)	qëlloj	[cətój]

to shout (vi)	bërtas	[bərtás]
to show (vt)	tregoj	[trɛgój]
to sign (document)	nënshkruaj	[nənʃkrúaj]
to sit down (vi)	ulem	[úlɛm]

to smile (vi)	buzëqesh	[buzəcéʃ]
to speak (vi, vt)	flas	[flas]
to steal (money, etc.)	vjedh	[vjɛð]
to stop (for pause, etc.)	ndaloj	[ndalój]
to stop (please ~ calling me)	ndaloj	[ndalój]

to study (vt)	studioj	[studiój]
to swim (vi)	notoj	[notój]
to take (vt)	marr	[mar]
to think (vi, vt)	mendoj	[mɛndój]
to threaten (vt)	kërcënoj	[kərtsənój]

to touch (with hands)	prek	[prɛk]
to translate (vt)	përkthej	[pərkθéj]
to trust (vt)	besoj	[bɛsój]
to try (attempt)	përpiqem	[pərpícɛm]
to turn (e.g., ~ left)	kthej	[kθɛj]

| to underestimate (vt) | nënvlerësoj | [nənvlɛrəsój] |
| to understand (vt) | kuptoj | [kuptój] |

| to unite (vt) | bashkoj | [baʃkój] |
| to wait (vt) | pres | [prɛs] |

to want (wish, desire)	dëshiroj	[dəʃirój]
to warn (vt)	paralajmëroj	[paralajmərój]
to work (vi)	punoj	[punój]
to write (vt)	shkruaj	[ʃkrúaj]
to write down	mbaj shënim	[mbáj ʃəním]

12. Colors

color	ngjyrë (f)	[ɲɟýrə]
shade (tint)	nuancë (f)	[nuántsə]
hue	tonalitet (m)	[tonalitét]
rainbow	ylber (m)	[ylbér]

white (adj)	e bardhë	[ɛ bárðə]
black (adj)	e zezë	[ɛ zézə]
gray (adj)	gri	[gri]

green (adj)	jeshile	[jɛʃílɛ]
yellow (adj)	e verdhë	[ɛ vérðə]
red (adj)	e kuqe	[ɛ kúcɛ]

blue (adj)	blu	[blu]
light blue (adj)	bojëqielli	[bojəciéɬi]
pink (adj)	rozë	[rózə]
orange (adj)	portokalli	[portokáɬi]
violet (adj)	bojëvjollcë	[bojəvjóɬtsə]
brown (adj)	kafe	[káfɛ]

| golden (adj) | e artë | [ɛ ártə] |
| silvery (adj) | e argjendtë | [ɛ aɻɟéndtə] |

beige (adj)	bezhë	[béʒə]
cream (adj)	krem	[krɛm]
turquoise (adj)	e bruztë	[ɛ brúztə]
cherry red (adj)	qershi	[cɛrʃí]
lilac (adj)	jargavan	[jargaván]
crimson (adj)	e kuqe e thellë	[ɛ kúcɛ ɛ θéɬə]

light (adj)	e hapur	[ɛ hápur]
dark (adj)	e errët	[ɛ érət]
bright, vivid (adj)	e ndritshme	[ɛ ndrítʃmɛ]

colored (pencils)	e ngjyrosur	[ɛ ɲɟyrósur]
color (e.g., ~ film)	ngjyrë	[ɲɟýrə]
black-and-white (adj)	bardhë e zi	[bárðə ɛ zi]
plain (one-colored)	njëngjyrëshe	[ɲəɲɟýrəʃɛ]
multicolored (adj)	shumëngjyrëshe	[ʃuməɲɟýrəʃɛ]

13. Questions

Who?	Kush?	[kuʃ?]
What?	Çka?	[tʃká?]
Where? (at, in)	Ku?	[ku?]
Where (to)?	Për ku?	[pər ku?]
From where?	Nga ku?	[ŋa ku?]
When?	Kur?	[kur?]
Why? (What for?)	Pse?	[psɛ?]
Why? (~ are you crying?)	Pse?	[psɛ?]

What for?	Për çfarë arsye?	[pər tʃfárə arsýɛ?]
How? (in what way)	Si?	[si?]
What? (What kind of ...?)	Çfarë?	[tʃfárə?]
Which?	Cili?	[tsíli?]

To whom?	Kujt?	[kújt?]
About whom?	Për kë?	[pər kə?]
About what?	Për çfarë?	[pər tʃfárə?]
With whom?	Me kë?	[mɛ kə?]

How many? How much?	Sa?	[sa?]
Whose?	Të kujt?	[tə kujt?]

14. Function words. Adverbs. Part 1

Where? (at, in)	Ku?	[ku?]
here (adv)	këtu	[kətú]
there (adv)	atje	[atjé]

somewhere (to be)	diku	[dikú]
nowhere (not in any place)	askund	[askúnd]

by (near, beside)	afër	[áfər]
by the window	tek dritarja	[tɛk dritárja]

Where (to)?	Për ku?	[pər ku?]
here (e.g., come ~!)	këtu	[kətú]
there (e.g., to go ~)	atje	[atjé]
from here (adv)	nga këtu	[ŋa kətú]
from there (adv)	nga atje	[ŋa atjɛ]

close (adv)	pranë	[páranə]
far (adv)	larg	[larg]

near (e.g., ~ Paris)	afër	[áfər]
nearby (adv)	pranë	[páranə]
not far (adv)	jo larg	[jo lárg]
left (adj)	majtë	[májtə]

on the left	majtas	[májtas]
to the left	në të majtë	[nə tə májtə]
right (adj)	djathtë	[djáθtə]
on the right	djathtas	[djáθtas]
to the right	në të djathtë	[nə tə djáθtə]
in front (adv)	përballë	[pərbáɫə]
front (as adj)	i përparmë	[i pərpáɾmə]
ahead (the kids ran ~)	përpara	[pərpára]
behind (adv)	prapa	[prápa]
from behind	nga prapa	[ŋa prápa]
back (towards the rear)	pas	[pas]
middle	mes (m)	[mɛs]
in the middle	në mes	[nə mɛs]
at the side	në anë	[nə anə]
everywhere (adv)	kudo	[kúdo]
around (in all directions)	përreth	[pəréθ]
from inside	nga brenda	[ŋa brénda]
somewhere (to go)	diku	[dikú]
straight (directly)	drejt	[dréjt]
back (e.g., come ~)	pas	[pas]
from anywhere	nga kudo	[ŋa kúdo]
from somewhere	nga diku	[ŋa dikú]
firstly (adv)	së pari	[sə pári]
secondly (adv)	së dyti	[sə dýti]
thirdly (adv)	së treti	[sə tréti]
suddenly (adv)	befas	[béfas]
at first (in the beginning)	në fillim	[nə fiɫím]
for the first time	për herë të parë	[pər hérə tə párə]
long before …	shumë përpara …	[ʃúmə pərpára …]
anew (over again)	sërish	[səríʃ]
for good (adv)	një herë e mirë	[ɲə hérə ɛ mírə]
never (adv)	kurrë	[kúrə]
again (adv)	përsëri	[pərsərí]
now (at present)	tani	[táni]
often (adv)	shpesh	[ʃpɛʃ]
then (adv)	atëherë	[atəhérə]
urgently (quickly)	urgjent	[uɾɟént]
usually (adv)	zakonisht	[zakoníʃt]
by the way, …	meqë ra fjala, …	[méce ra fjála, …]
possibly	ndoshta	[ndóʃta]
probably (adv)	mundësisht	[mundəsíʃt]

maybe (adv)	mbase	[mbásɛ]
besides ...	përveç	[pərvétʃ]
that's why ...	ja përse ...	[ja pərsé ...]
in spite of ...	pavarësisht se ...	[pavarəsíʃt sɛ ...]
thanks to ...	falë ...	[fálə ...]

what (pron.)	çfarë	[tʃfárə]
that (conj.)	që	[cə]
something	diçka	[ditʃká]
anything (something)	ndonji gjë	[ndoɲí ɟə]
nothing	asgjë	[asɟé]

who (pron.)	kush	[kuʃ]
someone	dikush	[dikúʃ]
somebody	dikush	[dikúʃ]

nobody	askush	[askúʃ]
nowhere (a voyage to ~)	askund	[askúnd]
nobody's	i askujt	[i askújt]
somebody's	i dikujt	[i dikújt]

so (I'm ~ glad)	aq	[ác]
also (as well)	gjithashtu	[ɟiθaʃtú]
too (as well)	gjithashtu	[ɟiθaʃtú]

15. Function words. Adverbs. Part 2

Why?	Pse?	[psɛ?]
for some reason	për një arsye	[pər ɲə arsýɛ]
because ...	sepse ...	[sɛpsé ...]
for some purpose	për ndonjë shkak	[pər ndóɲə ʃkak]

and	dhe	[ðɛ]
or	ose	[ósɛ]
but	por	[por]
for (e.g., ~ me)	për	[pər]

too (~ many people)	tepër	[tépər]
only (exclusively)	vetëm	[vétəm]
exactly (adv)	pikërisht	[pikəríʃt]
about (more or less)	rreth	[rɛθ]

approximately (adv)	përafërsisht	[pərafərsíʃt]
approximate (adj)	përafërt	[pəráfərt]
almost (adv)	pothuajse	[poθúajsɛ]
the rest	mbetje (f)	[mbétjɛ]

the other (second)	tjetri	[tjétri]
other (different)	tjetër	[tjétər]
each (adj)	çdo	[tʃdo]

27

any (no matter which)	çfarëdo	[tʃfarədó]
many (adj)	disa	[disá]
much (adv)	shumë	[ʃúmə]
many people	shumë njerëz	[ʃúmə ɲérəz]
all (everyone)	të gjithë	[tə ɟíθə]

in return for …	në vend të …	[nə vénd tə …]
in exchange (adv)	në shkëmbim të …	[nə ʃkəmbím tə …]
by hand (made)	me dorë	[mɛ dórə]
hardly (negative opinion)	vështirë se …	[vəʃtírə sɛ …]

probably (adv)	mundësisht	[mundəsíʃt]
on purpose (intentionally)	me qëllim	[mɛ cəɫím]
by accident (adv)	aksidentalisht	[aksidɛntalíʃt]

very (adv)	shumë	[ʃúmə]
for example (adv)	për shembull	[pər ʃémbuɫ]
between	midis	[midís]
among	rreth	[rɛθ]
so much (such a lot)	kaq shumë	[kác ʃúmə]
especially (adv)	veçanërisht	[vɛtʃanəríʃt]

Basic concepts. Part 2

16. Weekdays

Monday	E hënë (f)	[ɛ hə́nə]
Tuesday	E martë (f)	[ɛ mártə]
Wednesday	E mërkurë (f)	[ɛ mərkúrə]
Thursday	E enjte (f)	[ɛ éɲtɛ]
Friday	E premte (f)	[ɛ prémtɛ]
Saturday	E shtunë (f)	[ɛ ʃtúnə]
Sunday	E dielë (f)	[ɛ díɛlə]

today (adv)	sot	[sot]
tomorrow (adv)	nesër	[nésər]
the day after tomorrow	pasnesër	[pasnésər]
yesterday (adv)	dje	[djé]
the day before yesterday	pardje	[pardjé]

day	ditë (f)	[dítə]
working day	ditë pune (f)	[dítə púnɛ]
public holiday	festë kombëtare (f)	[féstə kombətárɛ]
day off	ditë pushim (m)	[dítə puʃím]
weekend	fundjavë (f)	[fundjávə]

all day long	gjithë ditën	[ɟíθə dítən]
the next day (adv)	ditën pasardhëse	[dítən pasárðəsɛ]
two days ago	dy ditë më parë	[dy dítə mə párə]
the day before	një ditë më parë	[ɲə dítə mə párə]
daily (adj)	ditor	[ditór]
every day (adv)	çdo ditë	[tʃdo dítə]

week	javë (f)	[jávə]
last week (adv)	javën e kaluar	[jávən ɛ kalúar]
next week (adv)	javën e ardhshme	[jávən ɛ árðʃmɛ]
weekly (adj)	javor	[javór]
every week (adv)	çdo javë	[tʃdo jávə]
twice a week	dy herë në javë	[dy hérə nə jávə]
every Tuesday	çdo të martë	[tʃdo tə mártə]

17. Hours. Day and night

morning	mëngjes (m)	[mənɟés]
in the morning	në mëngjes	[nə mənɟés]
noon, midday	mesditë (f)	[mɛsdítə]

in the afternoon	pasdite	[pasdítɛ]
evening	mbrëmje (f)	[mbrə́mjɛ]
in the evening	në mbrëmje	[nə mbrə́mjɛ]
night	natë (f)	[nátə]
at night	natën	[nátən]
midnight	mesnatë (f)	[mɛsnátə]

second	sekondë (f)	[sɛkóndə]
minute	minutë (f)	[minútə]
hour	orë (f)	[órə]
half an hour	gjysmë ore (f)	[ɟýsmə órɛ]
a quarter-hour	çerek ore (m)	[tʃɛrék órɛ]
fifteen minutes	pesëmbëdhjetë minuta	[pɛsəmbəðjétə minúta]
24 hours	24 orë	[nəzét ɛ kátər órə]

sunrise	agim (m)	[agím]
dawn	agim (m)	[agím]
early morning	mëngjes herët (m)	[mənɟés hérət]
sunset	perëndim dielli (m)	[pɛrəndím diéɬi]

early in the morning	herët në mëngjes	[hérət nə mənɟés]
this morning	sot në mëngjes	[sot nə mənɟés]
tomorrow morning	nesër në mëngjes	[nésər nə mənɟés]

this afternoon	sot pasdite	[sot pasdítɛ]
in the afternoon	pasdite	[pasdítɛ]
tomorrow afternoon	nesër pasdite	[nésər pasdítɛ]

tonight (this evening)	sonte në mbrëmje	[sóntɛ nə mbrəmjɛ]
tomorrow night	nesër në mbrëmje	[nésər nə mbrə́mjɛ]

at 3 o'clock sharp	në orën 3 fiks	[nə órən trɛ fiks]
about 4 o'clock	rreth orës 4	[rɛθ órəs kátər]
by 12 o'clock	deri në orën 12	[déri nə órən dymbəðjétə]

in 20 minutes	për 20 minuta	[pər nəzét minúta]
in an hour	për një orë	[pər ɲə órə]
on time (adv)	në orar	[nə orár]

a quarter to ...	çerek ...	[tʃɛrék ...]
within an hour	brenda një ore	[brénda ɲə órɛ]
every 15 minutes	çdo 15 minuta	[tʃdo pɛsəmbəðjétə minúta]
round the clock	gjithë ditën	[ɟíθə dítən]

18. Months. Seasons

January	Janar (m)	[janár]
February	Shkurt (m)	[ʃkurt]
March	Mars (m)	[mars]
April	Prill (m)	[priɬ]

| May | **Maj** (m) | [maj] |
| June | **Qershor** (m) | [cɛrʃór] |

July	**Korrik** (m)	[korík]
August	**Gusht** (m)	[guʃt]
September	**Shtator** (m)	[ʃtatór]
October	**Tetor** (m)	[tɛtór]
November	**Nëntor** (m)	[nəntór]
December	**Dhjetor** (m)	[ðjɛtór]

spring	**pranverë** (f)	[pranvérə]
in spring	**në pranverë**	[nə pranvérə]
spring (as adj)	**pranveror**	[pranvɛrór]

summer	**verë** (f)	[vérə]
in summer	**në verë**	[nə vérə]
summer (as adj)	**veror**	[vɛrór]

fall	**vjeshtë** (f)	[vjéʃtə]
in fall	**në vjeshtë**	[nə vjéʃtə]
fall (as adj)	**vjeshtor**	[vjéʃtor]

winter	**dimër** (m)	[dímər]
in winter	**në dimër**	[nə dímər]
winter (as adj)	**dimëror**	[dimərór]

month	**muaj** (m)	[múaj]
this month	**këtë muaj**	[kətə múaj]
next month	**muajin tjetër**	[múajin tjétər]
last month	**muajin e kaluar**	[múajin ɛ kalúar]

a month ago	**para një muaji**	[pára ɲə múaji]
in a month (a month later)	**pas një muaji**	[pas ɲə múaji]
in 2 months (2 months later)	**pas dy muajsh**	[pas dy múajʃ]
the whole month	**gjithë muajin**	[ɟíθə múajin]
all month long	**gjatë gjithë muajit**	[ɟátə ɟíθə múajit]

monthly (~ magazine)	**mujor**	[mujór]
monthly (adv)	**mujor**	[mujór]
every month	**çdo muaj**	[tʃdo múaj]
twice a month	**dy herë në muaj**	[dy hérə nə múaj]

year	**vit** (m)	[vit]
this year	**këtë vit**	[kətə vít]
next year	**vitin tjetër**	[vítin tjétər]
last year	**vitin e kaluar**	[vítin ɛ kalúar]

a year ago	**para një viti**	[pára ɲə víti]
in a year	**për një vit**	[pər ɲə vit]
in two years	**për dy vite**	[pər dy vítɛ]
the whole year	**gjithë vitin**	[ɟíθə vítin]

all year long	gjatë gjithë vitit	[ɟátə ɟíθə vítit]
every year	çdo vit	[tʃdo vít]
annual (adj)	vjetor	[vjɛtór]
annually (adv)	çdo vit	[tʃdo vít]
4 times a year	4 herë në vit	[kátər hérə nə vit]

date (e.g., today's ~)	datë (f)	[dátə]
date (e.g., ~ of birth)	data (f)	[dáta]
calendar	kalendar (m)	[kalɛndár]

half a year	gjysmë viti	[ɟýsmə víti]
six months	gjashtë muaj	[ɟáʃtə múaj]
season (summer, etc.)	stinë (f)	[stínə]
century	shekull (m)	[ʃékuɫ]

19. Time. Miscellaneous

time	kohë (f)	[kóhə]
moment	çast, moment (m)	[tʃást], [momént]
instant (n)	çast (m)	[tʃást]
instant (adj)	i çastit	[i tʃástit]
lapse (of time)	interval (m)	[intɛrvál]
life	jetë (f)	[jétə]
eternity	përjetësi (f)	[pərjɛtəsí]

epoch	epokë (f)	[ɛpókə]
era	erë (f)	[érə]
cycle	cikël (m)	[tsíkəl]
period	periudhë (f)	[pɛriúðə]
term (short-~)	afat (m)	[afát]

the future	ardhmëria (f)	[arðməría]
future (as adj)	e ardhme	[ɛ árðmɛ]
next time	herën tjetër	[hérən tjétər]
the past	e shkuara (f)	[ɛ ʃkúara]
past (recent)	kaluar	[kalúar]
last time	herën e fundit	[hérən ɛ fúndit]

later (adv)	më vonë	[mə vónə]
after (prep.)	pas	[pas]
nowadays (adv)	në këto kohë	[nə kəto kóhə]
now (at this moment)	tani	[táni]
immediately (adv)	menjëherë	[mɛɲəhérə]
soon (adv)	së shpejti	[sə ʃpéjti]
in advance (beforehand)	paraprakisht	[paraprakíʃt]

a long time ago	para shumë kohësh	[pára ʃúmə kóhəʃ]
recently (adv)	së fundmi	[sə fúndmi]
destiny	fat (m)	[fat]
memories (childhood ~)	kujtime (pl)	[kujtímɛ]

archives	arkiva (f)	[arkíva]
during ...	gjatë ...	[ɟátə ...]
long, a long time (adv)	gjatë, kohë e gjatë	[ɟátə], [kóhə ɛ ɟátə]
not long (adv)	jo gjatë	[jo ɟátə]
early (in the morning)	herët	[hérət]
late (not early)	vonë	[vónə]

forever (for good)	përjetë	[pərjétə]
to start (begin)	filloj	[fiɫój]
to postpone (vt)	shtyj	[ʃtyj]

at the same time	njëkohësisht	[nəkohəsíʃt]
permanently (adv)	përhershëm	[pərhérʃəm]
constant (noise, pain)	vazhdueshme	[vaʒdúɛʃmɛ]
temporary (adj)	i përkohshëm	[i pərkóhʃəm]

sometimes (adv)	ndonjëherë	[ndoɲəhérə]
rarely (adv)	rrallë	[ráɫə]
often (adv)	shpesh	[ʃpɛʃ]

20. Opposites

rich (adj)	i pasur	[i pásur]
poor (adj)	i varfër	[i várfər]

ill, sick (adj)	i sëmurë	[i səmúrə]
well (not sick)	mirë	[mírə]

big (adj)	i madh	[i máð]
small (adj)	i vogël	[i vógəl]

quickly (adv)	shpejt	[ʃpɛjt]
slowly (adv)	ngadalë	[ŋadálə]

fast (adj)	i shpejtë	[i ʃpéjtə]
slow (adj)	i ngadaltë	[i ŋadáltə]

glad (adj)	i kënaqur	[i kənácur]
sad (adj)	i mërzitur	[i mərzítur]

together (adv)	së bashku	[sə báʃku]
separately (adv)	veç e veç	[vɛtʃ ɛ vɛtʃ]

aloud (to read)	me zë	[mɛ zə]
silently (to oneself)	pa zë	[pa zə]

tall (adj)	i lartë	[i lártə]
low (adj)	i ulët	[i úlət]
deep (adj)	i thellë	[i θéɫə]
shallow (adj)	i cekët	[i tsékət]

| yes | po | [po] |
| no | jo | [jo] |

| distant (in space) | i largët | [i lárgət] |
| nearby (adj) | afër | [áfər] |

| far (adv) | larg | [larg] |
| nearby (adv) | pranë | [pránə] |

| long (adj) | i gjatë | [i ɟátə] |
| short (adj) | i shkurtër | [i ʃkúrtər] |

| good (kindhearted) | i mirë | [i mírə] |
| evil (adj) | djallëzor | [djaɫəzór] |

| married (adj) | i martuar | [i martúar] |
| single (adj) | beqar | [bɛcár] |

| to forbid (vt) | ndaloj | [ndalój] |
| to permit (vt) | lejoj | [lɛjój] |

| end | fund (m) | [fund] |
| beginning | fillim (m) | [fiɫím] |

| left (adj) | majtë | [májtə] |
| right (adj) | djathtë | [djáθtə] |

| first (adj) | i pari | [i pári] |
| last (adj) | i fundit | [i fúndit] |

| crime | krim (m) | [krim] |
| punishment | ndëshkim (m) | [ndəʃkím] |

| to order (vt) | urdhëroj | [urðərój] |
| to obey (vi, vt) | bindem | [bíndɛm] |

| straight (adj) | i drejtë | [i dréjtə] |
| curved (adj) | i harkuar | [i harkúar] |

| paradise | parajsë (f) | [parájsə] |
| hell | ferr (m) | [fɛr] |

| to be born | lind | [lind] |
| to die (vi) | vdes | [vdɛs] |

| strong (adj) | i fortë | [i fórtə] |
| weak (adj) | i dobët | [i dóbət] |

old (adj)	plak	[plak]
young (adj)	i ri	[i rí]
old (adj)	i vjetër	[i vjétər]
new (adj)	i ri	[i rí]

hard (adj)	i fortë	[i fórtə]
soft (adj)	i butë	[i bútə]
warm (tepid)	ngrohtë	[ŋróhtə]
cold (adj)	i ftohtë	[i ftóhtə]
fat (adj)	i shëndoshë	[i ʃəndóʃə]
thin (adj)	i dobët	[i dóbət]
narrow (adj)	i ngushtë	[i ŋúʃtə]
wide (adj)	i gjerë	[i ɟérə]
good (adj)	i mirë	[i mírə]
bad (adj)	i keq	[i kéc]
brave (adj)	guximtar	[gudzimtár]
cowardly (adj)	frikacak	[frikatsák]

21. Lines and shapes

square	katror (m)	[katrór]
square (as adj)	katrore	[katrórɛ]
circle	rreth (m)	[rɛθ]
round (adj)	i rrumbullakët	[i rumbułákət]
triangle	trekëndësh (m)	[trékəndəʃ]
triangular (adj)	trekëndor	[trɛkəndór]
oval	oval (f)	[ovál]
oval (as adj)	ovale	[oválɛ]
rectangle	drejtkëndësh (m)	[drɛjtkéndəʃ]
rectangular (adj)	drejtkëndor	[drɛjtkəndór]
pyramid	piramidë (f)	[piramídə]
rhombus	romb (m)	[romb]
trapezoid	trapezoid (m)	[trapɛzoíd]
cube	kub (m)	[kub]
prism	prizëm (m)	[prízəm]
circumference	perimetër (m)	[pɛrimétər]
sphere	sferë (f)	[sférə]
ball (solid sphere)	top (m)	[top]
diameter	diametër (m)	[diamétər]
radius	sipërfaqe (f)	[sipərfácɛ]
perimeter (circle's ~)	perimetër (m)	[pɛrimétər]
center	qendër (f)	[céndər]
horizontal (adj)	horizontal	[horizontál]
vertical (adj)	vertikal	[vɛrtikál]
parallel (n)	paralele (f)	[paralélɛ]
parallel (as adj)	paralel	[paralél]

35

line	vijë (f)	[víjə]
stroke	vizë (f)	[vízə]
straight line	vijë e drejtë (f)	[víjə ɛ dréjtə]
curve (curved line)	kurbë (f)	[kúrbə]
thin (line, etc.)	e hollë	[ɛ hółə]
contour (outline)	kontur (f)	[kontúr]

intersection	kryqëzim (m)	[krycəzím]
right angle	kënd i drejtë (m)	[kənd i dréjtə]
segment	segment (m)	[sɛgmént]
sector (circular ~)	sektor (m)	[sɛktór]
side (of triangle)	anë (f)	[ánə]
angle	kënd (m)	[kə́nd]

22. Units of measurement

weight	peshë (f)	[péʃə]
length	gjatësi (f)	[ɟatəsí]
width	gjerësi (f)	[ɟɛrəsí]
height	lartësi (f)	[lartəsí]
depth	thellësi (f)	[θɛłəsí]
volume	vëllim (m)	[vətím]
area	sipërfaqe (f)	[sipərfácɛ]

gram	gram (m)	[gram]
milligram	miligram (m)	[miligrám]
kilogram	kilogram (m)	[kilográm]
ton	ton (m)	[ton]
pound	paund (m)	[páund]
ounce	ons (m)	[ons]

meter	metër (m)	[métər]
millimeter	milimetër (m)	[milimétər]
centimeter	centimetër (m)	[tsɛntimétər]
kilometer	kilometër (m)	[kilométər]
mile	milje (f)	[míljɛ]

inch	inç (m)	[intʃ]
foot	këmbë (f)	[kə́mbə]
yard	jard (m)	[járd]

square meter	metër katror (m)	[métər katrór]
hectare	hektar (m)	[hɛktár]

liter	litër (m)	[lítər]
degree	gradë (f)	[grádə]
volt	volt (m)	[volt]
ampere	amper (m)	[ampér]
horsepower	kuaj-fuqi (f)	[kúaj-fucí]
quantity	sasi (f)	[sasí]

a little bit of ...	pak ...	[pak ...]
half	gjysmë (f)	[ɟýsmə]
dozen	dyzinë (f)	[dyzínə]
piece (item)	copë (f)	[tsópə]

size	madhësi (f)	[maðəsí]
scale (map ~)	shkallë (f)	[ʃkáɫə]

minimal (adj)	minimale	[minimálɛ]
the smallest (adj)	më i vogli	[mə i vógli]
medium (adj)	i mesëm	[i mésəm]
maximal (adj)	maksimale	[maksimálɛ]
the largest (adj)	më i madhi	[mə i máði]

23. Containers

canning jar (glass ~)	kavanoz (m)	[kavanóz]
can	kanoçe (f)	[kanótʃɛ]
bucket	kovë (f)	[kóvə]
barrel	fuçi (f)	[futʃí]

wash basin (e.g., plastic ~)	legen (m)	[lɛgén]
tank (100L water ~)	tank (m)	[tank]
hip flask	faqore (f)	[facórɛ]
jerrycan	bidon (m)	[bidón]
tank (e.g., tank car)	cisternë (f)	[tsistérnə]

mug	tas (m)	[tas]
cup (of coffee, etc.)	filxhan (m)	[fildʒán]
saucer	pjatë filxhani (f)	[pjátə fildʒáni]
glass (tumbler)	gotë (f)	[gótə]
wine glass	gotë vere (f)	[gótə vérɛ]
stock pot (soup pot)	tenxhere (f)	[tɛndʒérɛ]

bottle (~ of wine)	shishe (f)	[ʃíʃɛ]
neck (of the bottle, etc.)	grykë	[grýkə]

carafe (decanter)	brokë (f)	[brókə]
pitcher	shtambë (f)	[ʃtámbə]
vessel (container)	enë (f)	[énə]
pot (crock, stoneware ~)	enë (f)	[énə]
vase	vazo (f)	[vázo]

flacon, bottle (perfume ~)	shishe (f)	[ʃíʃɛ]
vial, small bottle	shishkë (f)	[ʃíʃkə]
tube (of toothpaste)	tubet (f)	[tubét]

sack (bag)	thes (m)	[θɛs]
bag (paper ~, plastic ~)	qese (f)	[césɛ]
pack (of cigarettes, etc.)	paketë (f)	[pakétə]

box (e.g., shoebox)	kuti (f)	[kutí]
crate	arkë (f)	[árkə]
basket	shportë (f)	[ʃpórtə]

24. Materials

material	material (m)	[matɛriál]
wood (n)	dru (m)	[dru]
wood-, wooden (adj)	prej druri	[prɛj drúri]

| glass (n) | qelq (m) | [cɛlc] |
| glass (as adj) | prej qelqi | [prɛj célci] |

| stone (n) | gur (m) | [guɾ] |
| stone (as adj) | guror | [guróɾ] |

| plastic (n) | plastikë (f) | [plastíkə] |
| plastic (as adj) | plastike | [plastíkɛ] |

| rubber (n) | gomë (f) | [gómə] |
| rubber (as adj) | prej gome | [prɛj gómɛ] |

| cloth, fabric (n) | pëlhurë (f) | [pəlhúrə] |
| fabric (as adj) | nga pëlhura | [ŋa pəlhúra] |

| paper (n) | letër (f) | [létər] |
| paper (as adj) | prej letre | [prɛj létrɛ] |

| cardboard (n) | karton (m) | [kartón] |
| cardboard (as adj) | prej kartoni | [prɛj kartóni] |

polyethylene	polietilen (m)	[poliétilɛn]
cellophane	celofan (m)	[tsɛlofán]
linoleum	linoleum (m)	[linolɛúm]
plywood	kompensatë (f)	[kompɛnsátə]

porcelain (n)	porcelan (m)	[portsɛlán]
porcelain (as adj)	prej porcelani	[prɛj portsɛláni]
clay (n)	argjilë (f)	[arɲílə]
clay (as adj)	prej argjile	[prɛj arɲílɛ]
ceramic (n)	qeramikë (f)	[cɛramíkə]
ceramic (as adj)	prej qeramike	[prɛj cɛramíkɛ]

25. Metals

metal (n)	metal (m)	[mɛtál]
metal (as adj)	prej metali	[prɛj mɛtáli]
alloy (n)	aliazh (m)	[aliáʒ]

gold (n)	**ar** (m)	[ár]
gold, golden (adj)	**prej ari**	[prɛj ári]
silver (n)	**argjend** (m)	[aɾɟénd]
silver (as adj)	**prej argjendi**	[prɛj aɾɟéndi]
iron (n)	**hekur** (m)	[hékuɾ]
iron-, made of iron (adj)	**prej hekuri**	[prɛj hékuɾi]
steel (n)	**çelik** (m)	[tʃɛlík]
steel (as adj)	**prej çeliku**	[prɛj tʃɛlíku]
copper (n)	**bakër** (m)	[bákəɾ]
copper (as adj)	**prej bakri**	[prɛj bákɾi]
aluminum (n)	**alumin** (m)	[alumín]
aluminum (as adj)	**prej alumini**	[prɛj alumíni]
bronze (n)	**bronz** (m)	[bronz]
bronze (as adj)	**prej bronzi**	[prɛj brónzi]
brass	**tunxh** (m)	[tundʒ]
nickel	**nikel** (m)	[nikél]
platinum	**platin** (m)	[platín]
mercury	**merkur** (m)	[mɛrkúɾ]
tin	**kallaj** (m)	[kaɫáj]
lead	**plumb** (m)	[plúmb]
zinc	**zink** (m)	[zink]

HUMAN BEING

Human being. The body

26. Humans. Basic concepts

human being	qenie njerëzore (f)	[cɛníɛ ɲɛrəzórɛ]
man (adult male)	burrë (m)	[búrə]
woman	grua (f)	[grúa]
child	fëmijë (f)	[fəmíjə]
girl	vajzë (f)	[vájzə]
boy	djalë (f)	[djálə]
teenager	adoleshent (m)	[adolɛʃént]
old man	plak (m)	[plak]
old woman	plakë (f)	[plákə]

27. Human anatomy

organism (body)	organizëm (m)	[organízəm]
heart	zemër (f)	[zémər]
blood	gjak (m)	[ɟak]
artery	arterie (f)	[artériɛ]
vein	venë (f)	[vénə]
brain	tru (m)	[tru]
nerve	nerv (m)	[nɛrv]
nerves	nerva (f)	[nérva]
vertebra	vertebër (f)	[vɛrtébər]
spine (backbone)	shtyllë kurrizore (f)	[ʃtýłə kurizórɛ]
stomach (organ)	stomak (m)	[stomák]
intestines, bowels	zorrët (f)	[zórət]
intestine (e.g., large ~)	zorrë (f)	[zórə]
liver	mëlçi (f)	[məltʃí]
kidney	veshkë (f)	[véʃkə]
bone	kockë (f)	[kótskə]
skeleton	skelet (m)	[skɛlét]
rib	brinjë (f)	[bríɲə]
skull	kafkë (f)	[káfkə]
muscle	muskul (m)	[múskul]
biceps	biceps (m)	[bitséps]

triceps	triceps (m)	[tritséps]
tendon	tendon (f)	[tɛndón]
joint	nyje (f)	[nýjɛ]
lungs	mushkëri (m)	[muʃkərí]
genitals	organe gjenitale (f)	[orgánɛ ɟɛnitálɛ]
skin	lëkurë (f)	[ləkúrə]

28. Head

head	kokë (f)	[kókə]
face	fytyrë (f)	[fytýrə]
nose	hundë (f)	[húndə]
mouth	gojë (f)	[gójə]

eye	sy (m)	[sy]
eyes	sytë	[sýtə]
pupil	bebëz (f)	[bébəz]
eyebrow	vetull (f)	[vétuɫ]
eyelash	qerpik (m)	[cɛrpík]
eyelid	qepallë (f)	[cɛpáɫə]

tongue	gjuhë (f)	[ɟúhə]
tooth	dhëmb (m)	[ðəmb]
lips	buzë (f)	[búzə]
cheekbones	mollëza (f)	[móɫəza]
gum	mishrat e dhëmbëve	[míʃrat ɛ ðəmbəvɛ]
palate	qiellzë (f)	[ciéɫzə]

nostrils	vrimat e hundës (pl)	[vrímat ɛ húndəs]
chin	mjekër (f)	[mjékər]
jaw	nofull (f)	[nófuɫ]
cheek	faqe (f)	[fácɛ]

forehead	ball (m)	[báɫ]
temple	tëmth (m)	[təmθ]
ear	vesh (m)	[vɛʃ]
back of the head	zverk (m)	[zvɛrk]
neck	qafë (f)	[cáfə]
throat	fyt (m)	[fyt]

hair	flokë (pl)	[flókə]
hairstyle	model flokësh (m)	[modél flókəʃ]
haircut	prerje flokësh (f)	[prérjɛ flókəʃ]
wig	paruke (f)	[parúkɛ]

mustache	mustaqe (f)	[mustácɛ]
beard	mjekër (f)	[mjékər]
to have (a beard, etc.)	lë mjekër	[lə mjékər]
braid	gërshet (m)	[gərʃét]
sideburns	baseta (f)	[baséta]

red-haired (adj)	flokëkuqe	[flokəkúcɛ]
gray (hair)	thinja	[θíɲa]
bald (adj)	qeros	[cɛrós]
bald patch	tullë (f)	[túłə]

| ponytail | bishtalec (m) | [biʃtaléts] |
| bangs | balluke (f) | [bałúkɛ] |

29. Human body

hand	dorë (f)	[dórə]
arm	krah (m)	[krah]
finger	gisht i dorës (m)	[gíʃt i dórəs]
toe	gisht i këmbës (m)	[gíʃt i kə́mbəs]
thumb	gishti i madh (m)	[gíʃti i máð]
little finger	gishti i vogël (m)	[gíʃti i vógəl]
nail	thua (f)	[θúa]

fist	grusht (m)	[grúʃt]
palm	pëllëmbë dore (f)	[pəłə́mbə dórɛ]
wrist	kyç (m)	[kytʃ]
forearm	parakrah (m)	[parakráh]
elbow	bërryl (m)	[bərýl]
shoulder	shpatull (f)	[ʃpátuł]

leg	këmbë (f)	[kə́mbə]
foot	shputë (f)	[ʃpútə]
knee	gju (m)	[ɟú]
calf (part of leg)	pulpë (f)	[púlpə]
hip	ijë (f)	[íjə]
heel	thembër (f)	[θémbər]

body	trup (m)	[trup]
stomach	stomak (m)	[stomák]
chest	kraharor (m)	[kraharór]
breast	gjoks (m)	[ɟóks]
flank	krah (m)	[krah]
back	kurriz (m)	[kuríz]
lower back	fundshpina (f)	[fundʃpína]
waist	beli (m)	[béli]

navel (belly button)	kërthizë (f)	[kərθízə]
buttocks	vithe (f)	[víθɛ]
bottom	prapanica (f)	[prapanítsa]

beauty mark	nishan (m)	[niʃán]
birthmark (café au lait spot)	shenjë lindjeje (f)	[ʃéɲə líndjɛjɛ]
tattoo	tatuazh (m)	[tatuáʒ]
scar	shenjë (f)	[ʃéɲə]

Clothing & Accessories

30. Outerwear. Coats

clothes	**rroba** (f)	[róba]
outerwear	**veshje e sipërme** (f)	[véʃjɛ ɛ sípərmɛ]
winter clothing	**veshje dimri** (f)	[véʃjɛ dímri]
coat (overcoat)	**pallto** (f)	[páɫto]
fur coat	**gëzof** (m)	[gəzóf]
fur jacket	**xhaketë lëkure** (f)	[dʒakétə ləkúrɛ]
down coat	**xhup** (m)	[dʒup]
jacket (e.g., leather ~)	**xhaketë** (f)	[dʒakétə]
raincoat (trenchcoat, etc.)	**pardesy** (f)	[pardɛsý]
waterproof (adj)	**kundër shiut**	[kúndər ʃiut]

31. Men's & women's clothing

shirt (button shirt)	**këmishë** (f)	[kəmíʃə]
pants	**pantallona** (f)	[pantaɫóna]
jeans	**xhinse** (f)	[dʒínsɛ]
suit jacket	**xhaketë kostumi** (f)	[dʒakétə kostúmi]
suit	**kostum** (m)	[kostúm]
dress (frock)	**fustan** (m)	[fustán]
skirt	**fund** (m)	[fund]
blouse	**bluzë** (f)	[blúzə]
knitted jacket (cardigan, etc.)	**xhaketë me thurje** (f)	[dʒakétə mɛ θúrjɛ]
jacket (of woman's suit)	**xhaketë femrash** (f)	[dʒakétə fémraʃ]
T-shirt	**bluzë** (f)	[blúzə]
shorts (short trousers)	**pantallona të shkurtra** (f)	[pantaɫóna tə ʃkúrtra]
tracksuit	**tuta sportive** (f)	[túta sportívɛ]
bathrobe	**peshqir trupi** (m)	[pɛʃcír trúpi]
pajamas	**pizhame** (f)	[piʒámɛ]
sweater	**triko** (f)	[tríko]
pullover	**pulovër** (m)	[pulóvər]
vest	**jelek** (m)	[jɛlék]
tailcoat	**frak** (m)	[frak]
tuxedo	**smoking** (m)	[smokíŋ]

uniform	uniformë (f)	[unifórmə]
workwear	rroba pune (f)	[róba púnɛ]
overalls	kominoshe (f)	[kominóʃɛ]
coat (e.g., doctor's smock)	uniformë (f)	[unifórmə]

32. Clothing. Underwear

underwear	të brendshme (f)	[tə bréndʃmɛ]
boxers, briefs	boksera (f)	[bokséra]
panties	brekë (f)	[brékə]
undershirt (A-shirt)	fanellë (f)	[fanétə]
socks	çorape (pl)	[tʃorápɛ]

nightdress	këmishë nate (f)	[kəmíʃə nátɛ]
bra	sytjena (f)	[sytjéna]
knee highs (knee-high socks)	çorape déri tek gjuri (pl)	[tʃorápɛ déri ték ɟúri]

pantyhose	geta (f)	[géta]
stockings (thigh highs)	çorape të holla (pl)	[tʃorápɛ tə hóła]
bathing suit	rrobë banje (f)	[róbə báɲɛ]

33. Headwear

hat	kapelë (f)	[kapélə]
fedora	kapelë republike (f)	[kapélə ɾɛpublíkɛ]
baseball cap	kapelë bejsbolli (f)	[kapélə bɛjsbóɬi]
flatcap	kapelë e sheshtë (f)	[kapélə ɛ ʃéʃtə]

beret	beretë (f)	[bɛrétə]
hood	kapuç (m)	[kapútʃ]
panama hat	kapelë panama (f)	[kapélə panamá]
knit cap (knitted hat)	kapuç leshi (m)	[kapútʃ léʃi]

headscarf	shami (f)	[ʃamí]
women's hat	kapelë femrash (f)	[kapélə fémraʃ]
hard hat	helmetë (f)	[hɛlmétə]
garrison cap	kapelë ushtrie (f)	[kapélə uʃtríɛ]
helmet	helmetë (f)	[hɛlmétə]

| derby | kapelë derby (f) | [kapélə dérby] |
| top hat | kapelë cilindër (f) | [kapélə tsilíndər] |

34. Footwear

| footwear | këpucë (pl) | [kəpútsə] |
| shoes (men's shoes) | këpucë burrash (pl) | [kəpútsə búraʃ] |

shoes (women's shoes)	këpucë grash (pl)	[kəpútsə gráʃ]
boots (e.g., cowboy ~)	çizme (pl)	[tʃízmɛ]
slippers	pantofla (pl)	[pantófla]

tennis shoes (e.g., Nike ~)	atlete tenisi (pl)	[atlétɛ tɛnísi]
sneakers (e.g., Converse ~)	atlete (pl)	[atlétɛ]
sandals	sandale (pl)	[sandálɛ]

cobbler (shoe repairer)	këpucëtar (m)	[kəputsətár]
heel	takë (f)	[tákə]
pair (of shoes)	palë (f)	[pálə]

shoestring	lidhëse këpucësh (f)	[líðəsɛ kəpútsəʃ]
to lace (vt)	lidh këpucët	[lið kəpútsət]
shoehorn	lugë këpucësh (f)	[lúgə kəpútsəʃ]
shoe polish	bojë këpucësh (f)	[bójə kəpútsəʃ]

35. Textile. Fabrics

cotton (n)	pambuk (m)	[pambúk]
cotton (as adj)	i pambuktë	[i pambúktə]
flax (n)	li (m)	[li]
flax (as adj)	prej liri	[prɛj líri]

silk (n)	mëndafsh (m)	[məndáfʃ]
silk (as adj)	i mëndafshtë	[i məndáfʃtə]
wool (n)	lesh (m)	[lɛʃ]
wool (as adj)	i leshtë	[i léʃtə]

velvet	kadife (f)	[kadífɛ]
suede	kamosh (m)	[kamóʃ]
corduroy	kadife me riga (f)	[kadífɛ mɛ ríga]

nylon (n)	najlon (m)	[najlón]
nylon (as adj)	prej najloni	[prɛj najlóni]
polyester (n)	poliestër (m)	[poliéstər]
polyester (as adj)	prej poliestri	[prɛj poliéstri]

leather (n)	lëkurë (f)	[ləkúrə]
leather (as adj)	prej lëkure	[prɛj ləkúrɛ]
fur (n)	gëzof (m)	[gəzóf]
fur (e.g., ~ coat)	prej gëzofi	[prɛj gəzófi]

36. Personal accessories

gloves	dorëza (pl)	[dórəza]
mittens	doreza (f)	[doréza]

scarf (muffler)	shall (m)	[ʃaɬ]
glasses (eyeglasses)	syze (f)	[sýzɛ]
frame (eyeglass ~)	skelet syzesh (m)	[skɛlét sýzɛʃ]
umbrella	çadër (f)	[tʃádər]
walking stick	bastun (m)	[bastún]
hairbrush	furçë flokësh (f)	[fúrtʃə flókəʃ]
fan	erashkë (f)	[ɛráʃkə]

tie (necktie)	kravatë (f)	[kravátə]
bow tie	papion (m)	[papión]
suspenders	aski (pl)	[askí]
handkerchief	shami (f)	[ʃamí]

comb	krehër (m)	[kréhər]
barrette	kapëse flokësh (f)	[kápəsɛ flókəʃ]
hairpin	karficë (f)	[karfítsə]
buckle	tokëz (f)	[tókəz]

| belt | rrip (m) | [rip] |
| shoulder strap | rrip supi (m) | [rip súpi] |

bag (handbag)	çantë dore (f)	[tʃántə dórɛ]
purse	çantë (f)	[tʃántə]
backpack	çantë shpine (f)	[tʃántə ʃpínɛ]

37. Clothing. Miscellaneous

fashion	modë (f)	[módə]
in vogue (adj)	në modë	[nə módə]
fashion designer	stilist (m)	[stilíst]

collar	jakë (f)	[jákə]
pocket	xhep (m)	[dʒɛp]
pocket (as adj)	i xhepit	[i dʒépit]
sleeve	mëngë (f)	[mə́ŋə]
hanging loop	hallkë për varje (f)	[háɬkə pər várjɛ]
fly (on trousers)	zinxhir (m)	[zindʒír]

zipper (fastener)	zinxhir (m)	[zindʒír]
fastener	kapëse (f)	[kápəsɛ]
button	kopsë (f)	[kópsə]
buttonhole	vrimë kopse (f)	[vrímə kópsɛ]
to come off (ab. button)	këputet	[kəpútɛt]

to sew (vi, vt)	qep	[cɛp]
to embroider (vi, vt)	qëndis	[cəndís]
embroidery	qëndisje (f)	[cəndísjɛ]
sewing needle	gjilpërë për qepje (f)	[ɟilpə́rə pər cépjɛ]
thread	pe (m)	[pɛ]
seam	tegel (m)	[tɛgél]

to get dirty (vi)	**bëhem pis**	[béhɛm pis]
stain (mark, spot)	**njollë** (f)	[ɲótə]
to crease, crumple (vi)	**zhubros**	[ʒubrós]
to tear, to rip (vt)	**gris**	[gris]
clothes moth	**molë rrobash** (f)	[mólə róbaʃ]

38. Personal care. Cosmetics

toothpaste	**pastë dhëmbësh** (f)	[pástə ðémbəʃ]
toothbrush	**furçë dhëmbësh** (f)	[fúrtʃə ðémbəʃ]
to brush one's teeth	**laj dhëmbët**	[laj ðémbət]
razor	**brisk** (m)	[brísk]
shaving cream	**pastë rroje** (f)	[pástə rójɛ]
to shave (vi)	**rruhem**	[rúhɛm]
soap	**sapun** (m)	[sapún]
shampoo	**shampo** (f)	[ʃampó]
scissors	**gërshërë** (f)	[gərʃérə]
nail file	**limë thonjsh** (f)	[límə θóɲʃ]
nail clippers	**prerëse thonjsh** (f)	[prérəsɛ θóɲʃ]
tweezers	**piskatore vetullash** (f)	[piskatórɛ vétuɫaʃ]
cosmetics	**kozmetikë** (f)	[kozmɛtíkə]
face mask	**maskë fytyre** (f)	[máskə fytýrɛ]
manicure	**manikyr** (m)	[manikýr]
to have a manicure	**bëj manikyr**	[bəj manikýr]
pedicure	**pedikyr** (m)	[pɛdikýr]
make-up bag	**çantë kozmetike** (f)	[tʃántə kozmɛtíkɛ]
face powder	**pudër fytyre** (f)	[púdər fytýrɛ]
powder compact	**pudër kompakte** (f)	[púdər kompáktɛ]
blusher	**ruzh** (m)	[ruʒ]
perfume (bottled)	**parfum** (m)	[parfúm]
toilet water (lotion)	**parfum** (m)	[parfúm]
lotion	**krem** (m)	[krɛm]
cologne	**kolonjë** (f)	[kolóɲə]
eyeshadow	**rimel** (m)	[rimél]
eyeliner	**laps për sy** (m)	[láps pər sy]
mascara	**rimel** (m)	[rimél]
lipstick	**buzëkuq** (m)	[buzəkúc]
nail polish, enamel	**llak për thonj** (m)	[ɫak pər θóɲ]
hair spray	**llak flokësh** (m)	[ɫak flókəʃ]
deodorant	**deodorant** (m)	[dɛodoránt]
cream	**krem** (m)	[krɛm]
face cream	**krem për fytyrë** (m)	[krɛm pər fytýrə]

hand cream	krem për duar (m)	[krɛm pər dúar]
anti-wrinkle cream	krem kundër rrudhave (m)	[krɛm kúndər rúðavɛ]
day cream	krem dite (m)	[krɛm dítɛ]
night cream	krem nate (m)	[krɛm nátɛ]
day (as adj)	dite	[dítɛ]
night (as adj)	nate	[nátɛ]

tampon	tampon (m)	[tampón]
toilet paper (toilet roll)	letër higjienike (f)	[létər hiɉiɛníkɛ]
hair dryer	tharëse flokësh (f)	[θárəsɛ flókəʃ]

39. Jewelry

jewelry, jewels	bizhuteri (f)	[biʒutɛrí]
precious (e.g., ~ stone)	i çmuar	[i tʃmúar]
hallmark stamp	vulë dalluese (f)	[vúlə datúɛsɛ]

ring	unazë (f)	[unázə]
wedding ring	unazë martese (f)	[unázə martésɛ]
bracelet	byzylyk (m)	[byzylýk]

earrings	vathë (pl)	[váθə]
necklace (~ of pearls)	gjerdan (m)	[ɉɛrdán]
crown	kurorë (f)	[kurórə]
bead necklace	qafore me rruaza (f)	[cafórɛ mɛ ruáza]

diamond	diamant (m)	[diamánt]
emerald	smerald (m)	[smɛráld]
ruby	rubin (m)	[rubín]
sapphire	safir (m)	[safír]
pearl	perlë (f)	[pérlə]
amber	qelibar (m)	[cɛlibár]

40. Watches. Clocks

watch (wristwatch)	orë dore (f)	[órə dórɛ]
dial	faqe e orës (f)	[fácɛ ɛ órəs]
hand (of clock, watch)	akrep (m)	[akrép]
metal watch band	rrip metalik ore (m)	[rip mɛtalík órɛ]
watch strap	rrip ore (m)	[rip órɛ]

battery	bateri (f)	[batɛrí]
to be dead (battery)	e shkarkuar	[ɛ ʃkarkúar]
to change a battery	ndërroj baterinë	[ndərój batɛrínə]
to run fast	kalon shpejt	[kalón ʃpéjt]
to run slow	ngel prapa	[ŋɛl prápa]
wall clock	orë muri (f)	[órə múri]
hourglass	orë rëre (f)	[órə rərɛ]

sundial	orë diellore (f)	[órə diɛłórɛ]
alarm clock	orë me zile (f)	[órə mɛ zílɛ]
watchmaker	orëndreqës (m)	[orəndrécəs]
to repair (vt)	ndreq	[ndréc]

Food. Nutricion

41. Food

meat	**mish** (m)	[miʃ]
chicken	**pulë** (f)	[púlə]
Rock Cornish hen (poussin)	**mish pule** (m)	[miʃ púlɛ]
duck	**rosë** (f)	[rósə]
goose	**patë** (f)	[pátə]
game	**gjah** (m)	[ɟáh]
turkey	**mish gjel deti** (m)	[miʃ ɟɛl déti]
pork	**mish derri** (m)	[miʃ déri]
veal	**mish viçi** (m)	[miʃ vítʃi]
lamb	**mish qengji** (m)	[miʃ cénɟi]
beef	**mish lope** (m)	[miʃ lópɛ]
rabbit	**mish lepuri** (m)	[miʃ lépuri]
sausage (bologna, etc.)	**salsiçe** (f)	[salsítʃɛ]
vienna sausage (frankfurter)	**salsiçe vjeneze** (f)	[salsítʃɛ vjɛnézɛ]
bacon	**proshutë** (f)	[proʃútə]
ham	**sallam** (m)	[saɫám]
gammon	**kofshë derri** (f)	[kófʃə déri]
pâté	**pate** (f)	[paté]
liver	**mëlçi** (f)	[məltʃí]
hamburger (ground beef)	**hamburger** (m)	[hamburgér]
tongue	**gjuhë** (f)	[ɟúhə]
egg	**ve** (f)	[vɛ]
eggs	**vezë** (pl)	[vézə]
egg white	**e bardhë veze** (f)	[ɛ bárðə vézɛ]
egg yolk	**e verdhë veze** (f)	[ɛ vérðə vézɛ]
fish	**peshk** (m)	[pɛʃk]
seafood	**fruta deti** (pl)	[frúta déti]
crustaceans	**krustace** (pl)	[krustátsɛ]
caviar	**havjar** (m)	[havjár]
crab	**gaforre** (f)	[gafórɛ]
shrimp	**karkalec** (m)	[karkaléts]
oyster	**midhje** (f)	[míðjɛ]
spiny lobster	**karavidhe** (f)	[karavíðɛ]
octopus	**oktapod** (m)	[oktapód]

squid	kallamarë (f)	[kałamárǝ]
sturgeon	bli (m)	[blí]
salmon	salmon (m)	[salmón]
halibut	shojzë e Atlantikut Verior (f)	[ʃójzǝ ɛ atlantíkut vɛriór]
cod	merluc (m)	[mɛrlúts]
mackerel	skumbri (m)	[skúmbri]
tuna	tunë (f)	[túnǝ]
eel	ngjalë (f)	[ɲálǝ]
trout	troftë (f)	[tróftǝ]
sardine	sardele (f)	[sardélɛ]
pike	mlysh (m)	[mlýʃ]
herring	harengë (f)	[haréɲǝ]
bread	bukë (f)	[búkǝ]
cheese	djath (m)	[djáθ]
sugar	sheqer (m)	[ʃɛcér]
salt	kripë (f)	[krípǝ]
rice	oriz (m)	[oríz]
pasta (macaroni)	makarona (f)	[makaróna]
noodles	makarona petë (f)	[makaróna pétǝ]
butter	gjalp (m)	[ɟalp]
vegetable oil	vaj vegjetal (m)	[vaj vɛɟɛtál]
sunflower oil	vaj luledielli (m)	[vaj lulɛdiéłi]
margarine	margarinë (f)	[margarínǝ]
olives	ullinj (pl)	[ułíɲ]
olive oil	vaj ulliri (m)	[vaj ułíri]
milk	qumësht (m)	[cúmǝʃt]
condensed milk	qumësht i kondensuar (m)	[cúmǝʃt i kondɛnsúar]
yogurt	kos (m)	[kos]
sour cream	salcë kosi (f)	[sáltsǝ kosi]
cream (of milk)	krem qumështi (m)	[krɛm cúmǝʃti]
mayonnaise	majonezë (f)	[majonézǝ]
buttercream	krem gjalpi (m)	[krɛm ɟálpi]
groats (barley ~, etc.)	drithëra (pl)	[dríθǝra]
flour	miell (m)	[míɛł]
canned food	konserva (f)	[konsérva]
cornflakes	kornfleiks (m)	[kornfléiks]
honey	mjaltë (f)	[mjáltǝ]
jam	reçel (m)	[rɛtʃél]
chewing gum	çamçakëz (m)	[tʃamtʃakéz]

42. Drinks

water	ujë (m)	[újə]
drinking water	ujë i pijshëm (m)	[újə i píʃʃəm]
mineral water	ujë mineral (m)	[újə minɛrál]
still (adj)	ujë natyral	[újə natyrál]
carbonated (adj)	ujë i karbonuar	[újə i karbonúar]
sparkling (adj)	ujë i gazuar	[újə i gazúar]
ice	akull (m)	[ákuɫ]
with ice	me akull	[mɛ ákuɫ]
non-alcoholic (adj)	jo alkoolik	[jo alkoolík]
soft drink	pije e lehtë (f)	[píjɛ ɛ léhtə]
refreshing drink	pije freskuese (f)	[píjɛ frɛskúɛsɛ]
lemonade	limonadë (f)	[limonádə]
liquors	likere (pl)	[likérɛ]
wine	verë (f)	[vérə]
white wine	verë e bardhë (f)	[vérə ɛ bárðə]
red wine	verë e kuqe (f)	[vérə ɛ kúcɛ]
liqueur	liker (m)	[likér]
champagne	shampanjë (f)	[ʃampáɲə]
vermouth	vermut (m)	[vɛrmút]
whiskey	uiski (m)	[víski]
vodka	vodkë (f)	[vódkə]
gin	xhin (m)	[dʒin]
cognac	konjak (m)	[koɲák]
rum	rum (m)	[rum]
coffee	kafe (f)	[káfɛ]
black coffee	kafe e zezë (f)	[káfɛ ɛ zézə]
coffee with milk	kafe me qumësht (m)	[káfɛ mɛ cúməʃt]
cappuccino	kapuçino (m)	[kaputʃíno]
instant coffee	neskafe (f)	[nɛskáfɛ]
milk	qumësht (m)	[cúməʃt]
cocktail	koktej (m)	[koktéj]
milkshake	milkshake (f)	[milkʃákɛ]
juice	lëng frutash (m)	[ləŋ frútaʃ]
tomato juice	lëng domatesh (m)	[ləŋ domátɛʃ]
orange juice	lëng portokalli (m)	[ləŋ portokáɫi]
freshly squeezed juice	lëng frutash i freskët (m)	[ləŋ frútaʃ i fréskət]
beer	birrë (f)	[bírə]
light beer	birrë e lehtë (f)	[bírə ɛ léhtə]
dark beer	birrë e zezë (f)	[bírə ɛ zézə]
tea	çaj (m)	[tʃáj]

| black tea | çaj i zi (m) | [tʃáj i zí] |
| green tea | çaj jeshil (m) | [tʃáj jɛʃíl] |

43. Vegetables

| vegetables | perime (pl) | [pɛrímɛ] |
| greens | zarzavate (pl) | [zarzavátɛ] |

tomato	domate (f)	[domátɛ]
cucumber	kastravec (m)	[kastravéts]
carrot	karotë (f)	[karótə]
potato	patate (f)	[patátɛ]
onion	qepë (f)	[cépə]
garlic	hudhër (f)	[húðər]

cabbage	lakër (f)	[lákər]
cauliflower	lulelakër (f)	[lulɛlákər]
Brussels sprouts	lakër Brukseli (f)	[lákər brukséli]
broccoli	brokoli (m)	[brókoli]

beet	panxhar (m)	[pandʒár]
eggplant	patëllxhan (m)	[patəɫdʒán]
zucchini	kungulleshë (m)	[kuŋuɫéʃə]
pumpkin	kungull (m)	[kúŋuɫ]
turnip	rrepë (f)	[répə]

parsley	majdanoz (m)	[majdanóz]
dill	kopër (f)	[kópər]
lettuce	sallatë jeshile (f)	[saɫátə jɛʃílɛ]
celery	selino (f)	[sɛlíno]
asparagus	asparagus (m)	[asparágus]
spinach	spinaq (m)	[spinác]

pea	bizele (f)	[bizélɛ]
beans	fasule (f)	[fasúlɛ]
corn (maize)	misër (m)	[mísər]
kidney bean	groshë (f)	[gróʃə]

bell pepper	spec (m)	[spɛts]
radish	rrepkë (f)	[répkə]
artichoke	angjinare (f)	[anɟinárɛ]

44. Fruits. Nuts

fruit	frut (m)	[frut]
apple	mollë (f)	[móɫə]
pear	dardhë (f)	[dárðə]
lemon	limon (m)	[limón]

| orange | portokall (m) | [portokáɫ] |
| strawberry (garden ~) | luleshtrydhe (f) | [lulɛʃtrýðɛ] |

mandarin	mandarinë (f)	[mandarínə]
plum	kumbull (f)	[kúmbuɫ]
peach	pjeshkë (f)	[pjéʃkə]
apricot	kajsi (f)	[kajsí]
raspberry	mjedër (f)	[mjédər]
pineapple	ananas (m)	[ananás]

banana	banane (f)	[banánɛ]
watermelon	shalqi (m)	[ʃalcí]
grape	rrush (m)	[ruʃ]
sour cherry	qershi vishnje (f)	[cɛrʃí víʃɲɛ]
sweet cherry	qershi (f)	[cɛrʃí]
melon	pjepër (m)	[pjépər]

grapefruit	grejpfrut (m)	[grɛjpfrút]
avocado	avokado (f)	[avokádo]
papaya	papaja (f)	[papája]
mango	mango (f)	[máŋo]
pomegranate	shegë (f)	[ʃégə]

redcurrant	kaliboba e kuqe (f)	[kalibóba ɛ kúcɛ]
blackcurrant	kaliboba e zezë (f)	[kalibóba ɛ zézə]
gooseberry	kulumbri (f)	[kulumbrí]
bilberry	boronicë (f)	[boronítsə]
blackberry	manaferra (f)	[manaféra]

raisin	rrush i thatë (m)	[ruʃ i θátə]
fig	fik (m)	[fik]
date	hurmë (f)	[húrmə]

peanut	kikirik (m)	[kikirík]
almond	bajame (f)	[bajámɛ]
walnut	arrë (f)	[árə]
hazelnut	lajthi (f)	[lajθí]
coconut	arrë kokosi (f)	[árə kokósi]
pistachios	fëstëk (m)	[fəsték]

45. Bread. Candy

bakers' confectionery (pastry)	ëmbëlsira (pl)	[əmbəlsíra]
bread	bukë (f)	[búkə]
cookies	biskota (pl)	[biskóta]

chocolate (n)	çokollatë (f)	[tʃokoɫátə]
chocolate (as adj)	prej çokollate	[prɛj tʃokoɫátɛ]
candy (wrapped)	karamele (f)	[karamélɛ]

| cake (e.g., cupcake) | kek (m) | [kék] |
| cake (e.g., birthday ~) | tortë (f) | [tórtə] |

| pie (e.g., apple ~) | tortë (f) | [tórtə] |
| filling (for cake, pie) | mbushje (f) | [mbúʃɛ] |

jam (whole fruit jam)	reçel (m)	[rɛtʃél]
marmalade	marmelatë (f)	[marmɛlátə]
wafers	vafera (pl)	[vaféra]
ice-cream	akullore (f)	[akutórɛ]
pudding	puding (m)	[pudín]

46. Cooked dishes

course, dish	pjatë (f)	[pjátə]
cuisine	kuzhinë (f)	[kuʒínə]
recipe	recetë (f)	[rɛtsétə]
portion	racion (m)	[ratsión]

| salad | sallatë (f) | [satátə] |
| soup | supë (f) | [súpə] |

clear soup (broth)	lëng mishi (m)	[lən míʃi]
sandwich (bread)	sandviç (m)	[sandvítʃ]
fried eggs	vezë të skuqura (pl)	[vézə tə skúcura]

| hamburger (beefburger) | hamburger | [hamburgér] |
| beefsteak | biftek (m) | [bifték] |

side dish	garniturë (f)	[garnitúrə]
spaghetti	shpageti (pl)	[ʃpagéti]
mashed potatoes	pure patatesh (f)	[puré patátɛʃ]
pizza	pica (f)	[pítsa]
porridge (oatmeal, etc.)	qull (m)	[cut]
omelet	omëletë (f)	[omǝlétə]

boiled (e.g., ~ beef)	i zier	[i zíɛr]
smoked (adj)	i tymosur	[i tymósur]
fried (adj)	i skuqur	[i skúcur]
dried (adj)	i tharë	[i θárə]
frozen (adj)	i ngrirë	[i ŋrírə]
pickled (adj)	i marinuar	[i marinúar]

sweet (sugary)	i ëmbël	[i émbəl]
salty (adj)	i kripur	[i krípur]
cold (adj)	i ftohtë	[i ftóhtə]
hot (adj)	i nxehtë	[i ndzéhtə]
bitter (adj)	i hidhur	[i híður]
tasty (adj)	i shijshëm	[i ʃíʃəm]
to cook in boiling water	ziej	[zíɛj]

to cook (dinner)	**gatuaj**	[gatúaj]
to fry (vt)	**skuq**	[skuc]
to heat up (food)	**ngroh**	[ŋróh]

to salt (vt)	**hedh kripë**	[hɛð krípə]
to pepper (vt)	**hedh piper**	[hɛð pipér]
to grate (vt)	**rendoj**	[rɛndój]
peel (n)	**lëkurë** (f)	[ləkúrə]
to peel (vt)	**qëroj**	[cərój]

47. Spices

salt	**kripë** (f)	[krípə]
salty (adj)	**i kripur**	[i krípur]
to salt (vt)	**hedh kripë**	[hɛð krípə]

black pepper	**piper i zi** (m)	[pipér i zi]
red pepper (milled ~)	**piper i kuq** (m)	[pipér i kuc]

mustard	**mustardë** (f)	[mustárdə]
horseradish	**rrepë djegëse** (f)	[répə djégəsɛ]

condiment	**salcë** (f)	[sáltsə]
spice	**erëz** (f)	[érəz]
sauce	**salcë** (f)	[sáltsə]
vinegar	**uthull** (f)	[úθuɫ]

anise	**anisetë** (f)	[anisétə]
basil	**borzilok** (m)	[borzilók]
cloves	**karafil** (m)	[karafíl]

ginger	**xhenxhefil** (m)	[dʒɛndʒɛfíl]
coriander	**koriandër** (m)	[koriándər]
cinnamon	**kanellë** (f)	[kanéɫə]

sesame	**susam** (m)	[susám]
bay leaf	**gjeth dafine** (m)	[ɟɛθ dafínɛ]
paprika	**spec** (m)	[spɛts]
caraway	**kumin** (m)	[kumín]
saffron	**shafran** (m)	[ʃafrán]

48. Meals

food	**ushqim** (m)	[uʃcím]
to eat (vi, vt)	**ha**	[ha]

breakfast	**mëngjes** (m)	[mənɟés]
to have breakfast	**ha mëngjes**	[ha mənɟés]

| lunch | drekë (f) | [drékə] |
| to have lunch | ha drekë | [ha drékə] |

| dinner | darkë (f) | [dárkə] |
| to have dinner | ha darkë | [ha dárkə] |

| appetite | oreks (m) | [oréks] |
| Enjoy your meal! | Të bëftë mirë! | [tə bəftə mírə!] |

to open (~ a bottle)	hap	[hap]
to spill (liquid)	derdh	[dérð]
to spill out (vi)	derdhje	[dérðjɛ]

to boil (vi)	ziej	[zíɛj]
to boil (vt)	ziej	[zíɛj]
boiled (~ water)	i zier	[i zíɛr]
to chill, cool down (vt)	ftoh	[ftoh]
to chill (vi)	ftohje	[ftóhjɛ]

| taste, flavor | shije (f) | [ʃíjɛ] |
| aftertaste | shije (f) | [ʃíjɛ] |

to slim down (lose weight)	dobësohem	[dobəsóhɛm]
diet	dietë (f)	[diétə]
vitamin	vitaminë (f)	[vitamínə]
calorie	kalori (f)	[kalorí]
vegetarian (n)	vegjetarian (m)	[vɛɟɛtarián]
vegetarian (adj)	vegjetarian	[vɛɟɛtarián]

fats (nutrient)	yndyrë (f)	[yndýrə]
proteins	proteinë (f)	[protɛínə]
carbohydrates	karbohidrat (m)	[karbohidrát]

slice (of lemon, ham)	fetë (f)	[fétə]
piece (of cake, pie)	copë (f)	[tsópə]
crumb	dromcë (f)	[drómtsə]
(of bread, cake, etc.)		

49. Table setting

spoon	lugë (f)	[lúgə]
knife	thikë (f)	[θíkə]
fork	pirun (m)	[pirún]

| cup (e.g., coffee ~) | filxhan (m) | [fildʒán] |
| plate (dinner ~) | pjatë (f) | [pjátə] |

saucer	pjatë filxhani (f)	[pjátə fildʒáni]
napkin (on table)	pecetë (f)	[pɛtsétə]
toothpick	kruajtëse dhëmbësh (f)	[krúajtəsɛ ðémbəʃ]

50. Restaurant

restaurant	**restorant** (m)	[rɛstoránt]
coffee house	**kafene** (f)	[kafɛné]
pub, bar	**pab** (m), **pijetore** (f)	[pab], [pijɛtórɛ]
tearoom	**çajtore** (f)	[tʃajtórɛ]
waiter	**kamerier** (m)	[kamɛriér]
waitress	**kameriere** (f)	[kamɛriérɛ]
bartender	**banakier** (m)	[banakiér]
menu	**menu** (f)	[mɛnú]
wine list	**menu verërash** (f)	[mɛnú vérəraʃ]
to book a table	**rezervoj një tavolinë**	[rɛzɛrvój ɲə tavolínə]
course, dish	**pjatë** (f)	[pjátə]
to order (meal)	**porosis**	[porosís]
to make an order	**bëj porosinë**	[bəj porosínə]
aperitif	**aperitiv** (m)	[apɛritív]
appetizer	**antipastë** (f)	[antipástə]
dessert	**ëmbëlsirë** (f)	[əmbəlsírə]
check	**faturë** (f)	[fatúrə]
to pay the check	**paguaj faturën**	[pagúaj fatúrən]
to give change	**jap kusur**	[jap kusúr]
tip	**bakshish** (m)	[bakʃíʃ]

Family, relatives and friends

51. Personal information. Forms

name (first name)	**emër** (m)	[émər]
surname (last name)	**mbiemër** (m)	[mbiémər]
date of birth	**datëlindje** (f)	[datəlíndjɛ]
place of birth	**vendlindje** (f)	[vɛndlíndjɛ]
nationality	**kombësi** (f)	[kombəsí]
place of residence	**vendbanim** (m)	[vɛndbaním]
country	**shtet** (m)	[ʃtɛt]
profession (occupation)	**profesion** (m)	[profɛsión]
gender, sex	**gjinia** (f)	[ɟinía]
height	**gjatësia** (f)	[ɟatəsía]
weight	**peshë** (f)	[péʃə]

52. Family members. Relatives

mother	**nënë** (f)	[nénə]
father	**baba** (f)	[babá]
son	**bir** (m)	[bir]
daughter	**bijë** (f)	[bíjə]
younger daughter	**vajza e vogël** (f)	[vájza ɛ vógəl]
younger son	**djali i vogël** (m)	[djáli i vógəl]
eldest daughter	**vajza e madhe** (f)	[vájza ɛ máðɛ]
eldest son	**djali i vogël** (m)	[djáli i vógəl]
brother	**vëlla** (m)	[vəɬá]
elder brother	**vëllai i madh** (m)	[vəɬái i mað]
younger brother	**vëllai i vogël** (m)	[vəɬai i vógəl]
sister	**motër** (f)	[mótər]
elder sister	**motra e madhe** (f)	[mótra ɛ máðɛ]
younger sister	**motra e vogël** (f)	[mótra ɛ vógəl]
cousin (masc.)	**kushëri** (m)	[kuʃərí]
cousin (fem.)	**kushërirë** (f)	[kuʃərírə]
mom, mommy	**mami** (f)	[mámi]
dad, daddy	**babi** (m)	[bábi]
parents	**prindër** (pl)	[príndər]
child	**fëmijë** (f)	[fəmíjə]

children	fëmijë (pl)	[fəmíjə]
grandmother	gjyshe (f)	[ɟýʃɛ]
grandfather	gjysh (m)	[ɟyʃ]
grandson	nip (m)	[nip]
granddaughter	mbesë (f)	[mbésə]
grandchildren	nipër e mbesa (pl)	[nípər ɛ mbésa]

uncle	dajë (f)	[dájə]
aunt	teze (f)	[tézɛ]
nephew	nip (m)	[nip]
niece	mbesë (f)	[mbésə]

mother-in-law (wife's mother)	vjehrrë (f)	[vjéhrə]
father-in-law (husband's father)	vjehrri (m)	[vjéhri]
son-in-law (daughter's husband)	dhëndër (m)	[ðə́ndər]

stepmother	njerkë (f)	[ɲérkə]
stepfather	njerk (m)	[ɲérk]

infant	foshnjë (f)	[fóʃɲə]
baby (infant)	fëmijë (f)	[fəmíjə]
little boy, kid	djalosh (m)	[djalóʃ]

wife	bashkëshorte (f)	[baʃkəʃórtɛ]
husband	bashkëshort (m)	[baʃkəʃórt]

spouse (husband)	bashkëshort (m)	[baʃkəʃórt]
spouse (wife)	bashkëshorte (f)	[baʃkəʃórtɛ]

married (masc.)	i martuar	[i martúar]
married (fem.)	e martuar	[ɛ martúar]
single (unmarried)	beqar	[bɛcár]
bachelor	beqar (m)	[bɛcár]
divorced (masc.)	i divorcuar	[i divortsúar]

widow	vejushë (f)	[vɛjúʃə]
widower	vejan (m)	[vɛján]

relative	kushëri (m)	[kuʃərí]
close relative	kushëri i afërt (m)	[kuʃərí i áfərt]

distant relative	kushëri i largët (m)	[kuʃərí i lárgət]
relatives	kushërinj (pl)	[kuʃəríɲ]

orphan (boy)	jetim (m)	[jɛtím]
orphan (girl)	jetime (f)	[jɛtímɛ]
guardian (of a minor)	kujdestar (m)	[kujdɛstár]
to adopt (a boy)	adoptoj	[adoptój]
to adopt (a girl)	adoptoj	[adoptój]

53. Friends. Coworkers

friend (masc.)	mik (m)	[mik]
friend (fem.)	mike (f)	[míkɛ]
friendship	miqësi (f)	[micəsí]
to be friends	të miqësohem	[tə micəsóhɛm]
buddy (masc.)	shok (m)	[ʃok]
buddy (fem.)	shoqe (f)	[ʃócɛ]
partner	partner (m)	[partnér]
chief (boss)	shef (m)	[ʃɛf]
superior (n)	epror (m)	[ɛprór]
owner, proprietor	pronar (m)	[pronár]
subordinate (n)	vartës (m)	[vártəs]
colleague	koleg (m)	[kolég]
acquaintance (person)	i njohur (m)	[i ɲóhur]
fellow traveler	bashkudhëtar (m)	[baʃkuðətár]
classmate	shok klase (m)	[ʃok klásɛ]
neighbor (masc.)	komshi (m)	[komʃí]
neighbor (fem.)	komshike (f)	[komʃíkɛ]
neighbors	komshinj (pl)	[komʃíɲ]

54. Man. Woman

woman	grua (f)	[grúa]
girl (young woman)	vajzë (f)	[vájzə]
bride	nuse (f)	[núsɛ]
beautiful (adj)	i bukur	[i búkur]
tall (adj)	i gjatë	[i ɟátə]
slender (adj)	i hollë	[i hółə]
short (adj)	i shkurtër	[i ʃkúrtər]
blonde (n)	bionde (f)	[bióndɛ]
brunette (n)	zeshkane (f)	[zɛʃkánɛ]
ladies' (adj)	për femra	[pər fémra]
virgin (girl)	virgjëreshë (f)	[virɟəréʃə]
pregnant (adj)	shtatzënë	[ʃtatzénə]
man (adult male)	burrë (m)	[búrə]
blond (n)	biond (m)	[biónd]
brunet (n)	zeshkan (m)	[zɛʃkán]
tall (adj)	i gjatë	[i ɟátə]
short (adj)	i shkurtër	[i ʃkúrtər]
rude (rough)	i vrazhdë	[i vráʒdə]

stocky (adj)	trupngjeshur	[trupɲéʃur]
robust (adj)	i fuqishëm	[i fucíʃəm]
strong (adj)	i fortë	[i fórtə]
strength	forcë (f)	[fórtsə]

stout, fat (adj)	bullafiq	[buɫafíc]
swarthy (adj)	zeshkan	[zɛʃkán]
slender (well-built)	i hollë	[i hóɫə]
elegant (adj)	elegant	[ɛlɛgánt]

55. Age

age	moshë (f)	[móʃə]
youth (young age)	rini (f)	[riní]
young (adj)	i ri	[i rí]

younger (adj)	më i ri	[mə i rí]
older (adj)	më i vjetër	[mə i vjétər]

young man	djalë i ri (m)	[djálə i rí]
teenager	adoleshent (m)	[adolɛʃént]
guy, fellow	djalë (f)	[djálə]

old man	plak (m)	[plak]
old woman	plakë (f)	[plákə]

adult (adj)	i rritur	[i rítur]
middle-aged (adj)	mesoburrë	[mɛsobúrə]
elderly (adj)	i moshuar	[i moʃúar]
old (adj)	i vjetër	[i vjétər]

retirement	pension (m)	[pɛnsión]
to retire (from job)	dal në pension	[dál nə pɛnsión]
retiree	pensionist (m)	[pɛnsioníst]

56. Children

child	fëmijë (f)	[fəmíjə]
children	fëmijë (pl)	[fəmíjə]
twins	binjakë (pl)	[biɲákə]

cradle	djep (m)	[djép]
rattle	rraketake (f)	[rakɛtákɛ]
diaper	pelenë (f)	[pɛlénə]

pacifier	biberon (m)	[bibɛrón]
baby carriage	karrocë për bebe (f)	[karótsə pər bébɛ]
kindergarten	kopsht fëmijësh (m)	[kópʃt fəmíjəʃ]

babysitter	dado (f)	[dádo]
childhood	fëmijëri (f)	[fəmijərí]
doll	kukull (f)	[kúkuɫ]
toy	lodër (f)	[lódər]
construction set (toy)	lodër për ndërtim (m)	[lódər pər ndərtím]

well-bred (adj)	i edukuar	[i ɛdukúar]
ill-bred (adj)	i paedukuar	[i paɛdukúar]
spoiled (adj)	i llastuar	[i ɫastúar]

to be naughty	trazovaç	[trazovátʃ]
mischievous (adj)	mistrec	[mistréts]
mischievousness	shpirtligësi (f)	[ʃpirtligəsí]
mischievous child	fëmijë mistrec (m)	[fəmíjə mistréts]

| obedient (adj) | i bindur | [i bíndur] |
| disobedient (adj) | i pabindur | [i pabíndur] |

docile (adj)	i butë	[i bútə]
clever (smart)	i zgjuar	[i zɟúar]
child prodigy	fëmijë gjeni (m)	[fəmíjə ɟɛní]

57. Married couples. Family life

to kiss (vt)	puth	[puθ]
to kiss (vi)	puthem	[púθɛm]
family (n)	familje (f)	[famíljɛ]
family (as adj)	familjare	[familjárɛ]
couple	çift (m)	[tʃíft]
marriage (state)	martesë (f)	[martésə]
hearth (home)	vatra (f)	[vátra]
dynasty	dinasti (f)	[dinastí]

| date | takim (m) | [takím] |
| kiss | puthje (f) | [púθjɛ] |

love (for sb)	dashuri (f)	[daʃurí]
to love (sb)	dashuroj	[daʃurój]
beloved	i dashur	[i dáʃur]

tenderness	ndjeshmëri (f)	[ndjɛʃmərí]
tender (affectionate)	i ndjeshëm	[i ndjéʃəm]
faithfulness	besnikëri (f)	[bɛsnikərí]
faithful (adj)	besnik	[bɛsník]
care (attention)	kujdes (m)	[kujdés]
caring (~ father)	i dashur	[i dáʃur]
newlyweds	të porsamartuar (pl)	[tə porsamartúar]
honeymoon	muaj mjalti (m)	[múaj mjálti]
to get married (ab. woman)	martohem	[martóhɛm]

to get married (ab. man)	martohem	[martóhɛm]
wedding	dasmë (f)	[dásmə]
golden wedding	martesë e artë (f)	[martésə ɛ ártə]
anniversary	përvjetor (m)	[pərvjɛtór]

| lover (masc.) | dashnor (m) | [daʃnór] |
| mistress (lover) | dashnore (f) | [daʃnórɛ] |

adultery	tradhti bashkëshortore (f)	[traðtí baʃkəʃortórɛ]
to cheat on ... (commit adultery)	tradhtoj ...	[traðtój ...]
jealous (adj)	xheloz	[dʒɛlóz]
to be jealous	jam xheloz	[jam dʒɛlóz]
divorce	divorc (m)	[divórts]
to divorce (vi)	divorcoj	[divortsój]

to quarrel (vi)	grindem	[gríndɛm]
to be reconciled (after an argument)	pajtohem	[pajtóhɛm]
together (adv)	së bashku	[sə báʃku]
sex	seks (m)	[sɛks]

happiness	lumturi (f)	[lumturí]
happy (adj)	i lumtur	[i lúmtur]
misfortune (accident)	fatkeqësi (f)	[fatkɛcəsí]
unhappy (adj)	i trishtuar	[i triʃtúar]

Character. Feelings. Emotions

58. Feelings. Emotions

feeling (emotion)	**ndjenjë** (f)	[ndjéɲə]
feelings	**ndjenja** (pl)	[ndjéɲa]
to feel (vt)	**ndjej**	[ndjéj]
hunger	**uri** (f)	[urí]
to be hungry	**kam uri**	[kam urí]
thirst	**etje** (f)	[étjɛ]
to be thirsty	**kam etje**	[kam étjɛ]
sleepiness	**përgjumësi** (f)	[pəɲuməsí]
to feel sleepy	**përgjumje**	[pəɲúmjɛ]
tiredness	**lodhje** (f)	[lóðjɛ]
tired (adj)	**i lodhur**	[i lóðuɾ]
to get tired	**lodhem**	[lóðɛm]
mood (humor)	**humor** (m)	[humóɾ]
boredom	**mërzitje** (f)	[mərzítjɛ]
to be bored	**mërzitem**	[mərzítɛm]
seclusion	**izolim** (m)	[izolím]
to seclude oneself	**izolohem**	[izolóhɛm]
to worry (make anxious)	**shqetësoj**	[ʃcɛtəsój]
to be worried	**shqetësohem**	[ʃcɛtəsóhɛm]
worrying (n)	**shqetësim** (m)	[ʃcɛtəsím]
anxiety	**ankth** (m)	[ankθ]
preoccupied (adj)	**i merakosur**	[i mɛrakósuɾ]
to be nervous	**nervozohem**	[nɛrvozóhɛm]
to panic (vi)	**më zë paniku**	[mə zə paníku]
hope	**shpresë** (f)	[ʃprésə]
to hope (vi, vt)	**shpresoj**	[ʃprɛsój]
certainty	**siguri** (f)	[sigurí]
certain, sure (adj)	**i sigurt**	[i sígurt]
uncertainty	**pasiguri** (f)	[pasigurí]
uncertain (adj)	**i pasigurt**	[i pasígurt]
drunk (adj)	**i dehur**	[i déhuɾ]
sober (adj)	**i kthjellët**	[i kθjétət]
weak (adj)	**i dobët**	[i dóbət]
happy (adj)	**i lumtur**	[i lúmtur]
to scare (vt)	**tremb**	[trɛmb]

| fury (madness) | tërbim (m) | [tərbím] |
| rage (fury) | inat (m) | [inát] |

depression	depresion (m)	[dɛprɛsión]
discomfort (unease)	parehati (f)	[parɛhatí]
comfort	rehati (f)	[rɛhatí]
to regret (be sorry)	pendohem	[pɛndóhɛm]
regret	pendim (m)	[pɛndím]
bad luck	ters (m)	[tɛrs]
sadness	trishtim (m)	[triʃtím]

shame (remorse)	turp (m)	[turp]
gladness	gëzim (m)	[gəzím]
enthusiasm, zeal	entuziazëm (m)	[ɛntuziázəm]
enthusiast	entuziast (m)	[ɛntuziást]
to show enthusiasm	tregoj entuziazëm	[trɛgój ɛntuziázəm]

59. Character. Personality

character	karakter (m)	[karaktér]
character flaw	dobësi karakteri (f)	[dobəsí karaktéri]
mind	mendje (f)	[méndjɛ]
reason	arsye (f)	[arsýɛ]

conscience	ndërgjegje (f)	[ndərɟéɟɛ]
habit (custom)	zakon (m)	[zakón]
ability (talent)	aftësi (f)	[aftəsí]
can (e.g., ~ swim)	mund	[mund]

patient (adj)	i duruar	[i durúar]
impatient (adj)	i paduruar	[i padurúar]
curious (inquisitive)	kurioz	[kurióz]
curiosity	kuriozitet (m)	[kuriozitét]

modesty	modesti (f)	[modɛstí]
modest (adj)	modest	[modést]
immodest (adj)	i paturpshëm	[i patúrpʃəm]

laziness	dembeli (f)	[dɛmbɛlí]
lazy (adj)	dembel	[dɛmbél]
lazy person (masc.)	dembel (m)	[dɛmbél]

cunning (n)	dinakëri (f)	[dinakərí]
cunning (as adj)	dinak	[dinák]
distrust	mosbesim (m)	[mosbɛsím]
distrustful (adj)	mosbesues	[mosbɛsúɛs]

generosity	zemërgjerësi (f)	[zɛmərɟɛrəsí]
generous (adj)	zemërgjerë	[zɛmərɟérə]
talented (adj)	i talentuar	[i talɛntúar]

talent	talent (m)	[talént]
courageous (adj)	i guximshëm	[i gudzímʃəm]
courage	guxim (m)	[gudzím]
honest (adj)	i ndershëm	[i ndérʃəm]
honesty	ndershmëri (f)	[ndɛrʃmərí]

careful (cautious)	i kujdesshëm	[i kujdésʃəm]
brave (courageous)	trim, guximtar	[trim], [gudzimtár]
serious (adj)	serioz	[sɛrióz]
strict (severe, stern)	i rreptë	[i réptə]

decisive (adj)	i vendosur	[i vɛndósur]
indecisive (adj)	i pavendosur	[i pavɛndósur]
shy, timid (adj)	i turpshëm	[i túrpʃəm]
shyness, timidity	turp (m)	[turp]

confidence (trust)	besim në vetvete (m)	[bɛsím nə vɛtvétɛ]
to believe (trust)	besoj	[bɛsój]
trusting (credulous)	i besueshëm	[i bɛsúɛʃəm]

sincerely (adv)	sinqerisht	[síncɛriʃt]
sincere (adj)	i sinqertë	[i sincértə]
sincerity	sinqeritet (m)	[sincɛritét]
open (person)	i hapur	[i hápur]

calm (adj)	i qetë	[i cétə]
frank (sincere)	i dëlirë	[i dəlírə]
naïve (adj)	naiv	[naív]
absent-minded (adj)	i hutuar	[i hutúar]
funny (odd)	zbavitës	[zbavítəs]

greed, stinginess	lakmi (f)	[lakmí]
greedy, stingy (adj)	lakmues	[lakmúɛs]
stingy (adj)	koprrac	[kopráts]
evil (adj)	djallëzor	[djałəzór]
stubborn (adj)	kokëfortë	[kokəfórtə]
unpleasant (adj)	i pakëndshëm	[i pakəndʃəm]

selfish person (masc.)	egoist (m)	[ɛgoíst]
selfish (adj)	egoist	[ɛgoíst]
coward	frikacak (m)	[frikatsák]
cowardly (adj)	frikacak	[frikatsák]

60. Sleep. Dreams

to sleep (vi)	fle	[flɛ]
sleep, sleeping	gjumë (m)	[ɟúmə]
dream	ëndërr (m)	[éndər]
to dream (in sleep)	ëndërroj	[əndərój]
sleepy (adj)	përgjumshëm	[pərɟúmʃəm]

bed	shtrat (m)	[ʃtrat]
mattress	dyshek (m)	[dyʃék]
blanket (comforter)	mbulesë (f)	[mbulésə]
pillow	jastëk (m)	[jastëk]
sheet	çarçaf (m)	[tʃartʃáf]

insomnia	pagjumësi (f)	[paɟuməsí]
sleepless (adj)	i pagjumë	[i paɟúmə]
sleeping pill	ilaç gjumi (m)	[ilátʃ ɟúmi]
to take a sleeping pill	marr ilaç gjumi	[mar ilátʃ ɟúmi]

to feel sleepy	përgjumje	[pəɾɟúmjɛ]
to yawn (vi)	më hapet goja	[mə hápɛt gója]
to go to bed	shkoj të fle	[ʃkoj tə flɛ]
to make up the bed	rregulloj shtratin	[rɛguɫój ʃtrátin]
to fall asleep	më zë gjumi	[mə zə ɟúmi]

nightmare	ankth (m)	[ankθ]
snore, snoring	gërhitje (f)	[gərhítjɛ]
to snore (vi)	gërhas	[gərhás]

alarm clock	orë me zile (f)	[órə mɛ zílɛ]
to wake (vt)	zgjoj	[zɟoj]
to wake up	zgjohem nga gjumi	[zɟóhɛm ŋa ɟúmi]
to get up (vi)	ngrihem	[ŋríhɛm]
to wash up (wash face)	laj	[laj]

61. Humour. Laughter. Gladness

humor (wit, fun)	humor (m)	[humór]
sense of humor	sens humori (m)	[sɛns humóri]
to enjoy oneself	kënaqem	[kənácɛm]
cheerful (merry)	gëzueshëm	[gəzúɛʃəm]
merriment (gaiety)	gëzim (m)	[gəzím]

smile	buzëqeshje (f)	[buzəcéʃɛ]
to smile (vi)	buzëqesh	[buzəcéʃ]
to start laughing	filloj të qesh	[fiɫój tə céʃ]
to laugh (vi)	qesh	[cɛʃ]
laugh, laughter	qeshje (f)	[céʃɛ]

anecdote	anekdotë (f)	[anɛkdótə]
funny (anecdote, etc.)	për të qeshur	[pər tə céʃur]
funny (odd)	zbavitës	[zbavítəs]

to joke (vi)	bëj shaka	[bəj ʃaká]
joke (verbal)	shaka (f)	[ʃaká]
joy (emotion)	gëzim (m)	[gəzím]
to rejoice (vi)	ngazëllohem	[ŋazəɫóhɛm]
joyful (adj)	gazmor	[gazmór]

62. Discussion, conversation. Part 1

communication	komunikim (m)	[komunikím]
to communicate	komunikoj	[komunikój]
conversation	bisedë (f)	[bisédə]
dialog	dialog (m)	[dialóg]
discussion (discourse)	diskutim (m)	[diskutím]
dispute (debate)	mosmarrëveshje (f)	[mosmarəvéʃjɛ]
to dispute	kundërshtoj	[kundərʃtój]
interlocutor	bashkëbisedues (m)	[baʃkəbisɛdúɛs]
topic (theme)	temë (f)	[témə]
point of view	pikëpamje (f)	[pikəpámjɛ]
opinion (point of view)	opinion (m)	[opinión]
speech (talk)	fjalim (m)	[fjalím]
discussion (of report, etc.)	diskutim (m)	[diskutím]
to discuss (vt)	diskutoj	[diskutój]
talk (conversation)	bisedë (f)	[bisédə]
to talk (to chat)	bisedoj	[bisɛdój]
meeting (encounter)	takim (m)	[takím]
to meet (vi, vt)	takoj	[takój]
proverb	fjalë e urtë (f)	[fjálə ɛ úrtə]
saying	thënie (f)	[θéniɛ]
riddle (poser)	gjëegjëzë (f)	[ɟəéɟəzə]
to pose a riddle	them gjëegjëzë	[θɛm ɟəéɟəzə]
password	fjalëkalim (m)	[fjaləkalím]
secret	sekret (m)	[sɛkrét]
oath (vow)	betim (m)	[bɛtím]
to swear (an oath)	betohem	[bɛtóhɛm]
promise	premtim (m)	[prɛmtím]
to promise (vt)	premtoj	[prɛmtój]
advice (counsel)	këshillë (f)	[kəʃíłə]
to advise (vt)	këshilloj	[kəʃiłój]
to follow one's advice	ndjek këshillën	[ndjék kəʃíłən]
to listen to … (obey)	bindem …	[bíndɛm …]
news	lajme (f)	[lájmɛ]
sensation (news)	ndjesi (f)	[ndjɛsí]
information (report)	informacion (m)	[informatsión]
conclusion (decision)	përfundim (m)	[pərfundím]
voice	zë (f)	[zə]
compliment	kompliment (m)	[komplimént]
kind (nice)	i mirë	[i mírə]
word	fjalë (f)	[fjálə]
phrase	frazë (f)	[frázə]

answer	përgjigje (f)	[pərɟíɟɛ]
truth	e vërtetë (f)	[ɛ vərtétə]
lie	gënjeshtër (f)	[gəɲéʃtər]

thought	mendim (m)	[mɛndím]
idea (inspiration)	ide (f)	[idé]
fantasy	fantazi (f)	[fantazí]

63. Discussion, conversation. Part 2

respected (adj)	i nderuar	[i ndɛrúar]
to respect (vt)	nderoj	[ndɛrój]
respect	nder (m)	[ndér]
Dear ... (letter)	i dashur ...	[i dáʃur ...]

| to introduce (sb to sb) | prezantoj | [prɛzantój] |
| to make acquaintance | njoftoj | [ɲoftój] |

intention	qëllim (m)	[cəɫím]
to intend (have in mind)	kam ndërmend	[kam ndərménd]
wish	dëshirë (f)	[dəʃírə]
to wish (~ good luck)	dëshiroj	[dəʃirój]

surprise (astonishment)	surprizë (f)	[surprízə]
to surprise (amaze)	befasoj	[bɛfasój]
to be surprised	çuditem	[tʃudítɛm]

to give (vt)	jap	[jap]
to take (get hold of)	marr	[mar]
to give back	kthej	[kθɛj]
to return (give back)	rikthej	[rikθéj]

to apologize (vi)	kërkoj falje	[kərkój fáljɛ]
apology	falje (f)	[fáljɛ]
to forgive (vt)	fal	[fal]

to talk (speak)	flas	[flas]
to listen (vi)	dëgjoj	[dəɟój]
to hear out	tregoj vëmendje	[trɛgój vəméndjɛ]
to understand (vt)	kuptoj	[kuptój]

to show (to display)	tregoj	[trɛgój]
to look at ...	shikoj ...	[ʃikój ...]
to call (yell for sb)	thërras	[θərás]
to distract (disturb)	tërheq vëmendjen	[tərhéc vəméndjɛn]
to disturb (vt)	shqetësoj	[ʃcɛtəsój]
to pass (to hand sth)	jap	[jap]

| demand (request) | kërkesë (f) | [kərkésə] |
| to request (ask) | kërkoj | [kərkój] |

| demand (firm request) | kërkesë (f) | [kərkésə] |
| to demand (request firmly) | kërkoj | [kərkój] |

to tease (call names)	ngacmoj	[ŋatsmój]
to mock (make fun of)	tallem	[táɫɛm]
mockery, derision	tallje (f)	[tátjɛ]
nickname	pseudonim (m)	[psɛudoním]

insinuation	nënkuptim (m)	[nənkuptím]
to insinuate (imply)	nënkuptoj	[nənkuptój]
to mean (vt)	dua të them	[dúa tə θém]

description	përshkrim (m)	[pərʃkrím]
to describe (vt)	përshkruaj	[pərʃkrúaj]
praise (compliments)	lëvdatë (f)	[ləvdátə]
to praise (vt)	lavdëroj	[lavdərój]

disappointment	zhgënjim (m)	[ʒgəɲím]
to disappoint (vt)	zhgënjej	[ʒgəɲéj]
to be disappointed	zhgënjehem	[ʒgəɲéhɛm]

supposition	supozim (m)	[supozím]
to suppose (assume)	supozoj	[supozój]
warning (caution)	paralajmërim (m)	[paralajmərím]
to warn (vt)	paralajmëroj	[paralajmərój]

64. Discussion, conversation. Part 3

| to talk into (convince) | bind | [bínd] |
| to calm down (vt) | qetësoj | [cɛtəsój] |

silence (~ is golden)	heshtje (f)	[héʃtjɛ]
to be silent (not speaking)	i heshtur	[i héʃtur]
to whisper (vi, vt)	pëshpëris	[pəʃpərís]
whisper	pëshpërimë (f)	[pəʃpərímə]

| frankly, sincerely (adv) | sinqerisht | [síncɛriʃt] |
| in my opinion ... | sipas mendimit tim ... | [sipás mɛndímit tim ...] |

detail (of the story)	detaj (m)	[dɛtáj]
detailed (adj)	i detajuar	[i dɛtajúar]
in detail (adv)	hollësisht	[hoɫəsíʃt]

| hint, clue | sugjerim (m) | [suɟɛrím] |
| to give a hint | aludoj | [aludój] |

look (glance)	shikim (m)	[ʃikím]
to have a look	i hedh një sy	[i héð ɲə sý]
fixed (look)	i ngurtë	[i ŋúrtə]
to blink (vi)	hap e mbyll sytë	[hap ɛ mbýɫ sýtə]

| to wink (vi) | luaj syrin | [lúaj sýrin] |
| to nod (in assent) | pohoj me kokë | [pohój mε kókə] |

sigh	psherëtimë (f)	[pʃεrətímə]
to sigh (vi)	psherëtij	[pʃεrətíj]
to shudder (vi)	rrëqethem	[rəcéθεm]
gesture	gjest (m)	[ɟεst]
to touch (one's arm, etc.)	prek	[prεk]
to seize	kap	[kap]
(e.g., ~ by the arm)		
to tap (on the shoulder)	prek	[prεk]

Look out!	Kujdes!	[kujdés!]
Really?	Vërtet?	[vərtét?]
Are you sure?	Je i sigurt?	[jε i sígurt?]
Good luck!	Paç fat!	[patʃ fat!]
I see!	E kuptova!	[ε kuptóva!]
What a pity!	Sa keq!	[sa kεc!]

65. Agreement. Refusal

consent	leje (f)	[léjε]
to consent (vi)	lejoj	[lεjój]
approval	miratim (m)	[miratím]
to approve (vt)	miratoj	[miratój]
refusal	refuzim (m)	[rεfuzím]
to refuse (vi, vt)	refuzoj	[rεfuzój]

Great!	Të lumtë!	[tə lúmtə!]
All right!	Në rregull!	[nə réguɫ!]
Okay! (I agree)	Në rregull!	[nə réguɫ!]

forbidden (adj)	i ndaluar	[i ndalúar]
it's forbidden	është e ndaluar	[əʃtə ε ndalúar]
it's impossible	është e pamundur	[əʃtə ε pámundur]
incorrect (adj)	i pasaktë	[i pasáktə]

to reject (~ a demand)	hedh poshtë	[hεð póʃtə]
to support (cause, idea)	mbështes	[mbəʃtés]
to accept (~ an apology)	pranoj	[pranój]

to confirm (vt)	konfirmoj	[konfirmój]
confirmation	konfirmim (m)	[konfirmím]
permission	leje (f)	[léjε]
to permit (vt)	lejoj	[lεjój]
decision	vendim (m)	[vεndím]
to say nothing	nuk them asgjë	[nuk θεm ásɉə]
(hold one's tongue)		
condition (term)	kusht (m)	[kuʃt]
excuse (pretext)	justifikim (m)	[justifikím]

| praise (compliments) | lëvdata (f) | [ləvdáta] |
| to praise (vt) | lavdëroj | [lavdərój] |

66. Success. Good luck. Failure

success	sukses (m)	[suksés]
successfully (adv)	me sukses	[mε suksés]
successful (adj)	i suksesshëm	[i suksésʃəm]

luck (good luck)	fat (m)	[fat]
Good luck!	Paç fat!	[patʃ fat!]
lucky (e.g., ~ day)	me fat	[mε fat]
lucky (fortunate)	fatlum	[fatlúm]

failure	dështim (m)	[dəʃtím]
misfortune	fatkeqësi (f)	[fatkɛcəsí]
bad luck	ters (m)	[tɛrs]
unsuccessful (adj)	i pasuksesshëm	[i pasuksésʃəm]
catastrophe	katastrofë (f)	[katastrófə]

pride	krenari (f)	[krɛnarí]
proud (adj)	krenar	[krɛnár]
to be proud	jam krenar	[jam krɛnár]

winner	fitues (m)	[fitúɛs]
to win (vi)	fitoj	[fitój]
to lose (not win)	humb	[húmb]
try	përpjekje (f)	[pərpjékjɛ]
to try (vi)	përpiqem	[pərpícɛm]
chance (opportunity)	shans (m)	[ʃans]

67. Quarrels. Negative emotions

shout (scream)	britmë (f)	[brítmə]
to shout (vi)	bërtas	[bərtás]
to start to cry out	filloj të ulërij	[fiɫój tə uləríj]

quarrel	grindje (f)	[gríndjɛ]
to quarrel (vi)	grindem	[gríndɛm]
fight (squabble)	sherr (m)	[ʃɛr]
to make a scene	bëj skenë	[bəj skénə]
conflict	konflikt (m)	[konflíkt]
misunderstanding	keqkuptim (m)	[kɛckuptím]

insult	ofendim (m)	[ofɛndím]
to insult (vt)	fyej	[fýɛj]
insulted (adj)	i ofenduar	[i ofɛndúar]
resentment	fyerje (f)	[fýɛrjɛ]

| to offend (vt) | ofendoj | [ofɛndój] |
| to take offense | mbrohem | [mbróhɛm] |

indignation	indinjatë (f)	[indiɲátə]
to be indignant	zemërohem	[zɛməróhɛm]
complaint	ankesë (f)	[ankésə]
to complain (vi, vt)	ankohem	[ankóhɛm]

apology	falje (f)	[fáljɛ]
to apologize (vi)	kërkoj falje	[kərkój fáljɛ]
to beg pardon	kërkoj ndjesë	[kərkój ndjésə]

criticism	kritikë (f)	[kritíkə]
to criticize (vt)	kritikoj	[kritikój]
accusation (charge)	akuzë (f)	[akúzə]
to accuse (vt)	akuzoj	[akuzój]

revenge	hakmarrje (f)	[hakmárjɛ]
to avenge (get revenge)	hakmerrem	[hakmérɛm]
to pay back	shpaguaj	[ʃpagúaj]

disdain	përbuzje (f)	[pərbúzjɛ]
to despise (vt)	përbuz	[pərbúz]
hatred, hate	urrejtje (f)	[uréjtjɛ]
to hate (vt)	urrej	[uréj]

nervous (adj)	nervoz	[nɛrvóz]
to be nervous	nervozohem	[nɛrvozóhɛm]
angry (mad)	i zemëruar	[i zɛmərúar]
to make angry	zemëroj	[zɛmərój]

humiliation	poshtërim (m)	[poʃtərím]
to humiliate (vt)	poshtëroj	[poʃtərój]
to humiliate oneself	poshtërohem	[poʃtəróhɛm]

| shock | tronditje (f) | [trondítjɛ] |
| to shock (vt) | trondit | [trondít] |

| trouble (e.g., serious ~) | shqetësim (m) | [ʃcɛtəsím] |
| unpleasant (adj) | i pakëndshëm | [i pakéndʃəm] |

fear (dread)	frikë (f)	[fríkə]
terrible (storm, heat)	i tmerrshëm	[i tmérʃəm]
scary (e.g., ~ story)	i frikshëm	[i fríkʃəm]
horror	horror (m)	[horór]
awful (crime, news)	i tmerrshëm	[i tmérʃəm]

to begin to tremble	filloj të dridhem	[fiłój tə dríðɛm]
to cry (weep)	qaj	[caj]
to start crying	filloj të qaj	[fiłój tə cáj]
tear	lot (m)	[lot]
fault	faj (m)	[faj]

guilt (feeling)	faj (m)	[faj]
dishonor (disgrace)	turp (m)	[turp]
protest	protestë (f)	[protéstə]
stress	stres (m)	[strɛs]

to disturb (vt)	shqetësoj	[ʃcɛtəsój]
to be furious	tërbohem	[tərbóhɛm]
mad, angry (adj)	i inatosur	[i inatósur]
to end (~ a relationship)	përfundoj	[pərfundój]
to swear (at sb)	betohem	[bɛtóhɛm]

to scare (become afraid)	tremb	[trɛmb]
to hit (strike with hand)	qëlloj	[cəɫój]
to fight (street fight, etc.)	grindem	[gríndɛm]

to settle (a conflict)	zgjidh	[zɟið]
discontented (adj)	i pakënaqur	[i pakənácur]
furious (adj)	i xhindosur	[i dʒindósur]

| It's not good! | Nuk është mirë! | [nuk əʃtə mírə!] |
| It's bad! | Është keq! | [əʃtə kɛc!] |

Medicine

68. Diseases

sickness	sëmundje (f)	[səmúndjɛ]
to be sick	jam sëmurë	[jam səmúrə]
health	shëndet (m)	[ʃəndét]
runny nose (coryza)	rrifë (f)	[rífə]
tonsillitis	grykët (m)	[grýkət]
cold (illness)	ftohje (f)	[ftóhjɛ]
to catch a cold	ftohem	[ftóhɛm]
bronchitis	bronkit (m)	[bronkít]
pneumonia	pneumoni (f)	[pnɛumoní]
flu, influenza	grip (m)	[grip]
nearsighted (adj)	miop	[mióp]
farsighted (adj)	presbit	[prɛsbít]
strabismus (crossed eyes)	strabizëm (m)	[strabízəm]
cross-eyed (adj)	strabik	[strabík]
cataract	katarakt (m)	[katarákt]
glaucoma	glaukoma (f)	[glaukóma]
stroke	goditje (f)	[godítjɛ]
heart attack	sulm në zemër (m)	[sulm nə zémər]
myocardial infarction	infarkt miokardiak (m)	[infárkt miokardiák]
paralysis	paralizë (f)	[paralízə]
to paralyze (vt)	paralizoj	[paralizój]
allergy	alergji (f)	[alɛrɟí]
asthma	astmë (f)	[ástmə]
diabetes	diabet (m)	[diabét]
toothache	dhimbje dhëmbi (f)	[ðímbjɛ ðémbi]
caries	karies (m)	[kariés]
diarrhea	diarre (f)	[diaré]
constipation	kapsllëk (m)	[kapsɫə́k]
stomach upset	dispepsi (f)	[dispɛpsí]
food poisoning	helmim (m)	[hɛlmím]
to get food poisoning	helmohem nga ushqimi	[hɛlmóhɛm ŋa uʃcími]
arthritis	artrit (m)	[artrít]
rickets	rakit (m)	[rakít]
rheumatism	reumatizëm (m)	[rɛumatízəm]

atherosclerosis	arteriosklerozë (f)	[artɛriosklɛrózə]
gastritis	gastrit (m)	[gastrít]
appendicitis	apendicit (m)	[apɛnditsít]
cholecystitis	kolecistit (m)	[kolɛtsistít]
ulcer	ulcerë (f)	[ultsérə]

measles	fruth (m)	[fruθ]
rubella (German measles)	rubeola (f)	[rubɛóla]
jaundice	verdhëza (f)	[vérðəza]
hepatitis	hepatit (m)	[hɛpatít]

schizophrenia	skizofreni (f)	[skizofrɛní]
rabies (hydrophobia)	sëmundje e tërbimit (f)	[səmúndjɛ ɛ tərbímit]
neurosis	neurozë (f)	[nɛurózə]
concussion	tronditje (f)	[trondítjɛ]

cancer	kancer (m)	[kantsér]
sclerosis	sklerozë (f)	[sklɛrózə]
multiple sclerosis	sklerozë e shumëfishtë (f)	[sklɛrózə ɛ ʃuməfíʃtə]

alcoholism	alkoolizëm (m)	[alkoolízəm]
alcoholic (n)	alkoolik (m)	[alkoolík]
syphilis	sifiliz (m)	[sifilíz]
AIDS	SIDA (f)	[sída]

tumor	tumor (m)	[tumór]
malignant (adj)	malinj	[malíɲ]
benign (adj)	beninj	[bɛníɲ]

fever	ethe (f)	[éθɛ]
malaria	malarie (f)	[malaríɛ]
gangrene	gangrenë (f)	[gaɲrénə]
seasickness	sëmundje deti (f)	[səmúndjɛ déti]
epilepsy	epilepsi (f)	[ɛpilɛpsí]

epidemic	epidemi (f)	[ɛpidɛmí]
typhus	tifo (f)	[tífo]
tuberculosis	tuberkuloz (f)	[tubɛrkulóz]
cholera	kolerë (f)	[kolérə]
plague (bubonic ~)	murtaja (f)	[murtája]

69. Symptoms. Treatments. Part 1

symptom	simptomë (f)	[simptómə]
temperature	temperaturë (f)	[tɛmpɛratúrə]
high temperature (fever)	temperaturë e lartë (f)	[tɛmpɛratúrə ɛ lártə]
pulse (heartbeat)	puls (m)	[puls]

| dizziness (vertigo) | marrje mendsh (m) | [márjɛ méndʃ] |
| hot (adj) | i nxehtë | [i ndzéhtə] |

shivering	drithërima (f)	[driθəríma]
pale (e.g., ~ face)	i zbehur	[i zbéhur]
cough	kollë (f)	[kótə]
to cough (vi)	kollitem	[kotítɛm]
to sneeze (vi)	teshtij	[tɛʃtíj]
faint	të fikët (f)	[tə fíkət]
to faint (vi)	bie të fikët	[bíɛ tə fíkət]
bruise (hématome)	mavijosje (f)	[mavijósjɛ]
bump (lump)	gungë (f)	[gúŋə]
to bang (bump)	godas	[godás]
contusion (bruise)	lëndim (m)	[ləndím]
to get a bruise	lëndohem	[ləndóhɛm]
to limp (vi)	çaloj	[tʃalój]
dislocation	dislokim (m)	[dislokím]
to dislocate (vt)	del nga vendi	[dɛl ŋa véndi]
fracture	thyerje (f)	[θýɛrjɛ]
to have a fracture	thyej	[θýɛj]
cut (e.g., paper ~)	e prerë (f)	[ɛ prérə]
to cut oneself	pres veten	[prɛs vétɛn]
bleeding	rrjedhje gjaku (f)	[rjéðjɛ ɟáku]
burn (injury)	djegie (f)	[djégiɛ]
to get burned	digjem	[díɟɛm]
to prick (vt)	shpoj	[ʃpoj]
to prick oneself	shpohem	[ʃpóhɛm]
to injure (vt)	dëmtoj	[dəmtój]
injury	dëmtim (m)	[dəmtím]
wound	plagë (f)	[plágə]
trauma	traumë (f)	[traúmə]
to be delirious	fol përçart	[fól pərtʃárt]
to stutter (vi)	belbëzoj	[bɛlbəzój]
sunstroke	pikë e diellit (f)	[píkə ɛ diétit]

70. Symptoms. Treatments. Part 2

pain, ache	dhimbje (f)	[ðímbjɛ]
splinter (in foot, etc.)	cifël (f)	[tsífəl]
sweat (perspiration)	djersë (f)	[djérsə]
to sweat (perspire)	djersij	[djɛrsíj]
vomiting	të vjella (f)	[tə vjéła]
convulsions	konvulsione (f)	[konvulsiónɛ]
pregnant (adj)	shtatzënë	[ʃtatzénə]
to be born	lind	[lind]

delivery, labor	lindje (f)	[líndjɛ]
to deliver (~ a baby)	sjell në jetë	[sjɛt nə jétə]
abortion	abort (m)	[abórt]

breathing, respiration	frymëmarrje (f)	[fryməmárjɛ]
in-breath (inhalation)	mbajtje e frymës (f)	[mbájtjɛ ɛ frýməs]
out-breath (exhalation)	lëshim i frymës (m)	[ləʃím i frýməs]
to exhale (breathe out)	nxjerr frymën	[ndzjér frýmən]
to inhale (vi)	marr frymë	[mar frýmə]

disabled person	invalid (m)	[invalíd]
cripple	i gjymtuar (m)	[i ɟymtúar]
drug addict	narkoman (m)	[narkomán]

deaf (adj)	shurdh	[ʃurð]
mute (adj)	memec	[mɛméts]
deaf mute (adj)	shurdh-memec	[ʃurð-mɛméts]

mad, insane (adj)	i marrë	[i márə]
madman (demented person)	i çmendur (m)	[i tʃméndur]
madwoman	e çmendur (f)	[ɛ tʃméndur]
to go insane	çmendem	[tʃméndɛm]

gene	gen (m)	[gɛn]
immunity	imunitet (m)	[imunitét]
hereditary (adj)	e trashëguar	[ɛ traʃəgúar]
congenital (adj)	e lindur	[ɛ líndur]

virus	virus (m)	[virús]
microbe	mikrob (m)	[mikrób]
bacterium	bakterie (f)	[baktériɛ]
infection	infeksion (m)	[infɛksión]

71. Symptoms. Treatments. Part 3

| hospital | spital (m) | [spitál] |
| patient | pacient (m) | [patsiént] |

diagnosis	diagnozë (f)	[diagnózə]
cure	kurë (f)	[kúrə]
medical treatment	trajtim mjekësor (m)	[trajtím mjɛkəsór]
to get treatment	kurohem	[kuróhɛm]
to treat (~ a patient)	kuroj	[kurój]
to nurse (look after)	kujdesem	[kujdésɛm]
care (nursing ~)	kujdes (m)	[kujdés]

operation, surgery	operacion (m)	[opɛratsión]
to bandage (head, limb)	fashoj	[faʃój]
bandaging	fashim (m)	[faʃím]

vaccination	**vaksinim** (m)	[vaksiním]
to vaccinate (vt)	**vaksinoj**	[vaksinój]
injection, shot	**injeksion** (m)	[iɲɛksión]
to give an injection	**bëj injeksion**	[bəj iɲɛksíon]
attack	**atak** (m)	[aták]
amputation	**amputim** (m)	[amputím]
to amputate (vt)	**amputoj**	[amputój]
coma	**komë** (f)	[kómə]
to be in a coma	**jam në komë**	[jam nə kómə]
intensive care	**kujdes intensiv** (m)	[kujdés intɛnsív]
to recover (~ from flu)	**shërohem**	[ʃəróhɛm]
condition (patient's ~)	**gjendje** (f)	[ɟéndjɛ]
consciousness	**vetëdije** (f)	[vɛtədíjɛ]
memory (faculty)	**kujtesë** (f)	[kujtésə]
to pull out (tooth)	**heq**	[hɛc]
filling	**mbushje** (f)	[mbúʃɛ]
to fill (a tooth)	**mbush**	[mbúʃ]
hypnosis	**hipnozë** (f)	[hipnózə]
to hypnotize (vt)	**hipnotizim**	[hipnotizím]

72. Doctors

doctor	**mjek** (m)	[mjék]
nurse	**infermiere** (f)	[infɛrmiérɛ]
personal doctor	**mjek personal** (m)	[mjék pɛrsonál]
dentist	**dentist** (m)	[dɛntíst]
eye doctor	**okulist** (m)	[okulíst]
internist	**mjek i përgjithshëm** (m)	[mjék i pərɟíθʃəm]
surgeon	**kirurg** (m)	[kirúrg]
psychiatrist	**psikiatër** (m)	[psikiátər]
pediatrician	**pediatër** (m)	[pɛdiátər]
psychologist	**psikolog** (m)	[psikológ]
gynecologist	**gjinekolog** (m)	[ɟinɛkológ]
cardiologist	**kardiolog** (m)	[kardiológ]

73. Medicine. Drugs. Accessories

medicine, drug	**ilaç** (m)	[ilátʃ]
remedy	**mjekim** (m)	[mjɛkím]
to prescribe (vt)	**shkruaj recetë**	[ʃkrúaj rɛtsétə]
prescription	**recetë** (f)	[rɛtsétə]
tablet, pill	**pilulë** (f)	[pilúlə]

ointment	krem (m)	[krɛm]
ampule	ampulë (f)	[ampúlə]
mixture, solution	përzierje (f)	[pərzíɛrjɛ]
syrup	shurup (m)	[ʃurúp]
capsule	pilulë (f)	[pilúlə]
powder	pudër (f)	[púdər]
gauze bandage	fashë garze (f)	[faʃə gárzɛ]
cotton wool	pambuk (m)	[pambúk]
iodine	jod (m)	[jod]
Band-Aid	leukoplast (m)	[lɛukoplást]
eyedropper	pikatore (f)	[pikatórɛ]
thermometer	termometër (m)	[tɛrmométər]
syringe	shiringë (f)	[ʃiríŋə]
wheelchair	karrocë me rrota (f)	[karótsə mɛ róta]
crutches	paterica (f)	[patɛrítsa]
painkiller	qetësues (m)	[cɛtəsúɛs]
laxative	laksativ (m)	[laksatív]
spirits (ethanol)	alkool dezinfektues (m)	[alkoól dɛzinfɛktúɛs]
medicinal herbs	bimë mjekësore (f)	[bímə mjɛkəsórɛ]
herbal (~ tea)	çaj bimor	[tʃáj bimór]

74. Smoking. Tobacco products

tobacco	duhan (m)	[duhán]
cigarette	cigare (f)	[tsigárɛ]
cigar	puro (f)	[púro]
pipe	llullë (f)	[łúłə]
pack (of cigarettes)	pako cigaresh (m)	[páko tsigárɛʃ]
matches	shkrepëse (pl)	[ʃkrépəsɛ]
matchbox	kuti shkrepësesh (f)	[kutí ʃkrépəsɛʃ]
lighter	çakmak (m)	[tʃakmák]
ashtray	taketuke (f)	[takɛtúkɛ]
cigarette case	kuti cigaresh (f)	[kutí tsigárɛʃ]
cigarette holder	cigarishte (f)	[tsigaríʃtɛ]
filter (cigarette tip)	filtër (m)	[fíltər]
to smoke (vi, vt)	pi duhan	[pi duhán]
to light a cigarette	ndez një cigare	[ndɛz ɲə tsigárɛ]
smoking	pirja e duhanit (f)	[pírja ɛ duhánit]
smoker	duhanpirës (m)	[duhanpírəs]
stub, butt (of cigarette)	bishti i cigares (m)	[bíʃti i tsigárɛs]
smoke, fumes	tym (m)	[tym]
ash	hi (m)	[hi]

HUMAN HABITAT

City

75. City. Life in the city

city, town	**qytet** (m)	[cytét]
capital city	**kryeqytet** (m)	[kryɛcytét]
village	**fshat** (m)	[fʃát]
city map	**hartë e qytetit** (f)	[hártə ɛ cytétit]
downtown	**qendër e qytetit** (f)	[céndər ɛ cytétit]
suburb	**periferi** (f)	[pɛrifɛrí]
suburban (adj)	**periferik**	[pɛrifɛrík]
outskirts	**periferia** (f)	[pɛrifɛría]
environs (suburbs)	**periferia** (f)	[pɛrifɛría]
city block	**bllok pallatesh** (m)	[bɫók paɫátɛʃ]
residential block (area)	**bllok banimi** (m)	[bɫók baními]
traffic	**trafik** (m)	[trafík]
traffic lights	**semafor** (m)	[sɛmafór]
public transportation	**transport publik** (m)	[transpórt publík]
intersection	**kryqëzim** (m)	[krycəzím]
crosswalk	**kalim për këmbësorë** (m)	[kalím pər kəmbəsórə]
pedestrian underpass	**nënkalim për këmbësorë** (m)	[nənkalím pər kəmbəsórə]
to cross (~ the street)	**kapërcej**	[kapərtséj]
pedestrian	**këmbësor** (m)	[kəmbəsór]
sidewalk	**trotuar** (m)	[trotuár]
bridge	**urë** (f)	[úrə]
embankment (river walk)	**breg lumi** (m)	[brɛg lúmi]
fountain	**shatërvan** (m)	[ʃatərván]
allée (garden walkway)	**rrugëz** (m)	[rúgəz]
park	**park** (m)	[park]
boulevard	**bulevard** (m)	[bulɛvárd]
square	**shesh** (m)	[ʃɛʃ]
avenue (wide street)	**bulevard** (m)	[bulɛvárd]
street	**rrugë** (f)	[rúgə]
side street	**rrugë dytësore** (f)	[rúgə dytəsórɛ]
dead end	**rrugë pa krye** (f)	[rúgə pa krýɛ]
house	**shtëpi** (f)	[ʃtəpí]

| building | ndërtesë (f) | [ndərtésə] |
| skyscraper | qiellgërvishtës (m) | [ciɛɫgərvíʃtəs] |

facade	fasadë (f)	[fasádə]
roof	çati (f)	[tʃatí]
window	dritare (f)	[dritárɛ]
arch	hark (m)	[hárk]
column	kolonë (f)	[kolónə]
corner	kënd (m)	[kénd]

store window	vitrinë (f)	[vitrínə]
signboard (store sign, etc.)	tabelë (f)	[tabélə]
poster (e.g., playbill)	poster (m)	[postér]
advertising poster	afishe reklamuese (f)	[afíʃɛ rɛklamúɛsɛ]
billboard	tabelë reklamash (f)	[tabélə rɛklámaʃ]

garbage, trash	plehra (f)	[pléhra]
trash can (public ~)	kosh plehrash (m)	[koʃ pléhraʃ]
to litter (vi)	hedh mbeturina	[hɛð mbɛturína]
garbage dump	deponi plehrash (f)	[dɛponí pléhraʃ]

phone booth	kabinë telefonike (f)	[kabínə tɛlɛfoníkɛ]
lamppost	shtyllë dritash (f)	[ʃtýɬə drítaʃ]
bench (park ~)	stol (m)	[stol]

police officer	polic (m)	[políts]
police	polici (f)	[politsí]
beggar	lypës (m)	[lýpəs]
homeless (n)	i pastrehë (m)	[i pastréhə]

76. Urban institutions

store	dyqan (m)	[dycán]
drugstore, pharmacy	farmaci (f)	[farmatsí]
eyeglass store	optikë (f)	[optíkə]
shopping mall	qendër tregtare (f)	[céndər trɛgtárɛ]
supermarket	supermarket (m)	[supɛrmarkét]

bakery	furrë (f)	[fúrə]
baker	furrtar (m)	[furtár]
pastry shop	pastiçeri (f)	[pastitʃɛrí]
grocery store	dyqan ushqimor (m)	[dycán uʃcimór]
butcher shop	dyqan mishi (m)	[dycán míʃi]

| produce store | dyqan fruta-perimesh (m) | [dycán frúta-perímɛʃ] |
| market | treg (m) | [trɛg] |

coffee house	kafene (f)	[kafɛné]
restaurant	restorant (m)	[rɛstoránt]
pub, bar	pab (m), pijetore (f)	[pab], [pijɛtórɛ]

pizzeria	**piceri** (f)	[pitsɛrí]
hair salon	**parukeri** (f)	[parukɛrí]
post office	**zyrë postare** (f)	[zýrə postárɛ]
dry cleaners	**pastrim kimik** (m)	[pastrím kimík]
photo studio	**studio fotografike** (f)	[stúdio fotografíkɛ]

shoe store	**dyqan këpucësh** (m)	[dycán kəpútsəʃ]
bookstore	**librari** (f)	[librarí]
sporting goods store	**dyqan me mallra sportivë** (m)	[dycán mɛ máɫra sportívə]

clothes repair shop	**rrobaqepësi** (f)	[robacɛpəsí]
formal wear rental	**dyqan veshjesh me qira** (m)	[dycán véʃjɛʃ mɛ cirá]
video rental store	**dyqan videosh me qira** (m)	[dycán vídɛoʃ mɛ cirá]

circus	**cirk** (m)	[tsírk]
zoo	**kopsht zoologjik** (m)	[kópʃt zooloɟík]
movie theater	**kinema** (f)	[kinɛmá]
museum	**muze** (m)	[muzé]
library	**bibliotekë** (f)	[bibliotékə]

theater	**teatër** (m)	[tɛátər]
opera (opera house)	**opera** (f)	[opéra]
nightclub	**klub nate** (m)	[klúb nátɛ]
casino	**kazino** (f)	[kazíno]

mosque	**xhami** (f)	[dʒamí]
synagogue	**sinagogë** (f)	[sinagógə]
cathedral	**katedrale** (f)	[katɛdrálɛ]
temple	**tempull** (m)	[témpuɫ]
church	**kishë** (f)	[kíʃə]

college	**kolegj** (m)	[koléɟ]
university	**universitet** (m)	[univɛrsitét]
school	**shkollë** (f)	[ʃkóɫə]

prefecture	**prefekturë** (f)	[prɛfɛktúrə]
city hall	**bashki** (f)	[baʃkí]
hotel	**hotel** (m)	[hotél]
bank	**bankë** (f)	[bánkə]

embassy	**ambasadë** (f)	[ambasádə]
travel agency	**agjenci udhëtimesh** (f)	[aɟentsí uðətímɛʃ]
information office	**zyrë informacioni** (f)	[zýrə informatsióni]
currency exchange	**këmbim valutor** (m)	[kəmbím valutór]

subway	**metro** (f)	[mɛtró]
hospital	**spital** (m)	[spitál]
gas station	**pikë karburanti** (f)	[píkə karburánti]
parking lot	**parking** (m)	[parkíŋ]

77. Urban transportation

bus	autobus (m)	[autobús]
streetcar	tramvaj (m)	[tramváj]
trolley bus	autobus tramvaj (m)	[autobús tramváj]
route (of bus, etc.)	itinerar (m)	[itinɛrár]
number (e.g., bus ~)	numër (m)	[númər]
to go by ...	udhëtoj me ...	[uðətój mɛ ...]
to get on (~ the bus)	hip	[hip]
to get off ...	zbres ...	[zbrɛs ...]
stop (e.g., bus ~)	stacion (m)	[statsión]
next stop	stacioni tjetër (m)	[statsióni tjétər]
terminus	terminal (m)	[tɛrminál]
schedule	orar (m)	[orár]
to wait (vt)	pres	[prɛs]
ticket	biletë (f)	[bilétə]
fare	çmim bilete (m)	[tʃmím bilétɛ]
cashier (ticket seller)	shitës biletash (m)	[ʃítəs bilétaʃ]
ticket inspection	kontroll biletash (m)	[kontróɫ bilétaʃ]
ticket inspector	kontrollues biletash (m)	[kontroɫúɛs bilétaʃ]
to be late (for ...)	vonohem	[vonóhɛm]
to miss (~ the train, etc.)	humbas	[humbás]
to be in a hurry	nxitoj	[ndzitój]
taxi, cab	taksi (m)	[táksi]
taxi driver	shofer taksie (m)	[ʃofér taksíɛ]
by taxi	me taksi	[mɛ táksi]
taxi stand	stacion taksish (m)	[statsión táksiʃ]
to call a taxi	thërras taksi	[θərás táksi]
to take a taxi	marr taksi	[mar táksi]
traffic	trafik (m)	[trafík]
traffic jam	bllokim trafiku (m)	[bɫokím trafíku]
rush hour	orë e trafikut të rëndë (f)	[órə ɛ trafíkut tə rəndə]
to park (vi)	parkoj	[parkój]
to park (vt)	parkim	[parkím]
parking lot	parking (m)	[parkíŋ]
subway	metro (f)	[mɛtró]
station	stacion (m)	[statsión]
to take the subway	shkoj me metro	[ʃkoj mɛ métro]
train	tren (m)	[trɛn]
train station	stacion treni (m)	[statsión tréni]

78. Sightseeing

monument	monument (m)	[monumént]
fortress	kala (f)	[kalá]
palace	pallat (m)	[pałát]
castle	kështjellë (f)	[kəʃtjétə]
tower	kullë (f)	[kútə]
mausoleum	mauzoleum (m)	[mauzolɛúm]
architecture	arkitekturë (f)	[arkitɛktúrə]
medieval (adj)	mesjetare	[mɛsjɛtárɛ]
ancient (adj)	e lashtë	[ɛ láʃtə]
national (adj)	kombëtare	[kombətárɛ]
famous (monument, etc.)	i famshëm	[i fámʃəm]
tourist	turist (m)	[turíst]
guide (person)	udhërrëfyes (m)	[uðərəfýɛs]
excursion, sightseeing tour	ekskursion (m)	[ɛkskursión]
to show (vt)	tregoj	[trɛgój]
to tell (vt)	dëftoj	[dəftój]
to find (vt)	gjej	[ɟéj]
to get lost (lose one's way)	humbas	[humbás]
map (e.g., subway ~)	hartë (f)	[hártə]
map (e.g., city ~)	hartë (f)	[hártə]
souvenir, gift	suvenir (m)	[suvɛnír]
gift shop	dyqan dhuratash (m)	[dycán ðurátaʃ]
to take pictures	bëj foto	[bəj fóto]
to have one's picture taken	bëj fotografi	[bəj fotografí]

79. Shopping

to buy (purchase)	blej	[blɛj]
purchase	blerje (f)	[blérjɛ]
to go shopping	shkoj për pazar	[ʃkoj pər pazár]
shopping	pazar (m)	[pazár]
to be open (ab. store)	hapur	[hápur]
to be closed	mbyllur	[mbýtur]
footwear, shoes	këpucë (f)	[kəpútsə]
clothes, clothing	veshje (f)	[véʃjɛ]
cosmetics	kozmetikë (f)	[kozmɛtíkə]
food products	mallra ushqimore (f)	[mátra uʃcimórɛ]
gift, present	dhuratë (f)	[ðurátə]
salesman	shitës (m)	[ʃítəs]
saleswoman	shitëse (f)	[ʃítəsɛ]

check out, cash desk	arkë (f)	[árkə]
mirror	pasqyrë (f)	[pascýrə]
counter (store ~)	banak (m)	[bának]
fitting room	dhomë prove (f)	[ðómə próvɛ]

to try on	provoj	[provój]
to fit (ab. dress, etc.)	më rri mirë	[mə ri mírə]
to like (I like ...)	pëlqej	[pəlcéj]

price	çmim (m)	[tʃmím]
price tag	etiketa e çmimit (f)	[ɛtikéta ɛ tʃmímit]
to cost (vt)	kushton	[kuʃtón]
How much?	Sa?	[sa?]
discount	ulje (f)	[úljɛ]

inexpensive (adj)	jo e shtrenjtë	[jo ɛ ʃtréɲtə]
cheap (adj)	e lirë	[ɛ lírə]
expensive (adj)	i shtrenjtë	[i ʃtréɲtə]
It's expensive	Është e shtrenjtë	[éʃtə ɛ ʃtréɲtə]

rental (n)	qiramarrje (f)	[ciramárjɛ]
to rent (~ a tuxedo)	marr me qira	[mar mɛ cirá]
credit (trade credit)	kredit (m)	[krɛdít]
on credit (adv)	me kredi	[mɛ krɛdí]

80. Money

money	para (f)	[pará]
currency exchange	këmbim valutor (m)	[kəmbím valutór]
exchange rate	kurs këmbimi (m)	[kurs kəmbími]
ATM	bankomat (m)	[bankomát]
coin	monedhë (f)	[monéðə]

| dollar | dollar (m) | [doɫár] |
| euro | euro (f) | [éuro] |

lira	lirë (f)	[lírə]
Deutschmark	Marka gjermane (f)	[márka ɟɛrmánɛ]
franc	franga (f)	[fráŋa]
pound sterling	sterlina angleze (f)	[stɛrlína aŋlézɛ]
yen	jen (m)	[jén]

debt	borxh (m)	[bórdʒ]
debtor	debitor (m)	[dɛbitór]
to lend (money)	jap hua	[jap huá]
to borrow (vi, vt)	marr hua	[mar huá]

bank	bankë (f)	[bánkə]
account	llogari (f)	[ɫogarí]
to deposit (vt)	depozitoj	[dɛpozitój]

| to deposit into the account | depozitoj në llogari | [dɛpozitój nə łogarí] |
| to withdraw (vt) | tërheq | [tərhéc] |

credit card	kartë krediti (f)	[kártə krɛdíti]
cash	kesh (m)	[kɛʃ]
check	çek (m)	[tʃɛk]
to write a check	lëshoj një çek	[ləʃój ɲə tʃék]
checkbook	bllok çeqesh (m)	[błók tʃécɛʃ]

wallet	portofol (m)	[portofól]
change purse	kuletë (f)	[kulétə]
safe	kasafortë (f)	[kasafórtə]

heir	trashëgimtar (m)	[traʃəgimtár]
inheritance	trashëgimi (f)	[traʃəgimí]
fortune (wealth)	pasuri (f)	[pasurí]

lease	qira (f)	[cirá]
rent (money)	qiraja (f)	[cirája]
to rent (sth from sb)	marr me qira	[mar mɛ cirá]

price	çmim (m)	[tʃmím]
cost	kosto (f)	[kósto]
sum	shumë (f)	[ʃúmə]

to spend (vt)	shpenzoj	[ʃpɛnzój]
expenses	shpenzime (f)	[ʃpɛnzímɛ]
to economize (vi, vt)	kursej	[kurséj]
economical	ekonomik	[ɛkonomík]

to pay (vi, vt)	paguaj	[pagúaj]
payment	pagesë (f)	[pagésə]
change (give the ~)	kusur (m)	[kusúr]

tax	taksë (f)	[táksə]
fine	gjobë (f)	[ɟóbə]
to fine (vt)	vendos gjobë	[vɛndós ɟóbə]

81. Post. Postal service

post office	zyrë postare (f)	[zýrə postárɛ]
mail (letters, etc.)	postë (f)	[póstə]
mailman	postier (m)	[postiér]
opening hours	orari i punës (m)	[orári i púnəs]

letter	letër (f)	[létər]
registered letter	letër rekomande (f)	[létər rɛkomándɛ]
postcard	kartolinë (f)	[kartolínə]
telegram	telegram (m)	[tɛlɛgrám]
package (parcel)	pako (f)	[páko]

money transfer	transfer parash (m)	[transfér paráʃ]
to receive (vt)	pranoj	[pranój]
to send (vt)	dërgoj	[dərgój]
sending	dërgesë (f)	[dərgésə]
address	adresë (f)	[adrésə]
ZIP code	kodi postar (m)	[kódi postáɾ]
sender	dërguesi (m)	[dərgúɛsi]
receiver	pranues (m)	[pranúɛs]
name (first name)	emër (m)	[émər]
surname (last name)	mbiemër (m)	[mbiémər]
postage rate	tarifë postare (f)	[tarífə postáɾɛ]
standard (adj)	standard	[standárd]
economical (adj)	ekonomike	[ɛkonomíkɛ]
weight	peshë (f)	[péʃə]
to weigh (~ letters)	peshoj	[pɛʃój]
envelope	zarf (m)	[zarf]
postage stamp	pullë postare (f)	[pútə postáɾɛ]
to stamp an envelope	vendos pullën postare	[vɛndós pútən postáɾɛ]

Dwelling. House. Home

82. House. Dwelling

house	shtëpi (f)	[ʃtəpí]
at home (adv)	në shtëpi	[nə ʃtəpí]
yard	oborr (m)	[obór]
fence (iron ~)	gardh (m)	[garð]

brick (n)	tullë (f)	[túłə]
brick (as adj)	me tulla	[mɛ túła]
stone (n)	gur (m)	[guɾ]
stone (as adj)	guror	[guɾór]
concrete (n)	çimento (f)	[tʃiménto]
concrete (as adj)	prej çimentoje	[pɾɛj tʃiméntojɛ]

new (new-built)	i ri	[i rí]
old (adj)	i vjetër	[i vjétəɾ]
decrepit (house)	e vjetruar	[ɛ vjɛtrúaɾ]
modern (adj)	moderne	[modérnɛ]
multistory (adj)	shumëkatëshe	[ʃumǝkátǝʃɛ]
tall (~ building)	e lartë	[ɛ láɾtǝ]

floor, story	kat (m)	[kat]
single-story (adj)	njëkatëshe	[ɲǝkátǝʃɛ]
1st floor	përdhese (f)	[pǝrðésɛ]
top floor	kati i fundit (m)	[káti i fúndit]

roof	çati (f)	[tʃatí]
chimney	oxhak (m)	[odʒák]

roof tiles	tjegulla (f)	[tjéguła]
tiled (adj)	me tjegulla	[mɛ tjéguła]
attic (storage place)	papafingo (f)	[papafíŋo]

window	dritare (f)	[dritárɛ]
glass	xham (m)	[dʒam]
window ledge	prag dritareje (m)	[prag dritárɛjɛ]
shutters	grila (f)	[gríła]

wall	mur (m)	[muɾ]
balcony	ballkon (m)	[bałkón]
downspout	ulluk (m)	[utúk]

upstairs (to be ~)	lart	[lart]
to go upstairs	ngjitem lart	[ɲitém láɾt]

to come down (the stairs)	zbres	[zbrɛs]
to move (to new premises)	lëviz	[ləvíz]

83. House. Entrance. Lift

entrance	hyrje (f)	[hýrjɛ]
stairs (stairway)	shkallë (f)	[ʃkátə]
steps	shkallë (f)	[ʃkátə]
banister	parmak (m)	[parmák]
lobby (hotel ~)	holl (m)	[hoɫ]

mailbox	kuti postare (f)	[kutí postárɛ]
garbage can	kazan mbeturinash (m)	[kazán mbɛturínaʃ]
trash chute	ashensor mbeturinash (m)	[aʃɛnsór mbɛturínaʃ]

elevator	ashensor (m)	[aʃɛnsór]
freight elevator	ashensor mallrash (m)	[aʃɛnsór máɫraʃ]
elevator cage	kabinë ashensori (f)	[kabínə aʃɛnsóri]
to take the elevator	marr ashensorin	[mar aʃɛnsórin]

apartment	apartament (m)	[apartamént]
residents (~ of a building)	banorë (pl)	[banórə]
neighbor (masc.)	komshi (m)	[komʃí]
neighbor (fem.)	komshike (f)	[komʃíkɛ]
neighbors	komshinj (pl)	[komʃíɲ]

84. House. Doors. Locks

door	derë (f)	[dérə]
gate (vehicle ~)	portik (m)	[portík]
handle, doorknob	dorezë (f)	[dorézə]
to unlock (unbolt)	zhbllokoj	[ʒbɫokój]
to open (vt)	hap	[hap]
to close (vt)	mbyll	[mbyɫ]

key	çelës (m)	[tʃéləs]
bunch (of keys)	tufë çelësash (f)	[túfə tʃéləsaʃ]
to creak (door, etc.)	kërcet	[kərtsét]
creak	kërcitje (f)	[kərtsítjɛ]
hinge (door ~)	menteshë (f)	[mɛntéʃə]
doormat	tapet hyrës (m)	[tapét hýrəs]

door lock	kyç (m)	[kytʃ]
keyhole	vrimë e çelësit (f)	[vrímə ɛ tʃéləsit]
crossbar (sliding bar)	shul (m)	[ʃul]
door latch	shul (m)	[ʃul]
padlock	dry (m)	[dry]

to ring (~ the door bell)	i bie ziles	[i bíɛ zílɛs]
ringing (sound)	tingulli i ziles (m)	[tíŋuɬi i zílɛs]
doorbell	zile (f)	[zílɛ]
doorbell button	çelësi i ziles (m)	[tʃéləsi i zílɛs]
knock (at the door)	trokitje (f)	[trokítjɛ]
to knock (vi)	trokas	[trokás]

code	kod (m)	[kod]
combination lock	kod (m)	[kod]
intercom	interkom (m)	[intɛrkóm]
number (on the door)	numër (m)	[númər]
doorplate	pllakë e emrit (f)	[pɬákə ɛ émrit]
peephole	vrimë përgjimi (f)	[vrímə pərɟími]

85. Country house

village	fshat (m)	[fʃát]
vegetable garden	kopsht zarzavatesh (m)	[kópʃt zarzavátɛʃ]
fence	gardh (m)	[garð]
picket fence	gardh kunjash	[garð kúɲaʃ]
wicket gate	portik (m)	[portík]

granary	hambar (m)	[hambár]
root cellar	qilar (m)	[cilár]
shed (garden ~)	kasolle (f)	[kasóɬɛ]
water well	pus (m)	[pus]

stove (wood-fired ~)	sobë (f)	[sóbə]
to stoke the stove	mbush sobën	[mbúʃ sóbən]
firewood	dru për zjarr (m)	[dru pər zjár]
log (firewood)	dru (m)	[dru]

veranda	verandë (f)	[vɛrándə]
deck (terrace)	ballkon (m)	[baɬkón]
stoop (front steps)	prag i derës (m)	[prag i dérəs]
swing (hanging seat)	kolovajzë (f)	[kolovájzə]

86. Castle. Palace

castle	kështjellë (f)	[kəʃtjéɬə]
palace	pallat (m)	[paɬát]
fortress	kala (f)	[kalá]

wall (round castle)	mur rrethues (m)	[mur rɛθúɛs]
tower	kullë (f)	[kúɬə]
keep, donjon	kulla e parë (f)	[kúɬa ɛ párə]
portcullis	portë me hekura (f)	[pórtə mɛ hékura]
underground passage	nënkalim (m)	[nənkalím]

moat	kanal (m)	[kanál]
chain	zinxhir (m)	[zindʒír]
arrow loop	frëngji (f)	[frənɟí]

magnificent (adj)	e mrekullueshme	[ɛ mrɛkuɫúɛʃmɛ]
majestic (adj)	madhështore	[maðəʃtórɛ]
impregnable (adj)	e padepërtueshme	[ɛ padɛpərtúɛʃmɛ]
medieval (adj)	mesjetare	[mɛsjɛtárɛ]

87. Apartment

apartment	apartament (m)	[apartamént]
room	dhomë (f)	[ðómə]
bedroom	dhomë gjumi (f)	[ðómə ɟúmi]
dining room	dhomë ngrënie (f)	[ðómə ŋrəníɛ]
living room	dhomë ndeje (f)	[ðómə ndéjɛ]
study (home office)	dhomë pune (f)	[ðómə púnɛ]

| entry room | hyrje (f) | [hýrjɛ] |
| bathroom (room with a bath or shower) | banjo (f) | [báɲo] |

| half bath | tualet (m) | [tualét] |

ceiling	tavan (m)	[taván]
floor	dysheme (f)	[dyʃɛmé]
corner	qoshe (f)	[cóʃɛ]

88. Apartment. Cleaning

| to clean (vi, vt) | pastroj | [pastrój] |
| to put away (to stow) | vendos | [vɛndós] |

dust	pluhur (m)	[plúhur]
dusty (adj)	e pluhurosur	[ɛ pluhurósur]
to dust (vt)	marr pluhurat	[mar plúhurat]
vacuum cleaner	fshesë elektrike (f)	[fʃésə ɛlɛktríkɛ]
to vacuum (vt)	thith pluhurin	[θiθ plúhurin]

| to sweep (vi, vt) | fshij | [fʃíj] |
| sweepings | plehra (f) | [pléhra] |

| order | rregull (m) | [réguɫ] |
| disorder, mess | rrëmujë (f) | [rəmújə] |

mop	shtupë (f)	[ʃtúpə]
dust cloth	leckë (f)	[létskə]
short broom	fshesë (f)	[fʃésə]
dustpan	kaci (f)	[katsí]

89. Furniture. Interior

furniture	orendi (f)	[orɛndí]
table	tryezë (f)	[tryézə]
chair	karrige (f)	[karígɛ]
bed	shtrat (m)	[ʃtrat]
couch, sofa	divan (m)	[diván]
armchair	kolltuk (m)	[koɫtúk]
bookcase	raft librash (m)	[ráft líbraʃ]
shelf	sergjen (m)	[sɛɟén]
wardrobe	gardërobë (f)	[gardəróbə]
coat rack (wall-mounted ~)	varëse (f)	[várəsɛ]
coat stand	varëse xhaketash (f)	[várəsɛ dʒakétaʃ]
bureau, dresser	komodë (f)	[komódə]
coffee table	tryezë e ulët (f)	[tryézə ɛ úlət]
mirror	pasqyrë (f)	[pascýrə]
carpet	qilim (m)	[cilím]
rug, small carpet	tapet (m)	[tapét]
fireplace	oxhak (m)	[odʒák]
candle	qiri (m)	[círi]
candlestick	shandan (m)	[ʃandán]
drapes	perde (f)	[pérdɛ]
wallpaper	tapiceri (f)	[tapitsɛrí]
blinds (jalousie)	grila (f)	[gríla]
table lamp	llambë tavoline (f)	[ɫámbə tavolínɛ]
wall lamp (sconce)	llambadar muri (m)	[ɫambadár múri]
floor lamp	llambadar (m)	[ɫambadár]
chandelier	llambadar (m)	[ɫambadár]
leg (of chair, table)	këmbë (f)	[kə́mbə]
armrest	mbështetëse krahu (f)	[mbəʃtétəsɛ kráhu]
back (backrest)	mbështetëse (f)	[mbəʃtétəsɛ]
drawer	sirtar (m)	[sirtár]

90. Bedding

bedclothes	çarçafë (pl)	[tʃartʃáfə]
pillow	jastëk (m)	[jasték]
pillowcase	këllëf jastëku (m)	[kəɫə́f jastéku]
duvet, comforter	jorgan (m)	[jorgán]
sheet	çarçaf (m)	[tʃartʃáf]
bedspread	mbulesë (f)	[mbulésə]

91. Kitchen

kitchen	kuzhinë (f)	[kuʒínə]
gas	gaz (m)	[gaz]
gas stove (range)	sobë me gaz (f)	[sóbə mɛ gaz]
electric stove	sobë elektrike (f)	[sóbə ɛlɛktríkɛ]
oven	furrë (f)	[fúrə]
microwave oven	mikrovalë (f)	[mikroválə]
refrigerator	frigorifer (m)	[frigorifér]
freezer	frigorifer (m)	[frigorifér]
dishwasher	pjatalarëse (f)	[pjataláresɛ]
meat grinder	grirëse mishi (f)	[grírəsɛ míʃi]
juicer	shtrydhëse frutash (f)	[ʃtrýðəsɛ frútaʃ]
toaster	toster (m)	[tostér]
mixer	mikser (m)	[miksér]
coffee machine	makinë kafeje (f)	[makínə kaféjɛ]
coffee pot	kafetierë (f)	[kafɛtiérə]
coffee grinder	mulli kafeje (f)	[muɫí káfɛjɛ]
kettle	çajnik (m)	[tʃajník]
teapot	çajnik (m)	[tʃajník]
lid	kapak (m)	[kapák]
tea strainer	sitë çaji (f)	[sítə tʃáji]
spoon	lugë (f)	[lúgə]
teaspoon	lugë çaji (f)	[lúgə tʃáji]
soup spoon	lugë gjelle (f)	[lúgə ɟéɫɛ]
fork	pirun (m)	[pirún]
knife	thikë (f)	[θíkə]
tableware (dishes)	enë kuzhine (f)	[énə kuʒínɛ]
plate (dinner ~)	pjatë (f)	[pjátə]
saucer	pjatë filxhani (f)	[pjátə fildʒáni]
shot glass	potir (m)	[potír]
glass (tumbler)	gotë (f)	[gótə]
cup	filxhan (m)	[fildʒán]
sugar bowl	tas për sheqer (m)	[tas pər ʃɛcér]
salt shaker	kripore (f)	[kripórɛ]
pepper shaker	enë piperi (f)	[énə pipéri]
butter dish	pjatë gjalpi (f)	[pjátə ɟálpi]
stock pot (soup pot)	tenxhere (f)	[tɛndʒérɛ]
frying pan (skillet)	tigan (m)	[tigán]
ladle	garuzhdë (f)	[garúʒdə]
colander	kullesë (f)	[kuɫésə]
tray (serving ~)	tabaka (f)	[tabaká]

bottle	shishe (f)	[ʃíʃɛ]
jar (glass)	kavanoz (m)	[kavanóz]
can	kanoçe (f)	[kanótʃɛ]

bottle opener	hapëse shishesh (f)	[hapəsé ʃíʃɛʃ]
can opener	hapëse kanoçesh (f)	[hapəsé kanótʃɛʃ]
corkscrew	turjelë tapash (f)	[turjélə tápaʃ]
filter	filtër (m)	[fíltər]
to filter (vt)	filtroj	[filtrój]

| trash, garbage (food waste, etc.) | pleh (m) | [plɛh] |
| trash can (kitchen ~) | kosh plehrash (m) | [koʃ pléhraʃ] |

92. Bathroom

bathroom	banjo (f)	[báɲo]
water	ujë (m)	[újə]
faucet	rubinet (m)	[rubinét]
hot water	ujë i nxehtë (f)	[újə i ndzéhtə]
cold water	ujë i ftohtë (f)	[újə i ftóhtə]

toothpaste	pastë dhëmbësh (f)	[pástə ðə́mbəʃ]
to brush one's teeth	laj dhëmbët	[laj ðə́mbət]
toothbrush	furçë dhëmbësh (f)	[fúrtʃə ðə́mbəʃ]

to shave (vi)	rruhem	[rúhɛm]
shaving foam	shkumë rroje (f)	[ʃkumə rójɛ]
razor	brisk (m)	[brísk]

to wash (one's hands, etc.)	laj duart	[laj dúart]
to take a bath	lahem	[láhɛm]
shower	dush (m)	[duʃ]
to take a shower	bëj dush	[bəj dúʃ]
bathtub	vaskë (f)	[váskə]
toilet (toilet bowl)	tualet (m)	[tualét]
sink (washbasin)	lavaman (m)	[lavamán]

| soap | sapun (m) | [sapún] |
| soap dish | pjatë sapuni (f) | [pjátə sapúni] |

sponge	sfungjer (m)	[sfunɟér]
shampoo	shampo (f)	[ʃampó]
towel	peshqir (m)	[pɛʃcír]
bathrobe	peshqir trupi (m)	[pɛʃcír trúpi]

laundry (laundering)	larje (f)	[lárjɛ]
washing machine	makinë larëse (f)	[makínə lárəsɛ]
to do the laundry	laj rroba	[laj róba]
laundry detergent	detergjent (m)	[dɛtɛrɟént]

93. Household appliances

TV set	televizor (m)	[tɛlɛvizór]
tape recorder	inçizues me shirit (m)	[intʃizúɛs mɛ ʃirít]
VCR (video recorder)	video regjistrues (m)	[vídɛo rɛɟistrúɛs]
radio	radio (f)	[rádio]
player (CD, MP3, etc.)	kasetofon (m)	[kasɛtofón]
video projector	projektor (m)	[projɛktór]
home movie theater	kinema shtëpie (f)	[kinɛmá ʃtəpíɛ]
DVD player	DVD player (m)	[dividí plɛjər]
amplifier	amplifikator (m)	[amplifikatór]
video game console	konsol video loje (m)	[konsól vídɛo lójɛ]
video camera	videokamerë (f)	[vidɛokamérə]
camera (photo)	aparat fotografik (m)	[aparát fotografík]
digital camera	kamerë digjitale (f)	[kamérə diɟitálɛ]
vacuum cleaner	fshesë elektrike (f)	[fʃésə ɛlɛktríkɛ]
iron (e.g., steam ~)	hekur (m)	[hékur]
ironing board	tryezë për hekurosje (f)	[tryézə pər hɛkurósjɛ]
telephone	telefon (m)	[tɛlɛfón]
cell phone	celular (m)	[tsɛlulár]
typewriter	makinë shkrimi (f)	[makínə ʃkrími]
sewing machine	makinë qepëse (f)	[makínə cépəsɛ]
microphone	mikrofon (m)	[mikrofón]
headphones	kufje (f)	[kúfjɛ]
remote control (TV)	telekomandë (f)	[tɛlɛkomándə]
CD, compact disc	CD (f)	[tsɛdé]
cassette, tape	kasetë (f)	[kasétə]
vinyl record	pllakë gramafoni (f)	[pɬákə gramafóni]

94. Repairs. Renovation

renovations	renovim (m)	[rɛnovím]
to renovate (vt)	rinovoj	[rinovój]
to repair, to fix (vt)	riparoj	[riparój]
to put in order	rregulloj	[rɛguɬój]
to redo (do again)	ribëj	[ribéj]
paint	bojë (f)	[bójə]
to paint (~ a wall)	lyej	[lýɛj]
house painter	bojaxhi (m)	[bojadʒí]
paintbrush	furçë (f)	[fúrtʃə]
whitewash	gëlqere (f)	[gəlcérɛ]
to whitewash (vt)	lyej me gëlqere	[lýɛj mɛ gəlcérɛ]

wallpaper	tapiceri (f)	[tapitsɛrí]
to wallpaper (vt)	vendos tapiceri	[vɛndós tapitsɛrí]
varnish	llak (m)	[ɫak]
to varnish (vt)	lustroj	[lustrój]

95. Plumbing

water	ujë (m)	[újə]
hot water	ujë i nxehtë (f)	[újə i ndzéhtə]
cold water	ujë i ftohtë (f)	[újə i ftóhtə]
faucet	rubinet (m)	[rubinét]

drop (of water)	pikë uji (f)	[píkə úji]
to drip (vi)	pikon	[pikón]
to leak (ab. pipe)	rrjedh	[rjéð]
leak (pipe ~)	rrjedhje (f)	[rjéðjɛ]
puddle	pellg (m)	[pɛɫg]

pipe	gyp (m)	[gyp]
valve (e.g., ball ~)	valvulë (f)	[valvúlə]
to be clogged up	bllokohet	[bɫokóhɛt]

tools	vegla (pl)	[végla]
adjustable wrench	çelës anglez (m)	[tʃéləs aŋléz]
to unscrew (lid, filter, etc.)	zhvidhos	[ʒviðós]
to screw (tighten)	vidhos	[viðós]

to unclog (vt)	zhbllokoj	[ʒbɫokój]
plumber	hidraulik (m)	[hidraulík]
basement	qilar (m)	[cilár]
sewerage (system)	kanalizim (m)	[kanalizím]

96. Fire. Conflagration

fire (accident)	zjarr (m)	[zjar]
flame	flakë (f)	[flákə]
spark	shkëndijë (f)	[ʃkəndíjə]
smoke (from fire)	tym (m)	[tym]
torch (flaming stick)	pishtar (m)	[piʃtár]
campfire	zjarr kampingu (m)	[zjar kampíŋu]

gas, gasoline	benzinë (f)	[bɛnzínə]
kerosene (type of fuel)	vajgur (m)	[vajgúr]
flammable (adj)	djegëse	[djégəsɛ]
explosive (adj)	shpërthyese	[ʃpərθýɛsɛ]
NO SMOKING	NDALOHET DUHANI	[ndalóhɛt duháni]
safety	siguri (f)	[sigurí]
danger	rrezik (m)	[rɛzík]

98

dangerous (adj)	**i rrezikshëm**	[i rɛzíkʃəm]
to catch fire	**merr flakë**	[mɛr flákə]
explosion	**shpërthim** (m)	[ʃpərθím]
to set fire	**vë flakën**	[və flákən]
arsonist	**zjarrvënës** (m)	[zjarvénəs]
arson	**zjarrvënie e qëllimshme** (f)	[zjarvéniɛ ɛ cətímʃmɛ]
to blaze (vi)	**flakëron**	[flakərón]
to burn (be on fire)	**digjet**	[díɟɛt]
to burn down	**u dogj**	[u doɟ]
to call the fire department	**telefonoj zjarrfikësit**	[tɛlɛfonój zjarfíkəsit]
firefighter, fireman	**zjarrfikës** (m)	[zjarfíkəs]
fire truck	**kamion zjarrfikës** (m)	[kamión zjarfíkəs]
fire department	**zjarrfikës** (m)	[zjarfíkəs]
fire truck ladder	**shkallë e zjarrfikëses** (f)	[ʃkáłə ɛ zjarfíkəsɛs]
fire hose	**pompë e ujit** (f)	[pómpə ɛ újit]
fire extinguisher	**bombolë kundër zjarrit** (f)	[bombólə kúndər zjárit]
helmet	**helmetë** (f)	[hɛlmétə]
siren	**alarm** (m)	[alárm]
to cry (for help)	**bërtas**	[bərtás]
to call for help	**thërras për ndihmë**	[θərás pər ndíhmə]
rescuer	**shpëtimtar** (m)	[ʃpətimtár]
to rescue (vt)	**shpëtoj**	[ʃpətój]
to arrive (vi)	**arrij**	[aríj]
to extinguish (vt)	**shuaj**	[ʃúaj]
water	**ujë** (m)	[újə]
sand	**rërë** (f)	[rérə]
ruins (destruction)	**gërmadhë** (f)	[gərmáðə]
to collapse (building, etc.)	**shembet**	[ʃémbɛt]
to fall down (vi)	**rrëzohem**	[rəzóhɛm]
to cave in (ceiling, floor)	**shembet**	[ʃémbɛt]
piece of debris	**mbetje** (f)	[mbétjɛ]
ash	**hi** (m)	[hi]
to suffocate (die)	**asfiksim**	[asfiksím]
to be killed (perish)	**vdes**	[vdɛs]

HUMAN ACTIVITIES

Job. Business. Part 1

97. Banking

bank	**bankë** (f)	[bánkə]
branch (of bank, etc.)	**degë** (f)	[dégə]
bank clerk, consultant	**punonjës banke** (m)	[punóɲəs bánkɛ]
manager (director)	**drejtor** (m)	[drɛjtór]
bank account	**llogari bankare** (f)	[ɫogarí bankárɛ]
account number	**numër llogarie** (m)	[númər ɫogaríɛ]
checking account	**llogari rrjedhëse** (f)	[ɫogarí rjéðəsɛ]
savings account	**llogari kursimesh** (f)	[ɫogarí kursímɛʃ]
to open an account	**hap një llogari**	[hap ɲə ɫogarí]
to close the account	**mbyll një llogari**	[mbýɫ ɲə ɫogarí]
to deposit into the account	**depozitoj në llogari**	[dɛpozitój nə ɫogarí]
to withdraw (vt)	**tërheq**	[tərhéc]
deposit	**depozitë** (f)	[dɛpozítə]
to make a deposit	**kryej një depozitim**	[krýɛj ɲə dɛpozitím]
wire transfer	**transfer bankar** (m)	[transfér bankár]
to wire, to transfer	**transferoj para**	[transfɛrój pará]
sum	**shumë** (f)	[ʃúmə]
How much?	**Sa?**	[sa?]
signature	**nënshkrim** (m)	[nənʃkrím]
to sign (vt)	**nënshkruaj**	[nənʃkrúaj]
credit card	**kartë krediti** (f)	[kártə krɛdíti]
code (PIN code)	**kodi PIN** (m)	[kódi pin]
credit card number	**numri i kartës**	[númri i kártəs
	së kreditit (m)	sə krɛdítit]
ATM	**bankomat** (m)	[bankomát]
check	**çek** (m)	[tʃɛk]
to write a check	**lëshoj një çek**	[ləʃój ɲə tʃék]
checkbook	**bllok çeqesh** (m)	[bɫók tʃécɛʃ]
loan (bank ~)	**kredi** (f)	[krɛdí]
to apply for a loan	**aplikoj për kredi**	[aplikój pər krɛdí]

to get a loan	marr kredi	[mar krɛdí]
to give a loan	jap kredi	[jap krɛdí]
guarantee	garanci (f)	[garantsí]

98. Telephone. Phone conversation

telephone	telefon (m)	[tɛlɛfón]
cell phone	celular (m)	[tsɛlulár]
answering machine	sekretari telefonike (f)	[sɛkrɛtarí tɛlɛfoníkɛ]

| to call (by phone) | telefonoj | [tɛlɛfonój] |
| phone call | telefonatë (f) | [tɛlɛfonátə] |

to dial a number	i bie numrit	[i bíɛ númrit]
Hello!	Përshëndetje!	[pərʃəndétjɛ!]
to ask (vt)	pyes	[pýɛs]
to answer (vi, vt)	përgjigjem	[pərɟíɟɛm]

to hear (vt)	dëgjoj	[dəɟój]
well (adv)	mirë	[mírə]
not well (adv)	jo mirë	[jo mírə]
noises (interference)	zhurmë (f)	[ʒúrmə]

receiver	marrës (m)	[márəs]
to pick up (~ the phone)	ngre telefonin	[ŋré tɛlɛfónin]
to hang up (~ the phone)	mbyll telefonin	[mbýɫ tɛlɛfónin]

busy (engaged)	i zënë	[i zénə]
to ring (ab. phone)	bie zilja	[bíɛ zílja]
telephone book	numerator telefonik (m)	[numɛratór tɛlɛfoník]

local (adj)	lokale	[lokálɛ]
local call	thirrje lokale (f)	[θírjɛ lokálɛ]
long distance (~ call)	distancë e largët	[distántsə ɛ lárgət]
long-distance call	thirrje në distancë (f)	[θírjɛ nə distántsə]
international (adj)	ndërkombëtar	[ndərkombətár]
international call	thirrje ndërkombëtare (f)	[θírjɛ ndərkombətárɛ]

99. Cell phone

cell phone	celular (m)	[tsɛlulár]
display	ekran (m)	[ɛkrán]
button	buton (m)	[butón]
SIM card	karta SIM (m)	[kárta sim]

battery	bateri (f)	[batɛrí]
to be dead (battery)	e shkarkuar	[ɛ ʃkarkúar]
charger	karikues (m)	[karikúɛs]

menu	menu (f)	[mɛnú]
settings	parametra (f)	[paramétra]
tune (melody)	melodi (f)	[mɛlodí]
to select (vt)	përzgjedh	[pərzɟéð]

calculator	makinë llogaritëse (f)	[makínə ɬogarítəsɛ]
voice mail	postë zanore (f)	[póstə zanórɛ]
alarm clock	alarm (m)	[alárm]
contacts	kontakte (pl)	[kontáktɛ]

| SMS (text message) | SMS (m) | [ɛsɛmɛs] |
| subscriber | abonent (m) | [abonént] |

100. Stationery

| ballpoint pen | stilolaps (m) | [stiloláps] |
| fountain pen | stilograf (m) | [stilográf] |

pencil	laps (m)	[láps]
highlighter	shënjues (m)	[ʃəɲúɛs]
felt-tip pen	tushë me bojë (f)	[túʃə mɛ bójə]

| notepad | bllok shënimesh (m) | [bɬók ʃənímɛʃ] |
| agenda (diary) | agjendë (f) | [aɟéndə] |

ruler	vizore (f)	[vizórɛ]
calculator	makinë llogaritëse (f)	[makínə ɬogarítəsɛ]
eraser	gomë (f)	[gómə]
thumbtack	pineskë (f)	[pinéskə]
paper clip	kapëse fletësh (f)	[kápəsɛ flétəʃ]

glue	ngjitës (m)	[ɲítəs]
stapler	ngjitës metalik (m)	[ɲítəs mɛtalík]
hole punch	hapës vrimash (m)	[hápəs vrímaʃ]
pencil sharpener	mprehëse lapsash (m)	[mpréhəsɛ lápsaʃ]

Job. Business. Part 2

101. Mass Media

newspaper	gazetë (f)	[gazétə]
magazine	revistë (f)	[rɛvístə]
press (printed media)	shtyp (m)	[ʃtyp]
radio	radio (f)	[rádio]
radio station	radio stacion (m)	[rádio statsión]
television	televizor (m)	[tɛlɛvizór]
presenter, host	prezantues (m)	[prɛzantúɛs]
newscaster	prezantues lajmesh (m)	[prɛzantúɛs lájmɛʃ]
commentator	komentues (m)	[komɛntúɛs]
journalist	gazetar (m)	[gazɛtár]
correspondent (reporter)	reporter (m)	[rɛportér]
press photographer	fotograf gazetar (m)	[fotográf gazɛtár]
reporter	reporter (m)	[rɛportér]
editor	redaktor (m)	[rɛdaktór]
editor-in-chief	kryeredaktor (m)	[kryɛrɛdaktór]
to subscribe (to …)	abonohem	[abonóhɛm]
subscription	abonim (m)	[aboním]
subscriber	abonent (m)	[abonént]
to read (vi, vt)	lexoj	[lɛdzój]
reader	lexues (m)	[lɛdzúɛs]
circulation (of newspaper)	qarkullim (m)	[carkułím]
monthly (adj)	mujore	[mujórɛ]
weekly (adj)	javor	[javór]
issue (edition)	edicion (m)	[ɛditsión]
new (~ issue)	i ri	[i rí]
headline	kryeradhë (f)	[kryɛráðə]
short article	artikull i shkurtër (m)	[artíkuł i ʃkúrtər]
column (regular article)	rubrikë (f)	[rubríkə]
article	artikull (m)	[artíkuł]
page	faqe (f)	[fácɛ]
reportage, report	reportazh (m)	[rɛportáʒ]
event (happening)	ceremoni (f)	[tsɛrɛmoní]
sensation (news)	ndjesi (f)	[ndjɛsí]
scandal	skandal (m)	[skandál]
scandalous (adj)	skandaloz	[skandalóz]

great (~ scandal)	i madh	[i máð]
show (e.g., cooking ~)	emision (m)	[ɛmisión]
interview	intervistë (f)	[intɛrvístə]
live broadcast	lidhje direkte (f)	[líðjɛ diréktɛ]
channel	kanal (m)	[kanál]

102. Agriculture

agriculture	agrikulturë (f)	[agrikultúrə]
peasant (masc.)	fshatar (m)	[fʃatár]
peasant (fem.)	fshatare (f)	[fʃatárɛ]
farmer	fermer (m)	[fɛrmér]

tractor (farm ~)	traktor (m)	[traktór]
combine, harvester	autokombajnë (f)	[autokombájnə]

plow	plug (m)	[plug]
to plow (vi, vt)	lëroj	[lərój]
plowland	tokë bujqësore (f)	[tókə bujcəsórɛ]
furrow (in field)	brazdë (f)	[brázdə]

to sow (vi, vt)	mbjell	[mbjéɫ]
seeder	mbjellës (m)	[mbjéɫəs]
sowing (process)	mbjellje (f)	[mbjéɫjɛ]

scythe	kosë (f)	[kósə]
to mow, to scythe	kosit	[kosít]

spade (tool)	lopatë (f)	[lopátə]
to till (vt)	lëroj	[lərój]

hoe	shat (m)	[ʃat]
to hoe, to weed	prashis	[praʃís]
weed (plant)	bar i keq (m)	[bar i kɛc]

watering can	vaditës (m)	[vadítəs]
to water (plants)	ujis	[ujís]
watering (act)	vaditje (f)	[vadítjɛ]

pitchfork	sfurk (m)	[sfúrk]
rake	grabujë (f)	[grabújə]

fertilizer	pleh (m)	[plɛh]
to fertilize (vt)	hedh pleh	[hɛð pléh]
manure (fertilizer)	pleh kafshësh (m)	[plɛh káfʃəʃ]

field	fushë (f)	[fúʃə]
meadow	lëndinë (f)	[ləndínə]
vegetable garden	kopsht zarzavatesh (m)	[kópʃt zarzavátɛʃ]
orchard (e.g., apple ~)	kopsht frutor (m)	[kópʃt frutór]

to graze (vt)	**kullos**	[kuɫós]
herder (herdsman)	**bari** (m)	[barí]
pasture	**kullota** (f)	[kuɫóta]
cattle breeding	**mbarështim bagëtish** (m)	[mbarəʃtím bagətíʃ]
sheep farming	**rritje e deleve** (f)	[rítjɛ ɛ délɛvɛ]
plantation	**plantacion** (m)	[plantatsión]
row (garden bed ~s)	**rresht** (m)	[réʃt]
hothouse	**serë** (f)	[sérə]
drought (lack of rain)	**thatësirë** (f)	[θatəsírə]
dry (~ summer)	**e thatë**	[ɛ θátə]
grain	**drithë** (m)	[dríθə]
cereal crops	**drithëra** (pl)	[dríθəra]
to harvest, to gather	**korr**	[kor]
miller (person)	**mullixhi** (m)	[muɫidʒí]
mill (e.g., gristmill)	**mulli** (m)	[muɫí]
to grind (grain)	**bluaj**	[blúaj]
flour	**miell** (m)	[míɛɫ]
straw	**kashtë** (f)	[káʃtə]

103. Building. Building process

construction site	**kantier ndërtimi** (m)	[kantiér ndərtími]
to build (vt)	**ndërtoj**	[ndərtój]
construction worker	**punëtor ndërtimi** (m)	[punətór ndərtími]
project	**projekt** (m)	[projékt]
architect	**arkitekt** (m)	[arkitékt]
worker	**punëtor** (m)	[punətór]
foundation (of a building)	**themel** (m)	[θɛmél]
roof	**çati** (f)	[tʃatí]
foundation pile	**shtyllë themeli** (f)	[ʃtýɫə θɛméli]
wall	**mur** (m)	[mur]
reinforcing bars	**shufra përforcuese** (pl)	[ʃúfra pərfortsúɛsɛ]
scaffolding	**skela** (f)	[skéla]
concrete	**beton** (m)	[bɛtón]
granite	**granit** (m)	[granít]
stone	**gur** (m)	[gur]
brick	**tullë** (f)	[túɫə]
sand	**rërë** (f)	[rérə]
cement	**çimento** (f)	[tʃiménto]
plaster (for walls)	**suva** (f)	[súva]

to plaster (vt)	suvatoj	[suvatój]
paint	bojë (f)	[bójə]
to paint (~ a wall)	lyej	[lýɛj]
barrel	fuçi (f)	[futʃí]

crane	vinç (m)	[vintʃ]
to lift, to hoist (vt)	ngreh	[ŋréh]
to lower (vt)	ul	[ul]

bulldozer	buldozer (m)	[buldozér]
excavator	ekskavator (m)	[ɛkskavatór]
scoop, bucket	goja e ekskavatorit (f)	[gója ɛ ɛkskavatórit]
to dig (excavate)	gërmoj	[gərmój]
hard hat	helmetë (f)	[hɛlmétə]

Professions and occupations

104. Job search. Dismissal

job	punë (f)	[púnə]
staff (work force)	staf (m)	[staf]
personnel	personel (m)	[pɛrsonél]
career	karrierë (f)	[kariérə]
prospects (chances)	mundësi (f)	[mundəsí]
skills (mastery)	aftësi (f)	[aftəsí]
selection (screening)	përzgjedhje (f)	[pərzɟéðjɛ]
employment agency	agjenci punësimi (f)	[aɟɛntsí punəsími]
résumé	resume (f)	[rɛsumé]
job interview	intervistë punësimi (f)	[intɛrvístə punəsími]
vacancy, opening	vend i lirë pune (m)	[vɛnd i lírə púnɛ]
salary, pay	rrogë (f)	[rógə]
fixed salary	rrogë fikse (f)	[rógə fíksɛ]
pay, compensation	pagesë (f)	[pagésə]
position (job)	post (m)	[post]
duty (of employee)	detyrë (f)	[dɛtýrə]
range of duties	lista e detyrave (f)	[lísta ɛ dɛtýravɛ]
busy (I'm ~)	i zënë	[i zénə]
to fire (dismiss)	pushoj nga puna	[puʃój ŋa púna]
dismissal	pushim nga puna (m)	[puʃím ŋa púna]
unemployment	papunësi (m)	[papunəsí]
unemployed (n)	i papunë (m)	[i papúnə]
retirement	pension (m)	[pɛnsión]
to retire (from job)	dal në pension	[dál nə pɛnsión]

105. Business people

director	drejtor (m)	[drɛjtór]
manager (director)	drejtor (m)	[drɛjtór]
boss	bos (m)	[bos]
superior	epror (m)	[ɛprór]
superiors	eprorët (pl)	[ɛprórət]
president	president (m)	[prɛsidént]

chairman	kryetar (m)	[kryɛtár]
deputy (substitute)	zëvendës (m)	[zəvéndəs]
assistant	ndihmës (m)	[ndíhməs]
secretary	sekretar (m)	[sɛkrɛtár]
personal assistant	ndihmës personal (m)	[ndíhməs pɛrsonál]

businessman	biznesmen (m)	[biznɛsmén]
entrepreneur	sipërmarrës (m)	[sipərmárəs]
founder	themelues (m)	[θɛmɛlúɛs]
to found (vt)	themeloj	[θɛmɛlój]

incorporator	bashkëthemelues (m)	[baʃkəθɛmɛlúɛs]
partner	partner (m)	[partnér]
stockholder	aksioner (m)	[aksionér]

millionaire	milioner (m)	[milionér]
billionaire	bilioner (m)	[bilionér]
owner, proprietor	pronar (m)	[pronár]
landowner	pronar tokash (m)	[pronár tókaʃ]

client	klient (m)	[kliént]
regular client	klient i rregullt (m)	[kliént i réguɫt]
buyer (customer)	blerës (m)	[blérəs]
visitor	vizitor (m)	[vizitór]

professional (n)	profesionist (m)	[profɛsioníst]
expert	ekspert (m)	[ɛkspért]
specialist	specialist (m)	[spɛtsialíst]

| banker | bankier (m) | [bankiér] |
| broker | komisioner (m) | [komisionér] |

cashier, teller	arkëtar (m)	[arkətár]
accountant	kontabilist (m)	[kontabilíst]
security guard	roje sigurimi (m)	[rójɛ sigurími]

investor	investitor (m)	[invɛstitór]
debtor	debitor (m)	[dɛbitór]
creditor	kreditor (m)	[krɛditór]
borrower	huamarrës (m)	[huamárəs]

| importer | importues (m) | [importúɛs] |
| exporter | eksportues (m) | [ɛksportúɛs] |

manufacturer	prodhues (m)	[proðúɛs]
distributor	distributor (m)	[distributór]
middleman	ndërmjetës (m)	[ndərmjétəs]

consultant	këshilltar (m)	[kəʃiɫtár]
sales representative	përfaqësues i shitjeve (m)	[pərfacəsúɛs i ʃitjévɛ]
agent	agjent (m)	[aɟént]
insurance agent	agjent sigurimesh (m)	[aɟént sigurímɛʃ]

106. Service professions

cook	kuzhinier (m)	[kuʒiniér]
chef (kitchen chef)	shef kuzhine (m)	[ʃɛf kuʒínɛ]
baker	furrtar (m)	[furtár]
bartender	banakier (m)	[banakiér]
waiter	kamerier (m)	[kamɛriér]
waitress	kameriere (f)	[kamɛriérɛ]
lawyer, attorney	avokat (m)	[avokát]
lawyer (legal expert)	jurist (m)	[juríst]
notary public	noter (m)	[notér]
electrician	elektricist (m)	[ɛlɛktritsíst]
plumber	hidraulik (m)	[hidraulík]
carpenter	marangoz (m)	[maraŋóz]
masseur	masazhist (m)	[masaʒíst]
masseuse	masazhiste (f)	[masaʒístɛ]
doctor	mjek (m)	[mjék]
taxi driver	shofer taksie (m)	[ʃofér taksíɛ]
driver	shofer (m)	[ʃofér]
delivery man	postier (m)	[postiér]
chambermaid	pastruese (f)	[pastrúɛsɛ]
security guard	roje sigurimi (m)	[rójɛ sigurími]
flight attendant (fem.)	stjuardesë (f)	[stjuardésə]
schoolteacher	mësues (m)	[məsúɛs]
librarian	punonjës biblioteke (m)	[punóɲəs bibliotékɛ]
translator	përkthyes (m)	[pərkθýɛs]
interpreter	përkthyes (m)	[pərkθýɛs]
guide	udhërrëfyes (m)	[uðərəfýɛs]
hairdresser	parukiere (f)	[parukiérɛ]
mailman	postier (m)	[postiér]
salesman (store staff)	shitës (m)	[ʃítəs]
gardener	kopshtar (m)	[kopʃtár]
domestic servant	shërbëtor (m)	[ʃərbətór]
maid (female servant)	shërbëtore (f)	[ʃərbətórɛ]
cleaner (cleaning lady)	pastruese (f)	[pastrúɛsɛ]

107. Military professions and ranks

private	ushtar (m)	[uʃtár]
sergeant	rreshter (m)	[rɛʃtér]

lieutenant	**toger** (m)	[togér]
captain	**kapiten** (m)	[kapitén]
major	**major** (m)	[majór]
colonel	**kolonel** (m)	[kolonél]
general	**gjeneral** (m)	[ɟɛnɛrál]
marshal	**marshall** (m)	[marʃáɫ]
admiral	**admiral** (m)	[admirál]
military (n)	**ushtri** (f)	[uʃtrí]
soldier	**ushtar** (m)	[uʃtár]
officer	**oficer** (m)	[ofitsér]
commander	**komandant** (m)	[komandánt]
border guard	**roje kufiri** (m)	[rójɛ kufíri]
radio operator	**radist** (m)	[radíst]
scout (searcher)	**eksplorues** (m)	[ɛksplorúɛs]
pioneer (sapper)	**xhenier** (m)	[dʒɛniér]
marksman	**shënjues** (m)	[ʃənúɛs]
navigator	**navigues** (m)	[navigúɛs]

108. Officials. Priests

king	**mbret** (m)	[mbrét]
queen	**mbretëreshë** (f)	[mbrɛtəréʃə]
prince	**princ** (m)	[prints]
princess	**princeshë** (f)	[printséʃə]
czar	**car** (m)	[tsár]
czarina	**carina** (f)	[tsarína]
president	**president** (m)	[prɛsidént]
Secretary (minister)	**ministër** (m)	[minístər]
prime minister	**kryeministër** (m)	[kryɛminístər]
senator	**senator** (m)	[sɛnatór]
diplomat	**diplomat** (m)	[diplomát]
consul	**konsull** (m)	[kónsuɫ]
ambassador	**ambasador** (m)	[ambasadór]
counselor (diplomatic officer)	**këshilltar diplomatik** (m)	[kəʃiɫtár diplomatík]
official, functionary (civil servant)	**zyrtar** (m)	[zyrtár]
prefect	**prefekt** (m)	[prɛfékt]
mayor	**kryetar komune** (m)	[kryɛtár komúnɛ]
judge	**gjykatës** (m)	[ɟykátəs]
prosecutor (e.g., district attorney)	**prokuror** (m)	[prokurór]

missionary	misionar (m)	[misionár]
monk	murg (m)	[murg]
abbot	abat (m)	[abát]
rabbi	rabin (m)	[rabín]

vizier	vezir (m)	[vɛzír]
shah	shah (m)	[ʃah]
sheikh	sheik (m)	[ʃéik]

109. Agricultural professions

beekeeper	bletar (m)	[blɛtár]
herder, shepherd	bari (m)	[barí]
agronomist	agronom (m)	[agronóm]
cattle breeder	rritës bagëtish (m)	[rítəs bagətíʃ]
veterinarian	veteriner (m)	[vɛtɛrinér]

farmer	fermer (m)	[fɛrmér]
winemaker	prodhues verërash (m)	[proðúɛs vérəraʃ]
zoologist	zoolog (m)	[zoológ]
cowboy	lopar (m)	[lopár]

110. Art professions

| actor | aktor (m) | [aktór] |
| actress | aktore (f) | [aktórɛ] |

| singer (masc.) | këngëtar (m) | [kəŋətár] |
| singer (fem.) | këngëtare (f) | [kəŋətárɛ] |

| dancer (masc.) | valltar (m) | [vaɫtár] |
| dancer (fem.) | valltare (f) | [vaɫtárɛ] |

| performer (masc.) | artist (m) | [artíst] |
| performer (fem.) | artiste (f) | [artístɛ] |

musician	muzikant (m)	[muzikánt]
pianist	pianist (m)	[pianíst]
guitar player	kitarist (m)	[kitaríst]

conductor (orchestra ~)	dirigjent (m)	[diriɟént]
composer	kompozitor (m)	[kompozitór]
impresario	organizator (m)	[organizatór]

film director	regjisor (m)	[rɛɟisór]
producer	producent (m)	[produtsént]
scriptwriter	skenarist (m)	[skɛnaríst]
critic	kritik (m)	[kritík]

writer	shkrimtar (m)	[ʃkrimtár]
poet	poet (m)	[poét]
sculptor	skulptor (m)	[skulptór]
artist (painter)	piktor (m)	[piktór]

juggler	zhongler (m)	[ʒoŋlér]
clown	kloun (m)	[kloún]
acrobat	akrobat (m)	[akrobát]
magician	magjistar (m)	[maɟistár]

111. Various professions

doctor	mjek (m)	[mjék]
nurse	infermiere (f)	[infɛrmiéɾɛ]
psychiatrist	psikiatër (m)	[psikiátər]
dentist	dentist (m)	[dɛntíst]
surgeon	kirurg (m)	[kirúrg]

astronaut	astronaut (m)	[astronaút]
astronomer	astronom (m)	[astronóm]
pilot	pilot (m)	[pilót]

driver (of taxi, etc.)	shofer (m)	[ʃofér]
engineer (train driver)	makinist (m)	[makiníst]
mechanic	mekanik (m)	[mɛkaník]

miner	minator (m)	[minatór]
worker	punëtor (m)	[punətór]
locksmith	bravandreqës (m)	[bravandrécəs]
joiner (carpenter)	marangoz (m)	[maraŋóz]
turner (lathe operator)	tornitor (m)	[tornitór]
construction worker	punëtor ndërtimi (m)	[punətór ndərtími]
welder	saldator (m)	[saldatór]

professor (title)	profesor (m)	[profɛsór]
architect	arkitekt (m)	[arkitékt]
historian	historian (m)	[historián]
scientist	shkencëtar (m)	[ʃkɛntsətár]
physicist	fizikant (m)	[fizikánt]
chemist (scientist)	kimist (m)	[kimíst]

archeologist	arkeolog (m)	[arkɛológ]
geologist	gjeolog (m)	[ɟɛológ]
researcher (scientist)	studiues (m)	[studiúɛs]

| babysitter | dado (f) | [dádo] |
| teacher, educator | mësues (m) | [məsúɛs] |

| editor | redaktor (m) | [rɛdaktór] |
| editor-in-chief | kryeredaktor (m) | [kryɛrɛdaktór] |

| correspondent | korrespondent (m) | [korɛspondént] |
| typist (fem.) | daktilografiste (f) | [daktilografístɛ] |

designer	projektues (m)	[projɛktúɛs]
computer expert	ekspert kompjuterësh (m)	[ɛkspért kompjutérəʃ]
programmer	programues (m)	[programúɛs]
engineer (designer)	inxhinier (m)	[indʒiniér]

sailor	marinar (m)	[marinár]
seaman	marinar (m)	[marinár]
rescuer	shpëtimtar (m)	[ʃpətimtár]

fireman	zjarrfikës (m)	[zjarfíkəs]
police officer	polic (m)	[políts]
watchman	roje (f)	[rójɛ]
detective	detektiv (m)	[dɛtɛktív]

customs officer	doganier (m)	[doganiér]
bodyguard	truprojë (f)	[truprójə]
prison guard	gardian burgu (m)	[gardián búrgu]
inspector	inspektor (m)	[inspɛktór]

sportsman	sportist (m)	[sportíst]
trainer, coach	trajner (m)	[trajnér]
butcher	kasap (m)	[kasáp]
cobbler (shoe repairer)	këpucëtar (m)	[kəputsətár]
merchant	tregtar (m)	[trɛgtár]
loader (person)	ngarkues (m)	[ŋarkúɛs]

| fashion designer | stilist (m) | [stilíst] |
| model (fem.) | modele (f) | [modélɛ] |

112. Occupations. Social status

| schoolboy | nxënës (m) | [ndzɛ́nəs] |
| student (college ~) | student (m) | [studént] |

philosopher	filozof (m)	[filozóf]
economist	ekonomist (m)	[ɛkonomíst]
inventor	shpikës (m)	[ʃpíkəs]

unemployed (n)	i papunë (m)	[i papúnə]
retiree	pensionist (m)	[pɛnsioníst]
spy, secret agent	spiun (m)	[spiún]

prisoner	i burgosur (m)	[i burgósur]
striker	grevist (m)	[grɛvíst]
bureaucrat	burokrat (m)	[burokrát]
traveler (globetrotter)	udhëtar (m)	[uðətár]
gay, homosexual (n)	homoseksual (m)	[homosɛksuál]

hacker	haker (m)	[hakér]
hippie	hipik (m)	[hipík]

bandit	bandit (m)	[bandít]
hit man, killer	vrasës (m)	[vrásəs]
drug addict	narkoman (m)	[narkomán]
drug dealer	trafikant droge (m)	[trafikánt drógɛ]
prostitute (fem.)	prostitutë (f)	[prostitútə]
pimp	tutor (m)	[tutór]

sorcerer	magjistar (m)	[maɟistár]
sorceress (evil ~)	shtrigë (f)	[ʃtrígə]
pirate	pirat (m)	[pirát]
slave	skllav (m)	[skɫav]
samurai	samurai (m)	[samurái]
savage (primitive)	i egër (m)	[i égər]

Sports

113. Kinds of sports. Sportspersons

sportsman	sportist (m)	[sportíst]
kind of sports	lloj sporti (m)	[łoj spórti]
basketball	basketboll (m)	[baskɛtbół]
basketball player	basketbollist (m)	[baskɛtbołíst]
baseball	bejsboll (m)	[bɛjsbół]
baseball player	lojtar bejsbolli (m)	[lojtár bɛjsbółi]
soccer	futboll (m)	[futbół]
soccer player	futbollist (m)	[futbołíst]
goalkeeper	portier (m)	[portiér]
hockey	hokej (m)	[hokéj]
hockey player	lojtar hokeji (m)	[lojtár hokéji]
volleyball	volejboll (m)	[volɛjbół]
volleyball player	volejbollist (m)	[volɛjbołíst]
boxing	boks (m)	[boks]
boxer	boksier (m)	[boksiér]
wrestling	mundje (f)	[múndjɛ]
wrestler	mundës (m)	[múndəs]
karate	karate (f)	[karátɛ]
karate fighter	karateist (m)	[karatɛíst]
judo	xhudo (f)	[dʒúdo]
judo athlete	xhudist (m)	[dʒudíst]
tennis	tenis (m)	[tɛnís]
tennis player	tenist (m)	[tɛníst]
swimming	not (m)	[not]
swimmer	notar (m)	[notár]
fencing	skerma (f)	[skérma]
fencer	skermist (m)	[skɛrmíst]
chess	shah (m)	[ʃah]
chess player	shahist (m)	[ʃahíst]

alpinism	alpinizëm (m)	[alpinízəm]
alpinist	alpinist (m)	[alpiníst]
running	vrapim (m)	[vrapím]
runner	vrapues (m)	[vrapúɛs]
athletics	atletikë (f)	[atlɛtíkə]
athlete	atlet (m)	[atlét]
horseback riding	kalërim (m)	[kalərím]
horse rider	kalorës (m)	[kalórəs]
figure skating	patinazh (m)	[patináʒ]
figure skater (masc.)	patinator (m)	[patinatór]
figure skater (fem.)	patinatore (f)	[patinatórɛ]
powerlifting	peshëngritje (f)	[pɛʃəŋrítjɛ]
powerlifter	peshëngritës (m)	[pɛʃəŋrítəs]
car racing	garë me makina (f)	[gárə mɛ makína]
racer (driver)	shofer garash (m)	[ʃofér gáraʃ]
cycling	çiklizëm (m)	[tʃiklízəm]
cyclist	çiklist (m)	[tʃiklíst]
broad jump	kërcim së gjati (m)	[kərtsím sə ɟáti]
pole vault	kërcim së larti (m)	[kərtsím sə lárti]
jumper	kërcyes (m)	[kərtsýɛs]

114. Kinds of sports. Miscellaneous

football	futboll amerikan (m)	[futbóɫ amɛrikán]
badminton	badminton (m)	[bádminton]
biathlon	biatlon (m)	[biatlón]
billiards	bilardo (f)	[bilárdo]
bobsled	bobsled (m)	[bobsléd]
bodybuilding	bodybuilding (m)	[bodybuildíŋ]
water polo	vaterpol (m)	[vatɛrpól]
handball	hendboll (m)	[hɛndbóɫ]
golf	golf (m)	[golf]
rowing, crew	kanotazh (m)	[kanotáʒ]
scuba diving	zhytje (f)	[ʒýtjɛ]
cross-country skiing	skijim nordik (m)	[skijím nordík]
table tennis (ping-pong)	ping pong (m)	[piŋ pón]
sailing	lundrim me vela (m)	[lundrím mɛ véla]
rally racing	garë rally (f)	[gárə ráɫy]
rugby	ragbi (m)	[rágbi]

| snowboarding | snoubord (m) | [snoubórd] |
| archery | gjuajtje me hark (f) | [ɟúajtjɛ mɛ hárk] |

115. Gym

| barbell | peshë (f) | [péʃə] |
| dumbbells | gira (f) | [gíra] |

training machine	makinë trajnimi (f)	[makínə trajními]
exercise bicycle	biçikletë ushtrimesh (f)	[bitʃiklétə uʃtrímɛʃ]
treadmill	makinë vrapi (f)	[makínə vrápi]

horizontal bar	tra horizontal (m)	[tra horizontál]
parallel bars	trarë paralele (pl)	[trárə paralélɛ]
vault (vaulting horse)	kaluç (m)	[kalútʃ]
mat (exercise ~)	tapet gjimnastike (m)	[tapét ɟimnastíkɛ]

jump rope	litar kërcimi (m)	[litár kərtsími]
aerobics	aerobik (m)	[aɛrobík]
yoga	joga (f)	[jóga]

116. Sports. Miscellaneous

Olympic Games	Lojërat Olimpike (pl)	[lójərat olimpíkɛ]
winner	fitues (m)	[fitúɛs]
to be winning	duke fituar	[dúkɛ fitúar]
to win (vi)	fitoj	[fitój]

| leader | lider (m) | [lidér] |
| to lead (vi) | udhëheq | [uðəhéc] |

first place	vendi i parë	[véndi i párə]
second place	vendi i dytë	[véndi i dýtə]
third place	vendi i tretë	[véndi i trétə]

medal	medalje (f)	[mɛdáljɛ]
trophy	trofe (f)	[trofé]
prize cup (trophy)	kupë (f)	[kúpə]
prize (in game)	çmim (m)	[tʃmím]
main prize	çmimi i parë (m)	[tʃmími i párə]

| record | rekord (m) | [rɛkórd] |
| to set a record | vendos rekord | [vɛndós rɛkórd] |

final	finale	[finálɛ]
final (adj)	finale	[finálɛ]
champion	kampion (m)	[kampión]
championship	kampionat (m)	[kampionát]

stadium	**stadium** (m)	[stadiúm]
stand (bleachers)	**tribunë** (f)	[tribúnə]
fan, supporter	**tifoz** (m)	[tifóz]
opponent, rival	**kundërshtar** (m)	[kundərʃtár]
start (start line)	**start** (m)	[start]
finish line	**cak** (m)	[tsák]
defeat	**humbje** (f)	[húmbjɛ]
to lose (not win)	**humb**	[húmb]
referee	**arbitër** (m)	[arbítər]
jury (judges)	**juri** (f)	[jurí]
score	**rezultat** (m)	[rɛzultát]
tie	**barazim** (m)	[barazím]
to tie (vi)	**barazoj**	[barazój]
point	**pikë** (f)	[píkə]
result (final score)	**rezultat** (m)	[rɛzultát]
period	**pjesë** (f)	[pjésə]
half-time	**pushim** (m)	[puʃím]
doping	**doping** (m)	[dopíŋ]
to penalize (vt)	**penalizoj**	[pɛnalizój]
to disqualify (vt)	**diskualifikoj**	[diskualifikój]
apparatus	**aparat** (m)	[aparát]
javelin	**hedhje e shtizës** (f)	[héðjɛ ɛ ʃtízəs]
shot (metal ball)	**gjyle** (f)	[ɟýlɛ]
ball (snooker, etc.)	**bile** (f)	[bílɛ]
aim (target)	**shënjestër** (f)	[ʃəɲéstər]
target	**shënjestër** (f)	[ʃəɲéstər]
to shoot (vi)	**qëlloj**	[cəɫój]
accurate (~ shot)	**e saktë**	[ɛ sáktə]
trainer, coach	**trajner** (m)	[trajnér]
to train (sb)	**stërvit**	[stərvít]
to train (vi)	**stërvitem**	[stərvítɛm]
training	**trajnim** (m)	[trajním]
gym	**palestër** (f)	[paléstər]
exercise (physical)	**ushtrime** (f)	[uʃtrímɛ]
warm-up (athlete ~)	**ngrohje** (f)	[ŋróhjɛ]

Education

117. School

school	**shkollë** (f)	[ʃkótə]
principal (headmaster)	**drejtor shkolle** (m)	[drɛjtór ʃkótɛ]
pupil (boy)	**nxënës** (m)	[ndzénəs]
pupil (girl)	**nxënëse** (f)	[ndzénəsɛ]
schoolboy	**nxënës** (m)	[ndzénəs]
schoolgirl	**nxënëse** (f)	[ndzénəsɛ]
to teach (sb)	**jap mësim**	[jap məsím]
to learn (language, etc.)	**mësoj**	[məsój]
to learn by heart	**mësoj përmendësh**	[məsój pərméndəʃ]
to learn (~ to count, etc.)	**mësoj**	[məsój]
to be in school	**jam në shkollë**	[jam nə ʃkótə]
to go to school	**shkoj në shkollë**	[ʃkoj nə ʃkótə]
alphabet	**alfabet** (m)	[alfabét]
subject (at school)	**lëndë** (f)	[léndə]
classroom	**klasë** (f)	[klásə]
lesson	**mësim** (m)	[məsím]
recess	**pushim** (m)	[puʃím]
school bell	**zile e shkollës** (f)	[zílɛ ɛ ʃkótəs]
school desk	**bankë e shkollës** (f)	[bánkə ɛ ʃkótəs]
chalkboard	**tabelë e zezë** (f)	[tabélə ɛ zézə]
grade	**notë** (f)	[nótə]
good grade	**notë e mirë** (f)	[nótə ɛ mírə]
bad grade	**notë e keqe** (f)	[nótə ɛ kécɛ]
to give a grade	**vendos notë**	[vɛndós nótə]
mistake, error	**gabim** (m)	[gabím]
to make mistakes	**bëj gabime**	[bəj gabímɛ]
to correct (an error)	**korrigjoj**	[koriɟój]
cheat sheet	**kopje** (f)	[kópjɛ]
homework	**detyrë shtëpie** (f)	[dɛtýrə ʃtəpíɛ]
exercise (in education)	**ushtrim** (m)	[uʃtrím]
to be present	**jam prezent**	[jam prɛzént]
to be absent	**mungoj**	[muŋój]
to miss school	**mungoj në shkollë**	[muŋój nə ʃkótə]

to punish (vt)	ndëshkoj	[ndəʃkój]
punishment	ndëshkim (m)	[ndəʃkím]
conduct (behavior)	sjellje (f)	[sjétjɛ]

report card	dëftesë (f)	[dəftésə]
pencil	laps (m)	[láps]
eraser	gomë (f)	[gómə]
chalk	shkumës (m)	[ʃkúməs]
pencil case	portofol lapsash (m)	[portofól lápsaʃ]

schoolbag	çantë shkolle (f)	[tʃántə ʃkótɛ]
pen	stilolaps (m)	[stiloláps]
school notebook	fletore (f)	[flɛtórɛ]
textbook	tekst mësimor (m)	[tɛkst məsimór]
drafting compass	kompas (m)	[kompás]

| to make technical drawings | vizatoj | [vizatój] |
| technical drawing | vizatim teknik (m) | [vizatím tɛkník] |

poem	poezi (f)	[poɛzí]
by heart (adv)	përmendësh	[pərméndəʃ]
to learn by heart	mësoj përmendësh	[məsój pərméndəʃ]

school vacation	pushimet e shkollës (m)	[puʃímɛt ɛ ʃkótəs]
to be on vacation	jam me pushime	[jam mɛ puʃímɛ]
to spend one's vacation	kaloj pushimet	[kalój puʃímɛt]

test (written math ~)	test (m)	[tɛst]
essay (composition)	ese (f)	[ɛsé]
dictation	diktim (m)	[diktím]
exam (examination)	provim (m)	[provím]
to take an exam	kam provim	[kam provím]
experiment (e.g., chemistry ~)	eksperiment (m)	[ɛkspɛrimént]

118. College. University

academy	akademi (f)	[akadɛmí]
university	universitet (m)	[univɛrsitét]
faculty (e.g., ~ of Medicine)	fakultet (m)	[fakultét]

student (masc.)	student (m)	[studént]
student (fem.)	studente (f)	[studéntɛ]
lecturer (teacher)	pedagog (m)	[pɛdagóg]

lecture hall, room	auditor (m)	[auditór]
graduate	i diplomuar (m)	[i diplomúar]
diploma	diplomë (f)	[diplómə]

dissertation	disertacion (m)	[disɛrtatsión]
study (report)	studim (m)	[studím]
laboratory	laborator (m)	[laboratór]

lecture	leksion (m)	[lɛksión]
coursemate	shok kursi (m)	[ʃok kúrsi]
scholarship	bursë (f)	[búrsə]
academic degree	diplomë akademike (f)	[diplómə akadɛmíkɛ]

119. Sciences. Disciplines

mathematics	matematikë (f)	[matɛmatíkə]
algebra	algjebër (f)	[alʲébər]
geometry	gjeometri (f)	[ɟɛomɛtrí]

astronomy	astronomi (f)	[astronomí]
biology	biologji (f)	[bioloɟí]
geography	gjeografi (f)	[ɟɛografí]
geology	gjeologji (f)	[ɟɛoloɟí]
history	histori (f)	[historí]

medicine	mjekësi (f)	[mjɛkəsí]
pedagogy	pedagogji (f)	[pɛdagoɟí]
law	drejtësi (f)	[drɛjtəsí]

physics	fizikë (f)	[fizíkə]
chemistry	kimi (f)	[kimí]
philosophy	filozofi (f)	[filozofí]
psychology	psikologji (f)	[psikoloɟí]

120. Writing system. Orthography

grammar	gramatikë (f)	[gramatíkə]
vocabulary	fjalor (m)	[fjalór]
phonetics	fonetikë (f)	[fonɛtíkə]

noun	emër (m)	[émər]
adjective	mbiemër (m)	[mbiémər]
verb	folje (f)	[fóljɛ]
adverb	ndajfolje (f)	[ndajfóljɛ]

pronoun	përemër (m)	[pərémər]
interjection	pasthirrmë (f)	[pasθírmə]
preposition	parafjalë (f)	[parafjálə]

root	rrënjë (f)	[réɲə]
ending	fundore (f)	[fundórɛ]
prefix	parashtesë (f)	[paraʃtésə]

| syllable | rrokje (f) | [rókjɛ] |
| suffix | prapashtesë (f) | [prapaʃtésə] |

| stress mark | theks (m) | [θɛks] |
| apostrophe | apostrof (m) | [apostróf] |

period, dot	pikë (f)	[píkə]
comma	presje (f)	[présjɛ]
semicolon	pikëpresje (f)	[pikəprésjɛ]
colon	dy pika (f)	[dy píka]
ellipsis	tre pika (f)	[trɛ píka]

| question mark | pikëpyetje (f) | [pikəpýɛtjɛ] |
| exclamation point | pikëçuditje (f) | [pikətʃudítjɛ] |

quotation marks	thonjëza (f)	[θóɲəza]
in quotation marks	në thonjëza	[nə θóɲəza]
parenthesis	kllapa (f)	[kɫápa]
in parenthesis	brenda kllapave	[brénda kɫápavɛ]

hyphen	vizë ndarëse (f)	[vízə ndárəsɛ]
dash	vizë (f)	[vízə]
space (between words)	hapësirë (f)	[hapəsírə]

| letter | shkronjë (f) | [ʃkróɲə] |
| capital letter | shkronjë e madhe (f) | [ʃkróɲə ɛ máðɛ] |

| vowel (n) | zanore (f) | [zanórɛ] |
| consonant (n) | bashkëtingëllore (f) | [baʃkətiŋəɫórɛ] |

sentence	fjali (f)	[fjalí]
subject	kryefjalë (f)	[kryɛfjálə]
predicate	kallëzues (m)	[kaɫəzúɛs]

line	rresht (m)	[réʃt]
on a new line	rresht i ri	[réʃt i rí]
paragraph	paragraf (m)	[paragráf]

word	fjalë (f)	[fjálə]
group of words	grup fjalësh (m)	[grup fjáləʃ]
expression	shprehje (f)	[ʃpréhjɛ]
synonym	sinonim (m)	[sinoním]
antonym	antonim (m)	[antoním]

rule	rregull (m)	[réguɫ]
exception	përjashtim (m)	[pərjaʃtím]
correct (adj)	saktë	[sáktə]

conjugation	lakim (m)	[lakím]
declension	rasë	[rásə]
nominal case	rasë emërore (f)	[rásə ɛmərórɛ]
question	pyetje (f)	[pýɛtjɛ]

| to underline (vt) | nënvijëzoj | [nənvijəzój] |
| dotted line | vijë me ndërprerje (f) | [víjə mɛ ndərprérjɛ] |

121. Foreign languages

language	gjuhë (f)	[ɟúhə]
foreign (adj)	huaj	[húaj]
foreign language	gjuhë e huaj (f)	[ɟúhə ɛ húaj]
to study (vt)	studioj	[studiój]
to learn (language, etc.)	mësoj	[məsój]

to read (vi, vt)	lexoj	[lɛdzój]
to speak (vi, vt)	flas	[flas]
to understand (vt)	kuptoj	[kuptój]
to write (vt)	shkruaj	[ʃkrúaj]

fast (adv)	shpejt	[ʃpɛjt]
slowly (adv)	ngadalë	[ŋadálə]
fluently (adv)	rrjedhshëm	[rjéðʃəm]

rules	rregullat (pl)	[réguɫat]
grammar	gramatikë (f)	[gramatíkə]
vocabulary	fjalor (m)	[fjalór]
phonetics	fonetikë (f)	[fonɛtíkə]

textbook	tekst mësimor (m)	[tɛkst məsimór]
dictionary	fjalor (m)	[fjalór]
teach-yourself book	libër i mësimit autodidakt (m)	[líbər i məsímit autodidákt]
phrasebook	libër frazeologjik (m)	[líbər frazɛoloɟík]

cassette, tape	kasetë (f)	[kasétə]
videotape	videokasetë (f)	[vidɛokasétə]
CD, compact disc	CD (f)	[tsɛdé]
DVD	DVD (m)	[dividí]

alphabet	alfabet (m)	[alfabét]
to spell (vt)	gërmëzoj	[gərməzój]
pronunciation	shqiptim (m)	[ʃciptím]

accent	aksent (m)	[aksént]
with an accent	me aksent	[mɛ aksént]
without an accent	pa aksent	[pa aksént]

| word | fjalë (f) | [fjálə] |
| meaning | kuptim (m) | [kuptím] |

course (e.g., a French ~)	kurs (m)	[kurs]
to sign up	regjistrohem	[rɛɟistróhɛm]
teacher	mësues (m)	[məsúɛs]

translation (process)	përkthim (m)	[pərkθím]
translation (text, etc.)	përkthim (m)	[pərkθím]
translator	përkthyes (m)	[pərkθýɛs]
interpreter	përkthyes (m)	[pərkθýɛs]

polyglot	poliglot (m)	[poliglót]
memory	kujtesë (f)	[kujtésə]

122. Fairy tale characters

Santa Claus	Santa Klaus (m)	[sánta kláus]
Cinderella	Hirushja (f)	[hirúʃja]
mermaid	sirenë (f)	[sirénə]
Neptune	Neptuni (m)	[nɛptúni]

magician, wizard	magjistar (m)	[maɉistár]
fairy	zanë (f)	[zánə]
magic (adj)	magjike	[maɉíkɛ]
magic wand	shkop magjik (m)	[ʃkop maɉík]

fairy tale	përrallë (f)	[pərátə]
miracle	mrekulli (f)	[mrɛkuɫí]
dwarf	xhuxh (m)	[dʒudʒ]
to turn into ...	shndërrohem ...	[ʃndəróhɛm ...]

ghost	fantazmë (f)	[fantázmə]
phantom	fantazmë (f)	[fantázmə]
monster	bishë (f)	[bíʃə]
dragon	dragua (m)	[dragúa]
giant	gjigant (m)	[ɟigánt]

123. Zodiac Signs

Aries	Dashi (m)	[dáʃi]
Taurus	Demi (m)	[démi]
Gemini	Binjakët (pl)	[biɲákət]
Cancer	Gaforrja (f)	[gafórja]
Leo	Luani (m)	[luáni]
Virgo	Virgjëresha (f)	[virɟəréʃa]

Libra	Peshorja (f)	[pɛʃórja]
Scorpio	Akrepi (m)	[akrépi]
Sagittarius	Shigjetari (m)	[ʃiɟɛtári]
Capricorn	Bricjapi (m)	[britsjápi]
Aquarius	Ujori (m)	[ujóri]
Pisces	Peshqit (pl)	[péʃcit]
character	karakter (m)	[karaktér]
character traits	tipare të karakterit (pl)	[tipárɛ tə karaktérit]

behavior	**sjellje** (f)	[sjétjɛ]
to tell fortunes	**parashikoj fatin**	[paraʃikój fátin]
fortune-teller	**lexuese e fatit** (f)	[lɛdzúɛsɛ ɛ fátit]
horoscope	**horoskop** (m)	[horoskóp]

Arts

124. Theater

theater	teatër (m)	[tɛátər]
opera	operë (f)	[opérə]
operetta	operetë (f)	[opɛrétə]
ballet	balet (m)	[balét]
theater poster	afishe teatri (f)	[afíʃɛ tɛátri]
troupe (theatrical company)	trupë teatrale (f)	[trúpə tɛatrálɛ]
tour	turne (f)	[turné]
to be on tour	jam në turne	[jam nə turné]
to rehearse (vi, vt)	bëj prova	[bəj próva]
rehearsal	provë (f)	[próvə]
repertoire	repertor (m)	[rɛpɛrtór]
performance	shfaqje (f)	[ʃfácjɛ]
theatrical show	shfaqje teatrale (f)	[ʃfácjɛ tɛatrálɛ]
play	dramë (f)	[drámə]
ticket	biletë (f)	[bilétə]
box office (ticket booth)	zyrë e shitjeve të biletave (f)	[zýrə ɛ ʃítjɛvɛ tə bilétavɛ]
lobby, foyer	holl (m)	[hoɫ]
coat check (cloakroom)	dhoma e xhaketave (f)	[ðóma ɛ dʒakétavɛ]
coat check tag	numri i xhaketës (m)	[númri i dʒakétəs]
binoculars	dylbi (f)	[dylbí]
usher	portier (m)	[portiér]
orchestra seats	plato (f)	[plató]
balcony	ballkon (m)	[baɫkón]
dress circle	galeria e parë (f)	[galɛría ɛ párə]
box	lozhë (f)	[lóʒə]
row	rresht (m)	[réʃt]
seat	karrige (f)	[karígɛ]
audience	publiku (m)	[publíku]
spectator	spektator (m)	[spɛktatór]
to clap (vi, vt)	duartrokas	[duartrokás]
applause	duartrokitje (f)	[duartrokítjɛ]
ovation	brohoritje (f)	[brohorítjɛ]
stage	skenë (f)	[skénə]
curtain	perde (f)	[pérdɛ]

scenery	skenografi (f)	[skɛnografí]
backstage	prapaskenë (f)	[prapaskénə]

scene (e.g., the last ~)	skenë (f)	[skénə]
act	akt (m)	[ákt]
intermission	pushim (m)	[puʃím]

125. Cinema

actor	aktor (m)	[aktór]
actress	aktore (f)	[aktórɛ]

movies (industry)	kinema (f)	[kinɛmá]
movie	film (m)	[film]
episode	episod (m)	[ɛpisód]

detective movie	triller (m)	[triłér]
action movie	aksion (m)	[aksión]
adventure movie	aventurë (f)	[avɛntúrə]
sci-fi movie	fanta-shkencë (f)	[fánta-ʃkéntsə]
horror movie	film horror (m)	[fílm horór]

comedy movie	komedi (f)	[komɛdí]
melodrama	melodramë (f)	[mɛlodrámə]
drama	dramë (f)	[drámə]

fictional movie	film fiktiv (m)	[fílm fiktív]
documentary	dokumentar (m)	[dokumɛntár]
cartoon	film vizatimor (m)	[fílm vizatimór]
silent movies	filma pa zë (m)	[fílma pa zə]

role (part)	rol (m)	[rol]
leading role	rol kryesor (m)	[rol kryɛsór]
to play (vi, vt)	luaj	[lúaj]

movie star	yll kinemaje (m)	[yɫ kinɛmájɛ]
well-known (adj)	i njohur	[i ɲóhur]
famous (adj)	i famshëm	[i fámʃəm]
popular (adj)	popullor	[popułór]

script (screenplay)	skenar (m)	[skɛnár]
scriptwriter	skenarist (m)	[skɛnaríst]
movie director	regjisor (m)	[rɛɟisór]
producer	producent (m)	[produtsént]
assistant	ndihmës (m)	[ndíhməs]
cameraman	kameraman (m)	[kamɛramán]
stuntman	dubla (f)	[dúbla]
double (stand-in)	dubla (f)	[dúbla]
to shoot a movie	xhiroj film	[dʒirój film]
audition, screen test	provë (f)	[próvə]

shooting	xhirim (m)	[dʒirím]
movie crew	ekip kinematografik (m)	[ɛkíp kinɛmatografík]
movie set	set kinematografik (m)	[sɛt kinɛmatografík]
camera	kamerë (f)	[kamérə]

movie theater	kinema (f)	[kinɛmá]
screen (e.g., big ~)	ekran (m)	[ɛkrán]
to show a movie	shfaq film	[ʃfac film]

soundtrack	muzikë e filmit (f)	[muzíkə ɛ filmit]
special effects	efekte speciale (pl)	[ɛféktɛ spɛtsiálɛ]
subtitles	titra (pl)	[títra]
credits	lista e pjesëmarrësve (f)	[lísta ɛ pjɛsəmárəsvɛ]
translation	përkthim (m)	[pərkθím]

126. Painting

art	art (m)	[art]
fine arts	artet e bukura (pl)	[ártɛt ɛ búkura]
art gallery	galeri arti (f)	[galɛrí árti]
art exhibition	ekspozitë (f)	[ɛkspozítə]

painting (art)	pikturë (f)	[piktúrə]
graphic art	art grafik (m)	[árt grafík]
abstract art	art abstrakt (m)	[árt abstrákt]
impressionism	impresionizëm (m)	[imprɛsionízəm]

picture (painting)	pikturë (f)	[piktúrə]
drawing	vizatim (m)	[vizatím]
poster	poster (m)	[postér]

illustration (picture)	ilustrim (m)	[ilustrím]
miniature	miniaturë (f)	[miniatúrə]
copy (of painting, etc.)	kopje (f)	[kópjɛ]
reproduction	riprodhim (m)	[riproðím]

mosaic	mozaik (m)	[mozaík]
stained glass window	pikturë në dritare (f)	[piktúrə nə dritárɛ]
fresco	afresk (m)	[afrésk]
engraving	gravurë (f)	[gravúrə]

bust (sculpture)	bust (m)	[búst]
sculpture	skulpturë (f)	[skulptúrə]
statue	statujë (f)	[statújə]
plaster of Paris	allçi (f)	[aɬtʃí]
plaster (as adj)	me allçi	[mɛ aɬtʃí]

portrait	portret (m)	[portrét]
self-portrait	autoportret (m)	[autoportrét]
landscape painting	peizazh (m)	[pɛizáʒ]

still life	natyrë e qetë (f)	[natýrə ɛ cétə]
caricature	karikaturë (f)	[karikatúrə]
sketch	skicë (f)	[skítsə]

paint	bojë (f)	[bójə]
watercolor paint	bojë uji (f)	[bójə úji]
oil (paint)	bojë vaji (f)	[bójə váji]
pencil	laps (m)	[láps]
India ink	bojë stilografi (f)	[bójə stilográfi]
charcoal	karbon (m)	[karbón]

| to draw (vi, vt) | vizatoj | [vizatój] |
| to paint (vi, vt) | pikturoj | [pikturój] |

to pose (vi)	pozoj	[pozój]
artist's model (masc.)	model (m)	[modél]
artist's model (fem.)	modele (f)	[modélɛ]

artist (painter)	piktor (m)	[piktór]
work of art	vepër arti (f)	[vépər árti]
masterpiece	kryevepër (f)	[kryɛvépər]
studio (artist's workroom)	studio (f)	[stúdio]

canvas (cloth)	kanavacë (f)	[kanavátsə]
easel	këmbalec (m)	[kəmbaléts]
palette	paletë (f)	[palétə]

frame (picture ~, etc.)	kornizë (f)	[kornízə]
restoration	restaurim (m)	[rɛstaurím]
to restore (vt)	restauroj	[rɛstaurój]

127. Literature & Poetry

literature	letërsi (f)	[lɛtərsí]
author (writer)	autor (m)	[autór]
pseudonym	pseudonim (m)	[psɛudoním]

book	libër (m)	[líbər]
volume	vëllim (m)	[vəłím]
table of contents	tabela e përmbajtjes (f)	[tabéla ɛ pərmbájtjɛs]
page	faqe (f)	[fácɛ]
main character	personazhi kryesor (m)	[pɛrsonáʒi kryɛsór]
autograph	autograf (m)	[autográf]

short story	tregim i shkurtër (m)	[trɛgím i ʃkúrtər]
story (novella)	novelë (f)	[novélə]
novel	roman (m)	[román]
work (writing)	vepër (m)	[vépər]
fable	fabula (f)	[fábula]
detective novel	roman policesk (m)	[román politsésk]

poem (verse)	vjershë (f)	[vjérʃə]
poetry	poezi (f)	[poɛzí]
poem (epic, ballad)	poemë (f)	[poémə]
poet	poet (m)	[poét]

fiction	trillim (m)	[tritím]
science fiction	fanta-shkencë (f)	[fánta-ʃkéntsə]
adventures	aventurë (f)	[avɛntúrə]
educational literature	letërsi edukative (f)	[lɛtərsí ɛdukatívɛ]
children's literature	letërsi për fëmijë (f)	[lɛtərsí pər fəmíjə]

128. Circus

circus	cirk (m)	[tsírk]
traveling circus	cirk udhëtues (m)	[tsírk uðətúɛs]
program	program (m)	[prográm]
performance	shfaqje (f)	[ʃfácjɛ]

| act (circus ~) | akt (m) | [ákt] |
| circus ring | arenë cirku (f) | [arénə tsírku] |

| pantomime (act) | pantomimë (f) | [pantomímə] |
| clown | kloun (m) | [kloún] |

acrobat	akrobat (m)	[akrobát]
acrobatics	akrobaci (f)	[akrobatsí]
gymnast	gjimnast (m)	[ɟimnást]
acrobatic gymnastics	gjimnastikë (f)	[ɟimnastíkə]
somersault	salto (f)	[sálto]
athlete (strongman)	atlet (m)	[atlét]
tamer (e.g., lion ~)	zbutës (m)	[zbútəs]
rider (circus horse ~)	kalorës (m)	[kalórəs]
assistant	ndihmës (m)	[ndíhməs]

stunt	akrobaci (f)	[akrobatsí]
magic trick	truk magjik (m)	[truk maɟík]
conjurer, magician	magjistar (m)	[maɟistár]

juggler	zhongler (m)	[ʒoŋlér]
to juggle (vi, vt)	luaj	[lúaj]
animal trainer	zbutës kafshësh (m)	[zbútəs káfʃəʃ]
animal training	zbutje kafshësh (f)	[zbútjɛ káfʃəʃ]
to train (animals)	stërvit	[stərvít]

129. Music. Pop music

| music | muzikë (f) | [muzíkə] |
| musician | muzikant (m) | [muzikánt] |

musical instrument	instrument muzikor (m)	[instrumént muzikór]
to play ...	i bie ...	[i bíɛ ...]
guitar	kitarë (f)	[kitárə]
violin	violinë (f)	[violínə]
cello	violonçel (m)	[violontʃél]
double bass	kontrabas (m)	[kontrabás]
harp	lira (f)	[líra]
piano	piano (f)	[piáno]
grand piano	pianoforte (f)	[pianofórtɛ]
organ	organo (f)	[orgáno]
wind instruments	instrumente frymore (pl)	[instruméntɛ frymórɛ]
oboe	oboe (f)	[obóɛ]
saxophone	saksofon (m)	[saksofón]
clarinet	klarinetë (f)	[klarinétə]
flute	flaut (m)	[flaút]
trumpet	trombë (f)	[trómbə]
accordion	fizarmonikë (f)	[fizarmoníkə]
drum	daulle (f)	[daúɬɛ]
duo	duet (m)	[duét]
trio	trio (f)	[trío]
quartet	kuartet (m)	[kuartét]
choir	kor (m)	[kor]
orchestra	orkestër (f)	[orkéstər]
pop music	muzikë pop (f)	[muzíkə pop]
rock music	muzikë rok (m)	[muzíkə rok]
rock group	grup rok (m)	[grup rók]
jazz	xhaz (m)	[dʒaz]
idol	idhull (m)	[íðuɬ]
admirer, fan	admirues (m)	[admirúɛs]
concert	koncert (m)	[kontsért]
symphony	simfoni (f)	[simfoní]
composition	kompozicion (m)	[kompozitsión]
to compose (write)	kompozoj	[kompozój]
singing (n)	këndim (m)	[kəndím]
song	këngë (f)	[kéŋə]
tune (melody)	melodi (f)	[mɛlodí]
rhythm	ritëm (m)	[rítəm]
blues	bluz (m)	[blúz]
sheet music	partiturë (f)	[partitúrə]
baton	shkopi i dirigjimit (m)	[ʃkopi i diriɟímit]
bow	hark (m)	[hárk]
string	tel (m)	[tɛl]
case (e.g., guitar ~)	kuti (f)	[kutí]

Rest. Entertainment. Travel

130. Trip. Travel

tourism, travel	**turizëm** (m)	[turízəm]
tourist	**turist** (m)	[turíst]
trip, voyage	**udhëtim** (m)	[uðətím]
adventure	**aventurë** (f)	[avɛntúrə]
trip, journey	**udhëtim** (m)	[uðətím]
vacation	**pushim** (m)	[puʃím]
to be on vacation	**jam me pushime**	[jam mɛ puʃímɛ]
rest	**pushim** (m)	[puʃím]
train	**tren** (m)	[trɛn]
by train	**me tren**	[mɛ trén]
airplane	**avion** (m)	[avión]
by airplane	**me avion**	[mɛ avión]
by car	**me makinë**	[mɛ makínə]
by ship	**me anije**	[mɛ aníjɛ]
luggage	**bagazh** (m)	[bagáʒ]
suitcase	**valixhe** (f)	[valídʒɛ]
luggage cart	**karrocë bagazhesh** (f)	[karótsə bagáʒɛʃ]
passport	**pasaportë** (f)	[pasapórtə]
visa	**vizë** (f)	[vízə]
ticket	**biletë** (f)	[bilétə]
air ticket	**biletë avioni** (f)	[bilétə avióni]
guidebook	**guidë turistike** (f)	[guídə turistíkɛ]
map (tourist ~)	**hartë** (f)	[hártə]
area (rural ~)	**zonë** (f)	[zónə]
place, site	**vend** (m)	[vɛnd]
exotica (n)	**ekzotikë** (f)	[ɛkzotíkə]
exotic (adj)	**ekzotik**	[ɛkzotík]
amazing (adj)	**mahnitëse**	[mahnítəsɛ]
group	**grup** (m)	[grup]
excursion, sightseeing tour	**ekskursion** (m)	[ɛkskursión]
guide (person)	**udhërrëfyes** (m)	[uðərəfýɛs]

131. Hotel

hotel, inn	hotel (m)	[hotél]
motel	motel (m)	[motél]
three-star (~ hotel)	me tre yje	[mɛ trɛ ýjɛ]
five-star	me pesë yje	[mɛ pésə ýjɛ]
to stay (in a hotel, etc.)	qëndroj	[cəndrój]
room	dhomë (f)	[ðómə]
single room	dhomë teke (f)	[ðómə tékɛ]
double room	dhomë dyshe (f)	[ðómə dýʃɛ]
to book a room	rezervoj një dhomë	[rɛzɛrvój ɲə ðómə]
half board	gjysmë-pension (m)	[ɟýsmə-pɛnsión]
full board	pension i plotë (m)	[pɛnsión i plótə]
with bath	me banjo	[mɛ báɲo]
with shower	me dush	[mɛ dúʃ]
satellite television	televizor satelitor (m)	[tɛlɛvizór satɛlitór]
air-conditioner	kondicioner (m)	[konditsionér]
towel	peshqir (m)	[pɛʃcír]
key	çelës (m)	[tʃéləs]
administrator	administrator (m)	[administratór]
chambermaid	pastruese (f)	[pastrúɛsɛ]
porter, bellboy	portier (m)	[portiér]
doorman	portier (m)	[portiér]
restaurant	restorant (m)	[rɛstoránt]
pub, bar	pab (m), pijetore (f)	[pab], [pijɛtórɛ]
breakfast	mëngjes (m)	[mənɟés]
dinner	darkë (f)	[dárkə]
buffet	bufe (f)	[bufé]
lobby	holl (m)	[hoɫ]
elevator	ashensor (m)	[aʃɛnsór]
DO NOT DISTURB	MOS SHQETËSONI	[mos ʃcɛtəsóni]
NO SMOKING	NDALOHET DUHANI	[ndalóhɛt duháni]

132. Books. Reading

book	libër (m)	[líbər]
author	autor (m)	[autór]
writer	shkrimtar (m)	[ʃkrimtár]
to write (~ a book)	shkruaj	[ʃkrúaj]
reader	lexues (m)	[lɛdzúɛs]
to read (vi, vt)	lexoj	[lɛdzój]

reading (activity)	**lexim** (m)	[lɛdzím]
silently (to oneself)	**pa zë**	[pa zə]
aloud (adv)	**me zë**	[mɛ zə]

to publish (vt)	**botoj**	[botój]
publishing (process)	**botim** (m)	[botím]
publisher	**botues** (m)	[botúɛs]
publishing house	**shtëpi botuese** (f)	[ʃtəpí botúɛsɛ]

to come out (be released)	**botohet**	[botóhɛt]
release (of a book)	**botim** (m)	[botím]
print run	**edicion** (m)	[ɛditsión]

bookstore	**librari** (f)	[librarí]
library	**bibliotekë** (f)	[bibliotékə]

story (novella)	**novelë** (f)	[novélə]
short story	**tregim i shkurtër** (m)	[trɛgím i ʃkúrtər]
novel	**roman** (m)	[román]
detective novel	**roman policesk** (m)	[román politsésk]

memoirs	**kujtime** (pl)	[kujtímɛ]
legend	**legjendë** (f)	[lɛɟéndə]
myth	**mit** (m)	[mit]

poetry, poems	**poezi** (f)	[poɛzí]
autobiography	**autobiografi** (f)	[autobiografí]
selected works	**vepra të zgjedhura** (f)	[vépra tə zɟéðura]
science fiction	**fanta-shkencë** (f)	[fánta-ʃkéntsə]

title	**titull** (m)	[títuɫ]
introduction	**hyrje** (f)	[hýrjɛ]
title page	**faqe e titullit** (f)	[fácɛ ɛ títuɫit]

chapter	**kreu** (m)	[kréu]
extract	**ekstrakt** (m)	[ɛkstrákt]
episode	**episod** (m)	[ɛpisód]

plot (storyline)	**fabul** (f)	[fábul]
contents	**përmbajtje** (f)	[pərmbájtjɛ]
table of contents	**tabela e përmbajtjes** (f)	[tabéla ɛ pərmbájtjɛs]
main character	**personazhi kryesor** (m)	[pɛrsonáʒi kryɛsór]

volume	**vëllim** (m)	[vəɫím]
cover	**kopertinë** (f)	[kopɛrtínə]
binding	**libërlidhje** (f)	[libərlíðjɛ]
bookmark	**shënjim** (m)	[ʃəɲím]
page	**faqe** (f)	[fácɛ]
to page through	**kaloj faqet**	[kalój fácɛt]
margins	**margjinat** (pl)	[marɟínat]
annotation	**shënim** (m)	[ʃəním]
(marginal note, etc.)		

footnote	fusnotë (f)	[fusnótə]
text	tekst (m)	[tɛkst]
type, font	lloji i shkrimit (m)	[tóji i ʃkrímit]
misprint, typo	gabim ortografik (m)	[gabím ortografík]

translation	përkthim (m)	[pərkθím]
to translate (vt)	përkthej	[pərkθéj]
original (n)	origjinal (m)	[oriɟinál]

famous (adj)	i famshëm	[i fámʃəm]
unknown (not famous)	i panjohur	[i paɲóhur]
interesting (adj)	interesant	[intɛrɛsánt]
bestseller	libër më i shitur (m)	[líbər mə i ʃítur]

dictionary	fjalor (m)	[fjalór]
textbook	tekst mësimor (m)	[tɛkst məsimór]
encyclopedia	enciklopedi (f)	[ɛntsiklopɛdí]

133. Hunting. Fishing

hunting	gjueti (f)	[ɟuɛtí]
to hunt (vi, vt)	dal për gjah	[dál pər ɟáh]
hunter	gjahtar (m)	[ɟahtár]

to shoot (vi)	qëlloj	[cətój]
rifle	pushkë (f)	[púʃkə]
bullet (shell)	fishek (m)	[fiʃék]
shot (lead balls)	plumb (m)	[plúmb]

steel trap	grackë (f)	[grátskə]
snare (for birds, etc.)	kurth (m)	[kurθ]
to fall into the steel trap	bie në grackë	[bíɛ nə grátskə]
to lay a steel trap	ngre grackë	[ŋré grátskə]

poacher	gjahtar i jashtëligjshëm (m)	[ɟahtár i jaʃtəlíɟʃəm]
game (in hunting)	gjah (m)	[ɟáh]
hound dog	zagar (m)	[zagár]
safari	safari (m)	[safári]
mounted animal	kafshë e balsamosur (f)	[káfʃə ɛ balsamósur]

fisherman, angler	peshkatar (m)	[pɛʃkatár]
fishing (angling)	peshkim (m)	[pɛʃkím]
to fish (vi)	peshkoj	[pɛʃkój]

fishing rod	kallam peshkimi (m)	[katám pɛʃkími]
fishing line	tojë peshkimi (f)	[tójə pɛʃkími]
hook	grep (m)	[grép]
float, bobber	tapë (f)	[tápə]
bait	karrem (m)	[karém]

to cast a line	hedh grepin	[hɛð grépin]
to bite (ab. fish)	bie në grep	[bíɛ nə grép]
catch (of fish)	kapje peshku (f)	[kápjɛ péʃku]
ice-hole	vrimë në akull (f)	[vrímə nə ákuɫ]

fishing net	rrjetë peshkimi (f)	[rjétə pɛʃkími]
boat	varkë (f)	[várkə]
to net (to fish with a net)	peshkoj me rrjeta	[pɛʃkój mɛ rjéta]
to cast[throw] the net	hedh rrjetat	[hɛð rjétat]
to haul the net in	tërheq rrjetat	[tərhéc rjétat]
to fall into the net	bie në rrjetë	[bíɛ nə rjétə]

whaler (person)	gjuetar balenash (m)	[ɟuɛtár balénaʃ]
whaleboat	balenagjuajtëse (f)	[balɛnaɟúajtəsɛ]
harpoon	fuzhnjë (f)	[fúʒɲə]

134. Games. Billiards

billiards	bilardo (f)	[bilárdo]
billiard room, hall	sallë bilardosh (f)	[sáɫə bilárdoʃ]
ball (snooker, etc.)	bile (f)	[bílɛ]

to pocket a ball	fus në vrimë	[fús nə vrímə]
cue	stekë (f)	[stékə]
pocket	xhep (m), vrimë (f)	[dʒɛp], [vrímə]

135. Games. Playing cards

diamonds	karo (f)	[káro]
spades	maç (m)	[matʃ]
hearts	kupë (f)	[kúpə]
clubs	spathi (m)	[spáθi]

ace	as (m)	[ás]
king	mbret (m)	[mbrét]
queen	mbretëreshë (f)	[mbrɛtəréʃə]
jack, knave	fant (m)	[fant]

playing card	letër (f)	[létər]
cards	letrat (pl)	[létrat]
trump	letër e fortë (f)	[létər ɛ fórtə]
deck of cards	set letrash (m)	[sɛt létraʃ]

point	pikë (f)	[píkə]
to deal (vi, vt)	ndaj	[ndáj]
to shuffle (cards)	përziej	[pərzíɛj]
lead, turn (n)	radha (f)	[ráða]
cardsharp	mashtrues (m)	[maʃtrúɛs]

136. Rest. Games. Miscellaneous

to stroll (vi, vt)	shëtitem	[ʃətítɛm]
stroll (leisurely walk)	shëtitje (f)	[ʃətítjɛ]
car ride	xhiro me makinë (f)	[dʒíro mɛ makínə]
adventure	aventurë (f)	[avɛntúrə]
picnic	piknik (m)	[pikník]
game (chess, etc.)	lojë (f)	[lójə]
player	lojtar (m)	[lojtár]
game (one ~ of chess)	një lojë (f)	[ɲə lójə]
collector (e.g., philatelist)	koleksionist (m)	[kolɛksioníst]
to collect (stamps, etc.)	koleksionoj	[kolɛksionój]
collection	koleksion (m)	[kolɛksión]
crossword puzzle	fjalëkryq (m)	[fjaləkrýc]
racetrack (horse racing venue)	hipodrom (m)	[hipodróm]
disco (discotheque)	disko (f)	[dísko]
sauna	sauna (f)	[saúna]
lottery	lotari (f)	[lotarí]
camping trip	kamping (m)	[kampíŋ]
camp	kamp (m)	[kamp]
tent (for camping)	çadër kampingu (f)	[tʃádər kampíŋu]
compass	kompas (m)	[kompás]
camper	kampinist (m)	[kampiníst]
to watch (movie, etc.)	shikoj	[ʃikój]
viewer	teleshikues (m)	[tɛlɛʃikúɛs]
TV show (TV program)	program televiziv (m)	[prográm tɛlɛvizív]

137. Photography

camera (photo)	aparat fotografik (m)	[aparát fotografík]
photo, picture	foto (f)	[fóto]
photographer	fotograf (m)	[fotográf]
photo studio	studio fotografike (f)	[stúdio fotografíkɛ]
photo album	album fotografik (m)	[albúm fotografík]
camera lens	objektiv (m)	[objɛktív]
telephoto lens	teleobjektiv (m)	[tɛlɛobjɛktív]
filter	filtër (m)	[fíltər]
lens	lente (f)	[léntɛ]
optics (high-quality ~)	optikë (f)	[optíkə]
diaphragm (aperture)	diafragma (f)	[diafrágma]

exposure time (shutter speed)	koha e ekspozimit (f)	[kóha ε εkspozímit]
viewfinder	tregues i kuadrit (m)	[trεgúεs i kuádrit]
digital camera	kamerë digjitale (f)	[kamérə diɟitálɛ]
tripod	tripod (m)	[tripód]
flash	blic (m)	[blits]
to photograph (vt)	fotografoj	[fotografój]
to take pictures	bëj foto	[bəj fóto]
to have one's picture taken	bëj fotografi	[bəj fotografí]
focus	fokus (m)	[fokús]
to focus	fokusoj	[fokusój]
sharp, in focus (adj)	i qartë	[i cártə]
sharpness	qartësi (f)	[cartəsí]
contrast	kontrast (m)	[kontrást]
contrast (as adj)	me kontrast	[mε kontrást]
picture (photo)	foto (f)	[fóto]
negative (n)	negativ (m)	[nεgatív]
film (a roll of ~)	film negativash (m)	[fílm nεgatívaʃ]
frame (still)	imazh (m)	[imáʒ]
to print (photos)	printoj	[printój]

138. Beach. Swimming

beach	plazh (m)	[plaʒ]
sand	rërë (f)	[rərə]
deserted (beach)	plazh i shkretë	[plaʒ i ʃkrétə]
suntan	nxirje nga dielli (f)	[ndzírjε ŋa díεɬi]
to get a tan	nxihem	[ndzíhεm]
tan (adj)	i nxirë	[i ndzírə]
sunscreen	krem dielli (f)	[krεm díεɬi]
bikini	bikini (m)	[bikíni]
bathing suit	rrobë banje (f)	[róbə báɲε]
swim trunks	mbathje banjo (f)	[mbáθjε báɲo]
swimming pool	pishinë (f)	[piʃínə]
to swim (vi)	notoj	[notój]
shower	dush (m)	[duʃ]
to change (one's clothes)	ndërroj	[ndərój]
towel	peshqir (m)	[pεʃcír]
boat	varkë (f)	[várkə]
motorboat	skaf (m)	[skaf]
water ski	ski ujor (m)	[ski ujór]

paddle boat	varkë me pedale (f)	[várkə mɛ pɛdálɛ]
surfing	surf (m)	[surf]
surfer	surfist (m)	[surfíst]

scuba set	komplet për skuba (f)	[komplét pər skúba]
flippers (swim fins)	këmbale noti (pl)	[kəmbálɛ nóti]
mask (diving ~)	maskë (f)	[máskə]
diver	zhytës (m)	[ʒýtəs]
to dive (vi)	zhytem	[ʒýtɛm]
underwater (adv)	nën ujë	[nən újə]

beach umbrella	çadër plazhi (f)	[tʃádər plázi]
sunbed (lounger)	shezlong (m)	[ʃɛzlón]
sunglasses	syze dielli (f)	[sýzɛ diéti]
air mattress	dyshek me ajër (m)	[dyʃék mɛ ájər]

| to play (amuse oneself) | loz | [loz] |
| to go for a swim | notoj | [notój] |

beach ball	top plazhi (m)	[top plázi]
to inflate (vt)	fryj	[fryj]
inflatable, air (adj)	që fryhet	[cə frýhɛt]

wave	dallgë (f)	[dátgə]
buoy (line of ~s)	tapë (f)	[tápə]
to drown (ab. person)	mbytem	[mbýtɛm]

to save, to rescue	shpëtoj	[ʃpətój]
life vest	jelek shpëtimi (m)	[jɛlék ʃpətími]
to observe, to watch	vëzhgoj	[vəʒgój]
lifeguard	rojë bregdetare (m)	[rójə brɛgdɛtárɛ]

TECHNICAL EQUIPMENT. TRANSPORTATION

Technical equipment

139. Computer

computer	kompjuter (m)	[kompjutér]
notebook, laptop	laptop (m)	[laptóp]
to turn on	ndez	[ndɛz]
to turn off	fik	[fik]
keyboard	tastiera (f)	[tastiéra]
key	çelës (m)	[tʃéləs]
mouse	maus (m)	[máus]
mouse pad	shtroje e mausit (f)	[ʃtrójɛ ɛ máusit]
button	buton (m)	[butón]
cursor	kursor (m)	[kursór]
monitor	monitor (m)	[monitór]
screen	ekran (m)	[ɛkrán]
hard disk	hard disk (m)	[hárd dísk]
hard disk capacity	kapaciteti i hard diskut (m)	[kapatsitéti i hárd dískut]
memory	memorie (f)	[mɛmóriɛ]
random access memory	memorie operative (f)	[mɛmóriɛ opɛratívɛ]
file	skedë (f)	[skédə]
folder	dosje (f)	[dósjɛ]
to open (vt)	hap	[hap]
to close (vt)	mbyll	[mbyɫ]
to save (vt)	ruaj	[rúaj]
to delete (vt)	fshij	[fʃij]
to copy (vt)	kopjoj	[kopjój]
to sort (vt)	sistemoj	[sistɛmój]
to transfer (copy)	transferoj	[transfɛrój]
program	program (m)	[prográm]
software	softuer (f)	[softuér]
programmer	programues (m)	[programúɛs]
to program (vt)	programoj	[programój]
hacker	haker (m)	[hakér]

password	fjalëkalim (m)	[fjaləkalím]
virus	virus (m)	[virús]
to find, to detect	zbuloj	[zbulój]

| byte | bajt (m) | [bájt] |
| megabyte | megabajt (m) | [mɛgabájt] |

| data | të dhënat (pl) | [tə ðénat] |
| database | databazë (f) | [databázə] |

cable (USB, etc.)	kabllo (f)	[kábɫo]
to disconnect (vt)	shkëpus	[ʃkəpús]
to connect (sth to sth)	lidh	[lið]

140. Internet. E-mail

Internet	internet (m)	[intɛrnét]
browser	shfletues (m)	[ʃflɛtúɛs]
search engine	makineri kërkimi (f)	[makinɛrí kərkími]
provider	ofrues (m)	[ofrúɛs]

webmaster	uebmaster (m)	[uɛbmástɛr]
website	ueb-faqe (f)	[uéb-fácɛ]
webpage	ueb-faqe (f)	[uéb-fácɛ]

| address (e-mail ~) | adresë (f) | [adrésə] |
| address book | libërth adresash (m) | [líbərθ adrésaʃ] |

mailbox	kuti postare (f)	[kutí postárɛ]
mail	postë (f)	[póstə]
full (adj)	i mbushur	[i mbúʃur]

message	mesazh (m)	[mɛsáʒ]
incoming messages	mesazhe të ardhura (pl)	[mɛsáʒɛ tə árðura]
outgoing messages	mesazhe të dërguara (pl)	[mɛsáʒɛ tə dərgúara]

sender	dërguesi (m)	[dərgúɛsi]
to send (vt)	dërgoj	[dərgój]
sending (of mail)	dërgesë (f)	[dərgésə]

| receiver | pranues (m) | [pranúɛs] |
| to receive (vt) | pranoj | [pranój] |

| correspondence | korrespondencë (f) | [korɛspondéntsə] |
| to correspond (vi) | komunikim | [komunikím] |

file	skedë (f)	[skédə]
to download (vt)	shkarkoj	[ʃkarkój]
to create (vt)	krijoj	[krijój]
to delete (vt)	fshij	[fʃíj]

deleted (adj)	e fshirë	[ɛ fʃírə]
connection (ADSL, etc.)	lidhje (f)	[líðjɛ]
speed	shpejtësi (f)	[ʃpɛjtəsí]
modem	modem (m)	[modém]
access	hyrje (f)	[hýrjɛ]
port (e.g., input ~)	port (m)	[port]

connection (make a ~)	lidhje (f)	[líðjɛ]
to connect to ... (vi)	lidhem me ...	[líðɛm mɛ ...]

to select (vt)	përzgjedh	[pərzɟéð]
to search (for ...)	kërkoj ...	[kərkój ...]

Transportation

141. Airplane

airplane	**avion** (m)	[avión]
air ticket	**biletë avioni** (f)	[bilétə avióni]
airline	**kompani ajrore** (f)	[kompaní ajrórɛ]
airport	**aeroport** (m)	[aɛropórt]
supersonic (adj)	**supersonik**	[supɛrsoník]
captain	**kapiten** (m)	[kapitén]
crew	**ekip** (m)	[ɛkíp]
pilot	**pilot** (m)	[pilót]
flight attendant (fem.)	**stjuardesë** (f)	[stjuardésə]
navigator	**navigues** (m)	[navigúɛs]
wings	**krahë** (pl)	[kráhə]
tail	**bisht** (m)	[biʃt]
cockpit	**kabinë** (f)	[kabínə]
engine	**motor** (m)	[motór]
undercarriage (landing gear)	**karrel** (m)	[karél]
turbine	**turbinë** (f)	[turbínə]
propeller	**helikë** (f)	[hɛlíkə]
black box	**kuti e zezë** (f)	[kutí ɛ zézə]
yoke (control column)	**timon** (m)	[timón]
fuel	**karburant** (m)	[karburánt]
safety card	**udhëzime sigurie** (pl)	[uðəzímɛ siguríɛ]
oxygen mask	**maskë oksigjeni** (f)	[máskə oksiɟéni]
uniform	**uniformë** (f)	[unifórmə]
life vest	**jelek shpëtimi** (m)	[jɛlék ʃpətími]
parachute	**parashutë** (f)	[paraʃútə]
takeoff	**ngritje** (f)	[ŋrítjɛ]
to take off (vi)	**fluturon**	[fluturón]
runway	**pista e fluturimit** (f)	[písta ɛ fluturímit]
visibility	**shikueshmëri** (f)	[ʃikuɛʃmərí]
flight (act of flying)	**fluturim** (m)	[fluturím]
altitude	**lartësi** (f)	[lartəsí]
air pocket	**xhep ajri** (m)	[dʒɛp ájri]
seat	**karrige** (f)	[karígɛ]
headphones	**kufje** (f)	[kúfjɛ]

folding tray (tray table)	**tabaka** (f)	[tabaká]
airplane window	**dritare avioni** (f)	[dritárɛ avióni]
aisle	**korridor** (m)	[koridór]

142. Train

train	**tren** (m)	[trɛn]
commuter train	**tren elektrik** (m)	[trɛn ɛlɛktrík]
express train	**tren ekspres** (m)	[trɛn ɛksprés]
diesel locomotive	**lokomotivë me naftë** (f)	[lokomótivǝ mɛ náftǝ]
steam locomotive	**lokomotivë me avull** (f)	[lokomótivǝ mɛ ávuɬ]

| passenger car | **vagon** (m) | [vagón] |
| dining car | **vagon restorant** (m) | [vagón rɛstoránt] |

rails	**shina** (pl)	[ʃína]
railroad	**hekurudhë** (f)	[hɛkurúðǝ]
railway tie	**traversë** (f)	[travérsǝ]

platform (railway ~)	**platformë** (f)	[platfórmǝ]
track (~ 1, 2, etc.)	**binar** (m)	[binár]
semaphore	**semafor** (m)	[sɛmafór]
station	**stacion** (m)	[statsión]

engineer (train driver)	**makinist** (m)	[makiníst]
porter (of luggage)	**portier** (m)	[portiér]
car attendant	**konduktor** (m)	[konduktór]
passenger	**pasagjer** (m)	[pasaɟér]
conductor (ticket inspector)	**konduktor** (m)	[konduktór]

| corridor (in train) | **korridor** (m) | [koridór] |
| emergency brake | **frena urgjence** (f) | [fréna urɟéntsɛ] |

compartment	**ndarje** (f)	[ndárjɛ]
berth	**kat** (m)	[kat]
upper berth	**kati i sipërm** (m)	[káti i sípǝrm]
lower berth	**kati i poshtëm** (m)	[káti i póʃtǝm]
bed linen, bedding	**shtroje shtrati** (pl)	[ʃtrójɛ ʃtráti]

ticket	**biletë** (f)	[bilétǝ]
schedule	**orar** (m)	[orár]
information display	**tabelë e informatave** (f)	[tabélǝ ɛ informátavɛ]

to leave, to depart	**niset**	[nísɛt]
departure (of train)	**nisje** (f)	[nísjɛ]
to arrive (ab. train)	**arrij**	[aríj]
arrival	**arritje** (f)	[arítjɛ]
to arrive by train	**arrij me tren**	[aríj mɛ trɛn]
to get on the train	**hip në tren**	[hip nǝ trén]

to get off the train	zbres nga treni	[zbrɛs ŋa tréni]
train wreck	aksident hekurudhor (m)	[aksidént hɛkuruðór]
to derail (vi)	del nga shinat	[dɛl ŋa ʃínat]

steam locomotive	lokomotivë me avull (f)	[lokomótivə mɛ ávuɫ]
stoker, fireman	mbikëqyrës i zjarrit (m)	[mbikəcýrəs i zjárit]
firebox	furrë (f)	[fúrə]
coal	qymyr (m)	[cymýr]

143. Ship

ship	anije (f)	[aníjɛ]
vessel	mjet lundrues (m)	[mjét lundrúɛs]

steamship	anije me avull (f)	[aníjɛ mɛ ávuɫ]
riverboat	anije lumi (f)	[aníjɛ lúmi]
cruise ship	krocierë (f)	[krotsiérə]
cruiser	anije luftarake (f)	[aníjɛ luftarákɛ]

yacht	jaht (m)	[jáht]
tugboat	anije rimorkiuese (f)	[aníjɛ rimorkiúɛsɛ]
barge	anije transportuese (f)	[aníjɛ transportúɛsɛ]
ferry	traget (m)	[tragét]

sailing ship	anije me vela (f)	[aníjɛ mɛ véla]
brigantine	brigantinë (f)	[brigantínə]

ice breaker	akullthyese (f)	[akuɫθýɛsɛ]
submarine	nëndetëse (f)	[nəndétəsɛ]

boat (flat-bottomed ~)	barkë (f)	[bárkə]
dinghy	gomone (f)	[gomónɛ]
lifeboat	varkë shpëtimi (f)	[várkə ʃpətími]
motorboat	skaf (m)	[skaf]

captain	kapiten (m)	[kapitén]
seaman	marinar (m)	[marinár]
sailor	marinar (m)	[marinár]
crew	ekip (m)	[ɛkíp]

boatswain	kryemarinar (m)	[kryɛmarinár]
ship's boy	djali i anijes (m)	[djáli i aníjɛs]
cook	kuzhinier (m)	[kuʒiniér]
ship's doctor	doktori i anijes (m)	[doktóri i aníjɛs]

deck	kuverta (f)	[kuvérta]
mast	direk (m)	[dirék]
sail	vela (f)	[véla]
hold	bagazh (m)	[bagáʒ]
bow (prow)	harku sipëror (m)	[hárku sipərór]

stern	pjesa e pasme (f)	[pjésa ɛ pásmɛ]
oar	rrem (m)	[rɛm]
screw propeller	helikë (f)	[hɛlíkə]
cabin	kabinë (f)	[kabínə]
wardroom	zyrë e oficerëve (m)	[zýrə ɛ ofitsérəvɛ]
engine room	salla e motorit (m)	[sáɫa ɛ motórit]
bridge	urë komanduese (f)	[úrə komandúɛsɛ]
radio room	kabina radiotelegrafike (f)	[kabína radiotɛlɛgrafíkɛ]
wave (radio)	valë (f)	[válə]
logbook	libri i shënimeve (m)	[líbri i ʃənímɛvɛ]
spyglass	dylbi (f)	[dylbí]
bell	këmbanë (f)	[kəmbánə]
flag	flamur (m)	[flamúr]
hawser (mooring ~)	pallamar (m)	[paɫamár]
knot (bowline, etc.)	nyjë (f)	[nýjə]
deckrails	parmakë (pl)	[parmákə]
gangway	shkallë (f)	[ʃkáɫə]
anchor	spirancë (f)	[spirántsə]
to weigh anchor	ngre spirancën	[ŋré spirántsən]
to drop anchor	hedh spirancën	[hɛð spirántsən]
anchor chain	zinxhir i spirancës (m)	[zindʒír i spirántsəs]
port (harbor)	port (m)	[port]
quay, wharf	skelë (f)	[skélə]
to berth (moor)	ankoroj	[ankorój]
to cast off	niset	[nísɛt]
trip, voyage	udhëtim (m)	[uðətím]
cruise (sea trip)	udhëtim me krocierë (f)	[uðətím mɛ krotsiérə]
course (route)	kursi i udhëtimit (m)	[kúrsi i uðətímit]
route (itinerary)	itinerar (m)	[itinɛrár]
fairway (safe water channel)	ujëra të lundrueshme (f)	[újəra tə lundrúɛʃmɛ]
shallows	cekëtinë (f)	[tsɛkətínə]
to run aground	bllokohet në rërë	[bɫokóhɛt nə rərə]
storm	stuhi (f)	[stuhí]
signal	sinjal (m)	[siɲál]
to sink (vi)	fundoset	[fundósɛt]
Man overboard!	Njeri në det!	[ɲɛrí nə dɛt!]
SOS (distress signal)	SOS (m)	[sos]
ring buoy	bovë shpëtuese (f)	[bóvə ʃpətúɛsɛ]

144. Airport

airport	aeroport (m)	[aɛropórt]
airplane	avion (m)	[avión]
airline	kompani ajrore (f)	[kompaní ajrórɛ]
air traffic controller	kontroll i trafikut ajror (m)	[kontróɫ i trafíkut ajrór]
departure	nisje (f)	[nísjɛ]
arrival	arritje (f)	[arítjɛ]
to arrive (by plane)	arrij me avion	[aríj mɛ avión]
departure time	nisja (f)	[nísja]
arrival time	arritja (f)	[arítja]
to be delayed	vonesë	[vonésə]
flight delay	vonesë avioni (f)	[vonésə avióni]
information board	ekrani i informacioneve (m)	[ɛkráni i informatsiónɛvɛ]
information	informacion (m)	[informatsión]
to announce (vt)	njoftoj	[ɲoftój]
flight (e.g., next ~)	fluturim (m)	[fluturím]
customs	doganë (f)	[dogánə]
customs officer	doganier (m)	[doganiér]
customs declaration	deklarim doganor (m)	[dɛklarím doganór]
to fill out (vt)	plotësoj	[plotəsój]
to fill out the declaration	plotësoj deklaratën	[plotəsój dɛklarátən]
passport control	kontroll pasaportash (m)	[kontróɫ pasapórtaʃ]
luggage	bagazh (m)	[bagáʒ]
hand luggage	bagazh dore (m)	[bagáʒ dórɛ]
luggage cart	karrocë bagazhesh (f)	[karótsə bagáʒɛʃ]
landing	aterrim (m)	[atɛrím]
landing strip	pistë aterrimi (f)	[pístə atɛrími]
to land (vi)	aterroj	[atɛrój]
airstair (passenger stair)	shkallë avioni (f)	[ʃkáɫə avióni]
check-in	regjistrim (m)	[rɛɟistrím]
check-in counter	sportel regjistrimi (m)	[sportél rɛɟistrími]
to check-in (vi)	regjistrohem	[rɛɟistróhɛm]
boarding pass	biletë e hyrjes (f)	[bilétə ɛ hýrjɛs]
departure gate	porta e nisjes (f)	[pórta ɛ nísjɛs]
transit	transit (m)	[transít]
to wait (vt)	pres	[prɛs]
departure lounge	salla e nisjes (f)	[sáɫa ɛ nísjɛs]
to see off	përcjell	[pərtsjéɫ]
to say goodbye	përshëndetem	[pərʃəndétɛm]

145. Bicycle. Motorcycle

bicycle	biçikletë (f)	[bitʃiklétə]
scooter	skuter (m)	[skutér]
motorcycle, bike	motoçikletë (f)	[mototʃiklétə]

to go by bicycle	shkoj me biçikletë	[ʃkoj mɛ bitʃiklétə]
handlebars	timon (m)	[timón]
pedal	pedale (f)	[pɛdálɛ]
brakes	frenat (pl)	[frénat]
bicycle seat (saddle)	shalë (f)	[ʃálə]

pump	pompë (f)	[pómpə]
luggage rack	mbajtëse (f)	[mbájtəsɛ]
front lamp	drita e përparme (f)	[dríta ɛ pərpármɛ]
helmet	helmetë (f)	[hɛlmétə]

wheel	rrotë (f)	[rótə]
fender	parafango (f)	[parafáŋo]
rim	rreth i jashtëm i rrotës (m)	[rɛθ i jáʃtəm i rótəs]
spoke	telat e diskut (m)	[télat ɛ dískut]

Cars

146. Types of cars

automobile, car	makinë (f)	[makínə]
sports car	makinë sportive (f)	[makínə sportívɛ]
limousine	limuzinë (f)	[limuzínə]
off-road vehicle	fuoristradë (f)	[fuoristrádə]
convertible (n)	kabriolet (m)	[kabriolét]
minibus	furgon (m)	[furgón]
ambulance	ambulancë (f)	[ambulántsə]
snowplow	borëpastruese (f)	[borəpastrúɛsɛ]
truck	kamion (m)	[kamión]
tanker truck	autocisternë (f)	[autotsistérnə]
van (small truck)	furgon mallrash (m)	[furgón máɬraʃ]
road tractor (trailer truck)	kamionçinë (f)	[kamiontʃínə]
trailer	rimorkio (f)	[rimórkio]
comfortable (adj)	i rehatshëm	[i rɛhátʃəm]
used (adj)	i përdorur	[i pərdórur]

147. Cars. Bodywork

hood	kofano (f)	[kófano]
fender	parafango (f)	[parafáŋo]
roof	çati (f)	[tʃatí]
windshield	xham i përparmë (m)	[dʒam i pərpármə]
rear-view mirror	pasqyrë për prapa (f)	[pascýrə pər prápa]
windshield washer	larëse xhami (f)	[lárəsɛ dʒámi]
windshield wipers	fshirëse xhami (f)	[fʃírəsɛ dʒámi]
side window	xham anësor (m)	[dʒam anəsór]
window lift (power window)	levë xhami (f)	[lévə dʒámi]
antenna	antenë (f)	[anténə]
sunroof	çati diellore (f)	[tʃatí diɛɬórɛ]
bumper	parakolp (m)	[parakólp]
trunk	bagazh (m)	[bagáʒ]
roof luggage rack	bagazh mbi çati (m)	[bagáʒ mbi tʃatí]
door	derë (f)	[dérə]

| door handle | doreza e derës (m) | [doréza ɛ dérəs] |
| door lock | kyç (m) | [kytʃ] |

license plate	targë makine (f)	[tárgə makínɛ]
muffler	silenciator (m)	[silɛntsiatór]
gas tank	serbator (m)	[sɛrbatór]
tailpipe	tub shkarkimi (m)	[tub ʃkarkími]

gas, accelerator	gaz (m)	[gaz]
pedal	këmbëz (f)	[kémbəz]
gas pedal	pedal i gazit (m)	[pɛdál i gázit]

brake	freni (m)	[fréni]
brake pedal	pedal i frenave (m)	[pɛdál i frénavɛ]
to brake (use the brake)	frenoj	[frɛnój]
parking brake	freni i dorës (m)	[fréni i dórəs]

clutch	friksion (m)	[friksión]
clutch pedal	pedal i friksionit (m)	[pɛdál i friksiónit]
clutch disc	disk i friksionit (m)	[dísk i friksiónit]
shock absorber	amortizator (m)	[amortizatór]

| wheel | rrotë (f) | [rótə] |
| spare tire | gomë rezervë (f) | [gómə rɛzérvə] |

| tire | gomë (f) | [gómə] |
| hubcap | mbulesë gome (f) | [mbulésə gómɛ] |

| driving wheels | rrota makine (f) | [róta makínɛ] |
| front-wheel drive (as adj) | me rrotat e përparme | [mɛ rotat ɛ pərpármɛ] |

| rear-wheel drive (as adj) | me rrotat e pasme | [mɛ rótat ɛ pásmɛ] |
| all-wheel drive (as adj) | me të gjitha rrotat | [mɛ tə ɟíθa rótat] |

| gearbox | kutia e marsheve (f) | [kutía ɛ márʃɛvɛ] |
| automatic (adj) | automatik | [automatík] |

| mechanical (adj) | mekanik | [mɛkaník] |
| gear shift | levë e marshit (f) | [lévə ɛ márʃit] |

| headlight | dritë e përparme (f) | [drítə ɛ pərpármɛ] |
| headlights | dritat e përparme (pl) | [drítat ɛ pərpármɛ] |

low beam	dritat e shkurtra (pl)	[drítat ɛ ʃkúrtra]
high beam	dritat e gjata (pl)	[drítat ɛ ɟáta]
brake light	dritat e frenave (pl)	[drítat ɛ frénavɛ]

parking lights	dritat për parkim (pl)	[drítat pər parkím]
hazard lights	sinjal për urgjencë (m)	[siɲál pər uɟéntsə]
fog lights	drita mjegulle (pl)	[dríta mjéguɫɛ]
turn signal	sinjali i kthesës (m)	[siɲáli i kθésəs]
back-up light	dritat e prapme (pl)	[drítat ɛ prápmɛ]

148. Cars. Passenger compartment

car inside (interior)	interier (m)	[intɛriér]
leather (as adj)	prej lëkure	[prɛj ləkúrɛ]
velour (as adj)	kadife	[kadífɛ]
upholstery	veshje (f)	[véʃjɛ]
instrument (gage)	instrument (m)	[instrumént]
dashboard	panel instrumentesh (m)	[panél instruméntɛʃ]
speedometer	matës i shpejtësisë (m)	[mátəs i ʃpɛjtəsísə]
needle (pointer)	shigjetë (f)	[ʃiɟétə]
odometer	kilometrazh (m)	[kilomɛtráʒ]
indicator (sensor)	indikator (m)	[indikatór]
level	nivel (m)	[nivél]
warning light	dritë paralajmëruese (f)	[drítə paralajmərúɛsɛ]
steering wheel	timon (m)	[timón]
horn	bori (f)	[borí]
button	buton (m)	[butón]
switch	çelës drite (m)	[tʃéləs drítɛ]
seat	karrige (f)	[karígɛ]
backrest	shpinore (f)	[ʃpinórɛ]
headrest	mbështetësja e kokës (m)	[mbəʃtétəsja ɛ kókəs]
seat belt	rrip i sigurimit (m)	[rip i sigurímit]
to fasten the belt	lidh rripin e sigurimit	[lið rípin ɛ sigurímit]
adjustment (of seats)	rregulloj (m)	[rɛguɫój]
airbag	jastëk ajri (m)	[jastək ájri]
air-conditioner	kondicioner (m)	[konditsionér]
radio	radio (f)	[rádio]
CD player	disk CD (m)	[dísk tsɛdé]
to turn on	ndez	[ndɛz]
antenna	antenë (f)	[anténə]
glove box	kroskot (m)	[kroskót]
ashtray	taketuke (f)	[takɛtúkɛ]

149. Cars. Engine

engine, motor	motor (m)	[motór]
diesel (as adj)	me naftë	[mɛ náftə]
gasoline (as adj)	me benzinë	[mɛ bɛnzínə]
engine volume	vëllim i motorit (m)	[vəɫím i motórit]
power	fuqi (f)	[fucí]
horsepower	kuaj-fuqi (f)	[kúaj-fucí]
piston	piston (m)	[pistón]

| cylinder | cilindër (m) | [tsilíndər] |
| valve | valvulë (f) | [valvúlə] |

injector	injektor (m)	[iɲɛktór]
generator (alternator)	gjenerator (m)	[ɟɛnɛratór]
carburetor	karburator (m)	[karburatór]
motor oil	vaj i motorit (m)	[vaj i motórit]

radiator	radiator (m)	[radiatór]
coolant	antifriz (m)	[antifríz]
cooling fan	ventilator (m)	[vɛntilatór]

battery (accumulator)	bateri (f)	[batɛrí]
starter	motorino (f)	[motoríno]
ignition	kuadër ndezës (m)	[kuádər ndézəs]
spark plug	kandelë (f)	[kandélə]

terminal (of battery)	morseta e baterisë (f)	[morséta ɛ batɛrísə]
positive terminal	kahu pozitiv (m)	[káhu pózitiv]
negative terminal	kahu negativ (m)	[káhu négativ]
fuse	siguresë (f)	[sigurésə]

air filter	filtri i ajrit (m)	[fíltri i ájrit]
oil filter	filtri i vajit (m)	[fíltri i vájit]
fuel filter	filtri i karburantit (m)	[fíltri i karburántit]

150. Cars. Crash. Repair

car crash	aksident (m)	[aksidént]
traffic accident	aksident rrugor (m)	[aksidént rúgor]
to crash (into the wall, etc.)	përplasem në mur	[pərplásɛm nə mur]
to get smashed up	aksident i rëndë	[aksidént i rəndə]
damage	dëm (m)	[dəm]
intact (unscathed)	pa dëmtime	[pa dəmtímɛ]

breakdown	avari (f)	[avarí]
to break down (vi)	prishet	[príʃet]
towrope	kabllo rimorkimi (f)	[kábło rimorkími]

puncture	shpim (m)	[ʃpim]
to be flat	shpohet	[ʃpóhɛt]
to pump up	fryj	[fryj]
pressure	presion (m)	[prɛsión]
to check (to examine)	kontrolloj	[kontrołój]

repair	riparim (m)	[riparím]
auto repair shop	auto servis (m)	[áuto sɛrvís]
spare part	pjesë këmbimi (f)	[pjésə kəmbími]
part	pjesë (f)	[pjésə]

bolt (with nut)	bulona (f)	[bulóna]
screw (fastener)	vida (f)	[vída]
nut	dado (f)	[dádo]
washer	rondelë (f)	[rondélə]
bearing (e.g., ball ~)	kushineta (f)	[kuʃinéta]

tube	tub (m)	[tub]
gasket (head ~)	rondelë (f)	[rondélə]
cable, wire	kabllo (f)	[kábɫo]

jack	krik (m)	[krik]
wrench	çelës (m)	[tʃéləs]
hammer	çekiç (m)	[tʃɛkítʃ]
pump	pompë (f)	[pómpə]
screwdriver	kaçavidë (f)	[katʃavídə]

| fire extinguisher | bombolë kundër zjarrit (f) | [bombólə kúndər zjárit] |
| warning triangle | trekëndësh paralajmërues (m) | [trékəndəʃ paralajmərúɛs] |

to stall (vi)	fiket	[fíkɛt]
stall (n)	fikje (f)	[fíkjɛ]
to be broken	prishet	[príʃɛt]

to overheat (vi)	nxehet	[ndzéhɛt]
to be clogged up	bllokohet	[bɫokóhɛt]
to freeze up (pipes, etc.)	ngrihet	[ŋríhɛt]
to burst (vi, ab. tube)	plas tubi	[plas túbi]

pressure	presion (m)	[prɛsión]
level	nivel (m)	[nivél]
slack (~ belt)	i lirshëm	[i lírʃəm]

dent	shtypje (f)	[ʃtýpjɛ]
knocking noise (engine)	zhurmë motori (f)	[ʒúrmə motóri]
crack	çarje (f)	[tʃárjɛ]
scratch	gërvishtje (f)	[gərvíʃtjɛ]

151. Cars. Road

road	rrugë (f)	[rúgə]
highway	autostradë (f)	[autostrádə]
freeway	autostradë (f)	[autostrádə]
direction (way)	drejtim (m)	[drɛjtím]
distance	largësi (f)	[largəsí]

bridge	urë (f)	[úrə]
parking lot	parking (m)	[parkíŋ]
square	shesh (m)	[ʃɛʃ]
interchange	kryqëzim rrugësh (m)	[krycəzím rúgəʃ]

tunnel	tunel (m)	[tunél]
gas station	pikë karburanti (f)	[píkə karburánti]
parking lot	parking (m)	[parkíŋ]
gas pump (fuel dispenser)	pompë karburanti (f)	[pómpə karburánti]
auto repair shop	auto servis (m)	[áuto sɛrvís]
to get gas (to fill up)	furnizohem me gaz	[furnizóhɛm mɛ gáz]
fuel	karburant (m)	[karburánt]
jerrycan	bidon (m)	[bidón]

asphalt	asfalt (m)	[asfált]
road markings	vijëzime të rrugës (pl)	[vijəzímɛ tə rúgəs]
curb	bordurë (f)	[bordúrə]
guardrail	parmakë të sigurisë (pl)	[parmákə tə sigurísə]
ditch	kanal (m)	[kanál]
roadside (shoulder)	shpatull rrugore (f)	[ʃpátuɫ rugórɛ]
lamppost	shtyllë dritash (f)	[ʃtýɫə drítaʃ]

to drive (a car)	ngas	[ŋas]
to turn (e.g., ~ left)	kthej	[kθɛj]
to make a U-turn	marr kthesë U	[mar kθésə u]
reverse (~ gear)	marsh prapa (m)	[marʃ prápa]

to honk (vi)	i bie borisë	[i bíɛ borísə]
honk (sound)	tyt (m)	[tyt]
to get stuck (in the mud, etc.)	ngec në baltë	[ŋɛts nə báltə]
to spin the wheels	xhiroj gomat	[dʒirój gómat]
to cut, to turn off (vt)	fik	[fik]

speed	shpejtësi (f)	[ʃpɛjtəsí]
to exceed the speed limit	kaloj minimumin e shpejtësisë	[kalój minimúmin ɛ ʃpɛjtəsísə]
to give a ticket	vë gjobë	[və ɟóbə]
traffic lights	semafor (m)	[sɛmafór]
driver's license	patentë shoferi (f)	[paténtə ʃoféri]

grade crossing	kalim hekurudhor (m)	[kalím hɛkuruðór]
intersection	kryqëzim (m)	[krycəzím]
crosswalk	kalim për këmbësorë (m)	[kalím pər kəmbəsórə]
bend, curve	kthesë (f)	[kθésə]
pedestrian zone	zonë këmbësorësh (f)	[zónə kəmbəsórəʃ]

PEOPLE. LIFE EVENTS

Life events

152. Holidays. Event

celebration, holiday	festë (f)	[féstə]
national day	festë kombëtare (f)	[féstə kombətárɛ]
public holiday	festë publike (f)	[féstə publíkɛ]
to commemorate (vt)	festoj	[fɛstój]
event (happening)	ceremoni (f)	[tsɛrɛmoní]
event (organized activity)	eveniment (m)	[ɛvɛnimént]
banquet (party)	banket (m)	[bankét]
reception (formal party)	pritje (f)	[prítjɛ]
feast	aheng (m)	[ahéŋ]
anniversary	përvjetor (m)	[pərvjɛtór]
jubilee	jubile (m)	[jubilé]
to celebrate (vt)	festoj	[fɛstój]
New Year	Viti i Ri (m)	[víti i rí]
Happy New Year!	Gëzuar Vitin e Ri!	[gəzúar vítin ɛ rí!]
Santa Claus	Santa Klaus (m)	[sánta kláus]
Christmas	Krishtlindje (f)	[kriʃtlíndjɛ]
Merry Christmas!	Gëzuar Krishtlindjen!	[gəzúar kriʃtlíndjɛn!]
Christmas tree	péma e Krishtlindjes (f)	[péma ɛ kriʃtlíndjɛs]
fireworks (fireworks show)	fishekzjarrë (m)	[fiʃɛkzjárə]
wedding	dasmë (f)	[dásmə]
groom	dhëndër (m)	[ðéndər]
bride	nuse (f)	[núsɛ]
to invite (vt)	ftoj	[ftoj]
invitation card	ftesë (f)	[ftésə]
guest	mysafir (m)	[mysafír]
to visit	vizitoj	[vizitój]
(~ your parents, etc.)		
to meet the guests	takoj të ftuarit	[takój tə ftúarit]
gift, present	dhuratë (f)	[ðurátə]
to give (sth as present)	dhuroj	[ðurój]
to receive gifts	marr dhurata	[mar ðuráta]

bouquet (of flowers)	buqetë (f)	[bucétə]
congratulations	urime (f)	[urímɛ]
to congratulate (vt)	përgëzoj	[pərgəzój]

greeting card	kartolinë (f)	[kartolínə]
to send a postcard	dërgoj kartolinë	[dərgój kartolínə]
to get a postcard	marr kartolinë	[mar kartolínə]

toast	dolli (f)	[doɫí]
to offer (a drink, etc.)	qeras	[cɛrás]
champagne	shampanjë (f)	[ʃampáɲə]

to enjoy oneself	kënaqem	[kənácɛm]
merriment (gaiety)	gëzim (m)	[gəzím]
joy (emotion)	gëzim (m)	[gəzím]

| dance | vallëzim (m) | [vaɫəzím] |
| to dance (vi, vt) | vallëzoj | [vaɫəzój] |

| waltz | vals (m) | [vals] |
| tango | tango (f) | [táŋo] |

153. Funerals. Burial

cemetery	varreza (f)	[varéza]
grave, tomb	varr (m)	[var]
cross	kryq (m)	[kryc]
gravestone	gur varri (m)	[gur vári]
fence	gardh (m)	[garð]
chapel	kishëz (m)	[kíʃəz]

death	vdekje (f)	[vdékjɛ]
to die (vi)	vdes	[vdɛs]
the deceased	i vdekuri (m)	[i vdékuri]
mourning	zi (f)	[zi]
to bury (vt)	varros	[varós]
funeral home	agjenci funeralesh (f)	[aɟɛntsí funɛrálɛʃ]
funeral	funeral (m)	[funɛrál]

wreath	kurorë (f)	[kurórə]
casket, coffin	arkivol (m)	[arkivól]
hearse	makinë funebre (f)	[makínə funébrɛ]
shroud	qefin (m)	[cɛfín]

funeral procession	kortezh (m)	[kortéʒ]
funerary urn	urnë (f)	[úrnə]
crematory	kremator (m)	[krɛmatór]
obituary	përkujtim (m)	[pərkujtím]
to cry (weep)	qaj	[caj]
to sob (vi)	qaj me dënesë	[caj mɛ dənésə]

154. War. Soldiers

platoon	togë (f)	[tógə]
company	kompani (f)	[kompaní]
regiment	regjiment (m)	[rɛɟimént]
army	ushtri (f)	[uʃtrí]
division	divizion (m)	[divizión]

| section, squad | skuadër (f) | [skuádər] |
| host (army) | armatë (f) | [armátə] |

| soldier | ushtar (m) | [uʃtár] |
| officer | oficer (m) | [ofitsér] |

private	ushtar (m)	[uʃtár]
sergeant	rreshter (m)	[rɛʃtér]
lieutenant	toger (m)	[togér]
captain	kapiten (m)	[kapitén]
major	major (m)	[majór]
colonel	kolonel (m)	[kolonél]
general	gjeneral (m)	[ɟɛnɛrál]

sailor	marinar (m)	[marinár]
captain	kapiten (m)	[kapitén]
boatswain	kryemarinar (m)	[kryɛmarinár]

artilleryman	artiljer (m)	[artiljér]
paratrooper	parashutist (m)	[paraʃutíst]
pilot	pilot (m)	[pilót]
navigator	navigues (m)	[navigúɛs]
mechanic	mekanik (m)	[mɛkaník]

pioneer (sapper)	xhenier (m)	[dʒɛniér]
parachutist	parashutist (m)	[paraʃutíst]
reconnaissance scout	agjent zbulimi (m)	[aɟént zbulími]
sniper	snajper (m)	[snajpér]

patrol (group)	patrullë (f)	[patrúɫə]
to patrol (vt)	patrulloj	[patruɫój]
sentry, guard	rojë (f)	[rójə]

warrior	luftëtar (m)	[luftətár]
patriot	patriot (m)	[patriót]
hero	hero (m)	[hɛró]
heroine	heroinë (f)	[hɛroínə]

| traitor | tradhtar (m) | [traðtár] |
| to betray (vt) | tradhtoj | [traðtój] |

| deserter | dezertues (m) | [dɛzɛrtúɛs] |
| to desert (vi) | dezertoj | [dɛzɛrtój] |

mercenary	mercenar (m)	[mɛrtsɛnár]
recruit	rekrut (m)	[rɛkrút]
volunteer	vullnetar (m)	[vuɫnɛtár]

dead (n)	vdekur (m)	[vdékur]
wounded (n)	i plagosur (m)	[i plagósur]
prisoner of war	rob lufte (m)	[rob lúftɛ]

155. War. Military actions. Part 1

war	luftë (f)	[lúftə]
to be at war	në luftë	[nə lúftə]
civil war	luftë civile (f)	[lúftə tsivílɛ]

treacherously (adv)	pabesisht	[pabɛsíʃt]
declaration of war	shpallje lufte (f)	[ʃpáɫjɛ lúftɛ]
to declare (~ war)	shpall	[ʃpaɫ]
aggression	agresion (m)	[agrɛsión]
to attack (invade)	sulmoj	[sulmój]

to invade (vt)	pushtoj	[puʃtój]
invader	pushtues (m)	[puʃtúɛs]
conqueror	pushtues (m)	[puʃtúɛs]

defense	mbrojtje (f)	[mbrójtjɛ]
to defend (a country, etc.)	mbroj	[mbrój]
to defend (against ...)	mbrohem	[mbróhɛm]

enemy	armik (m)	[armík]
foe, adversary	kundërshtar (m)	[kundərʃtár]
enemy (as adj)	armike	[armíkɛ]

| strategy | strategji (f) | [stratɛɟí] |
| tactics | taktikë (f) | [taktíkə] |

order	urdhër (m)	[úrðər]
command (order)	komandë (f)	[komándə]
to order (vt)	urdhëroj	[urðərój]
mission	mision (m)	[misión]
secret (adj)	sekret	[sɛkrét]

| battle, combat | betejë (f) | [bɛtéjə] |
| combat | luftim (m) | [luftím] |

attack	sulm (m)	[sulm]
charge (assault)	sulm (m)	[sulm]
to storm (vt)	sulmoj	[sulmój]
siege (to be under ~)	nën rrethim (m)	[nən rɛθím]
offensive (n)	sulm (m)	[sulm]
to go on the offensive	kaloj në sulm	[kalój nə súlm]

retreat	tërheqje (f)	[tərhécjɛ]
to retreat (vi)	tërhiqem	[tərhícɛm]

encirclement	rrethim (m)	[rɛθím]
to encircle (vt)	rrethoj	[rɛθój]

bombing (by aircraft)	bombardim (m)	[bombaɾdím]
to drop a bomb	hedh bombë	[hɛð bómbə]
to bomb (vt)	bombardoj	[bombaɾdój]
explosion	shpërthim (m)	[ʃpəɾθím]

shot	e shtënë (f)	[ɛ ʃténə]
to fire (~ a shot)	qëlloj	[cəɫój]
firing (burst of ~)	të shtëna (pl)	[tə ʃténa]

to aim (to point a weapon)	vë në shënjestër	[və nə ʃəɲéstəɾ]
to point (a gun)	drejtoj armën	[dɾɛjtój áɾmən]
to hit (the target)	qëlloj	[cəɫój]

to sink (~ a ship)	fundos	[fundós]
hole (in a ship)	vrimë (f)	[vrímə]
to founder, to sink (vi)	fundoset	[fundósɛt]

front (war ~)	front (m)	[front]
evacuation	evakuim (m)	[ɛvakuím]
to evacuate (vt)	evakuoj	[ɛvakuój]

trench	llogore (f)	[ɫogóɾɛ]
barbwire	tel me gjemba (m)	[tɛl mɛ ɟémba]
barrier (anti tank ~)	pengesë (f)	[pɛɲésə]
watchtower	kullë vrojtuese (f)	[kúɫə vrojtúɛsɛ]

military hospital	spital ushtarak (m)	[spitál uʃtarák]
to wound (vt)	plagos	[plagós]
wound	plagë (f)	[plágə]
wounded (n)	i plagosur (m)	[i plagósur]
to be wounded	jam i plagosur	[jam i plagósur]
serious (wound)	rëndë	[réndə]

156. Weapons

weapons	armë (f)	[áɾmə]
firearms	armë zjarri (f)	[áɾmə zjári]
cold weapons (knives, etc.)	armë të ftohta (pl)	[áɾmə tə ftóhta]

chemical weapons	armë kimike (f)	[áɾmə kimíkɛ]
nuclear (adj)	nukleare	[nuklɛáɾɛ]
nuclear weapons	armë nukleare (f)	[áɾmə nuklɛáɾɛ]
bomb	bombë (f)	[bómbə]

atomic bomb	bombë atomike (f)	[bómbə atomíkɛ]
pistol (gun)	pistoletë (f)	[pistolétə]
rifle	pushkë (f)	[púʃkə]
submachine gun	mitraloz (m)	[mitralóz]
machine gun	mitraloz (m)	[mitralóz]
muzzle	grykë (f)	[grýkə]
barrel	tytë pushke (f)	[týtə púʃkɛ]
caliber	kalibër (m)	[kalíbər]
trigger	këmbëz (f)	[kə́mbəz]
sight (aiming device)	shënjestër (f)	[ʃəɲéstər]
magazine	karikator (m)	[karikatór]
butt (shoulder stock)	qytë (f)	[cýtə]
hand grenade	bombë dore (f)	[bómbə dórɛ]
explosive	eksploziv (m)	[ɛksplozív]
bullet	plumb (m)	[plúmb]
cartridge	fishek (m)	[fiʃék]
charge	karikim (m)	[karikím]
ammunition	municion (m)	[munitsión]
bomber (aircraft)	avion bombardues (m)	[avión bombardúɛs]
fighter	avion luftarak (m)	[avión luftarák]
helicopter	helikopter (m)	[hɛlikoptér]
anti-aircraft gun	armë anti-ajrore (f)	[ármə ánti-ajrórɛ]
tank	tank (m)	[tank]
tank gun	top tanku (m)	[top tánku]
artillery	artileri (f)	[artilɛrí]
gun (cannon, howitzer)	top (m)	[top]
to lay (a gun)	vë në shënjestër	[və nə ʃəɲéstər]
shell (projectile)	mortajë (f)	[mortájə]
mortar bomb	bombë mortaje (f)	[bómbə mortájɛ]
mortar	mortajë (f)	[mortájə]
splinter (shell fragment)	copëz mortaje (f)	[tsópəz mortájɛ]
submarine	nëndetëse (f)	[nəndétəsɛ]
torpedo	silurë (f)	[silúrə]
missile	raketë (f)	[rakétə]
to load (gun)	mbush	[mbúʃ]
to shoot (vi)	qëlloj	[cəɬój]
to point at (the cannon)	drejtoj	[drɛjtój]
bayonet	bajonetë (f)	[bajonétə]
rapier	shpatë (f)	[ʃpátə]
saber (e.g., cavalry ~)	shpatë (f)	[ʃpátə]
spear (weapon)	shtizë (f)	[ʃtízə]

bow	hark (m)	[hárk]
arrow	shigjetë (f)	[ʃiɟétə]
musket	musketë (f)	[muskétə]
crossbow	pushkë-shigjetë (f)	[púʃkə-ʃiɟétə]

157. Ancient people

primitive (prehistoric)	prehistorik	[prɛhistorík]
prehistoric (adj)	prehistorike	[prɛhistoríkɛ]
ancient (~ civilization)	i lashtë	[i láʃtə]

Stone Age	Epoka e Gurit (f)	[ɛpóka ɛ gúrit]
Bronze Age	Epoka e Bronzit (f)	[ɛpóka ɛ brónzit]
Ice Age	Epoka e akullit (f)	[ɛpóka ɛ ákuɫit]

tribe	klan (m)	[klan]
cannibal	kanibal (m)	[kanibál]
hunter	gjahtar (m)	[ɟahtár]
to hunt (vi, vt)	dal për gjah	[dál pər ɟáh]
mammoth	mamut (m)	[mamút]

cave	shpellë (f)	[ʃpéɫə]
fire	zjarr (m)	[zjar]
campfire	zjarr kampingu (m)	[zjar kampíŋu]
cave painting	vizatim në shpella (m)	[vizatím nə ʃpéɫa]

tool (e.g., stone ax)	vegël (f)	[végəl]
spear	shtizë (f)	[ʃtízə]
stone ax	sëpatë guri (f)	[səpátə gúri]
to be at war	në luftë	[nə lúftə]
to domesticate (vt)	zbus	[zbus]

idol	idhull (m)	[íðuɫ]
to worship (vt)	adhuroj	[aðurój]
superstition	besëtytni (f)	[bɛsətytní]
rite	rit (m)	[rit]

evolution	evolucion (m)	[ɛvolutsión]
development	zhvillim (m)	[ʒviɫím]
disappearance (extinction)	zhdukje (f)	[ʒdúkjɛ]
to adapt oneself	përshtatem	[pərʃtátɛm]

archeology	arkeologji (f)	[arkɛoloʝí]
archeologist	arkeolog (m)	[arkɛológ]
archeological (adj)	arkeologjike	[arkɛoloʝíkɛ]

excavation site	vendi i gërmimeve (m)	[véndi i gərmímɛvɛ]
excavations	gërmime (pl)	[gərmímɛ]
find (object)	zbulim (m)	[zbulím]
fragment	fragment (m)	[fragmént]

158. Middle Ages

people (ethnic group)	popull (f)	[pópuɫ]
peoples	popuj (pl)	[pópuj]
tribe	klan (m)	[klan]
tribes	klane (pl)	[klánɛ]

barbarians	barbarë (pl)	[barbárə]
Gauls	Galët (pl)	[gálət]
Goths	Gotët (pl)	[gótət]
Slavs	Sllavët (pl)	[sɫávət]
Vikings	Vikingët (pl)	[vikíɲət]

Romans	Romakët (pl)	[romákət]
Roman (adj)	romak	[romák]

Byzantines	Bizantinët (pl)	[bizantínət]
Byzantium	Bizanti (m)	[bizánti]
Byzantine (adj)	bizantine	[bizantínɛ]

emperor	perandor (m)	[pɛrandór]
leader, chief (tribal ~)	prijës (m)	[príjəs]
powerful (~ king)	i fuqishëm	[i fucíʃəm]
king	mbret (m)	[mbrét]
ruler (sovereign)	sundimtar (m)	[sundimtár]

knight	kalorës (m)	[kalórəs]
feudal lord	lord feudal (m)	[lórd fɛudál]
feudal (adj)	feudal	[fɛudál]
vassal	vasal (m)	[vasál]

duke	dukë (f)	[dúkə]
earl	kont (m)	[kont]
baron	baron (m)	[barón]
bishop	peshkop (m)	[pɛʃkóp]

armor	parzmore (f)	[parzmórɛ]
shield	mburojë (f)	[mburójə]
sword	shpatë (f)	[ʃpátə]
visor	ballnik (m)	[baɫník]
chainmail	thurak (m)	[θurák]

Crusade	Kryqëzata (f)	[krycəzáta]
crusader	kryqtar (m)	[kryctár]

territory	territor (m)	[tɛritór]
to attack (invade)	sulmoj	[sulmój]
to conquer (vt)	mposht	[mpóʃt]
to occupy (invade)	pushtoj	[puʃtój]
siege (to be under ~)	nën rrethim (m)	[nən rɛθím]
besieged (adj)	i rrethuar	[i rɛθúar]

to besiege (vt)	rrethoj	[rrɛθój]
inquisition	inkuizicion (m)	[inkuizitsión]
inquisitor	inkuizitor (m)	[inkuizitór]
torture	torturë (f)	[tortúrə]
cruel (adj)	mizor	[mizór]
heretic	heretik (m)	[hɛrɛtík]
heresy	herezi (f)	[hɛrɛzí]

seafaring	lundrim (m)	[lundrím]
pirate	pirat (m)	[pirát]
piracy	pirateri (f)	[piratɛrí]
boarding (attack)	sulm me anije (m)	[sulm mɛ aníjɛ]
loot, booty	plaçkë (f)	[plátʃkə]
treasures	thesare (pl)	[θɛsárɛ]

discovery	zbulim (m)	[zbulím]
to discover (new land, etc.)	zbuloj	[zbulój]
expedition	ekspeditë (f)	[ɛkspɛdítə]

musketeer	musketar (m)	[muskɛtár]
cardinal	kardinal (m)	[kardinál]
heraldry	heraldikë (f)	[hɛraldíkə]
heraldic (adj)	heraldik	[hɛraldík]

159. Leader. Chief. Authorities

king	mbret (m)	[mbrét]
queen	mbretëreshë (f)	[mbrɛtəréʃə]
royal (adj)	mbretërore	[mbrɛtərórɛ]
kingdom	mbretëri (f)	[mbrɛtərí]

| prince | princ (m) | [prints] |
| princess | princeshë (f) | [printséʃə] |

president	president (m)	[prɛsidént]
vice-president	zëvendës president (m)	[zəvéndəs prɛsidént]
senator	senator (m)	[sɛnatór]

monarch	monark (m)	[monárk]
ruler (sovereign)	sundimtar (m)	[sundimtár]
dictator	diktator (m)	[diktatór]
tyrant	tiran (m)	[tirán]
magnate	manjat (m)	[maɲát]

director	drejtor (m)	[drɛjtór]
chief	udhëheqës (m)	[uðəhécəs]
manager (director)	drejtor (m)	[drɛjtór]
boss	bos (m)	[bos]
owner	pronar (m)	[pronár]
leader	lider (m)	[lidér]

head (~ of delegation)	kryetar (m)	[kryɛtár]
authorities	autoritetet (pl)	[autoritétɛt]
superiors	eprorët (pl)	[ɛprórət]

governor	guvernator (m)	[guvɛrnatór]
consul	konsull (m)	[kónsuɫ]
diplomat	diplomat (m)	[diplomát]
mayor	kryetar komune (m)	[kryɛtár komúnɛ]
sheriff	sherif (m)	[ʃɛríf]

emperor	perandor (m)	[pɛrandór]
tsar, czar	car (m)	[tsár]
pharaoh	faraon (m)	[faraón]
khan	khan (m)	[khán]

160. Breaking the law. Criminals. Part 1

bandit	bandit (m)	[bandít]
crime	krim (m)	[krim]
criminal (person)	kriminel (m)	[kriminél]

thief	hajdut (m)	[hajdút]
to steal (vi, vt)	vjedh	[vjɛð]
stealing, theft	vjedhje (f)	[vjéðjɛ]

to kidnap (vt)	rrëmbej	[rəmbéj]
kidnapping	rrëmbim (m)	[rəmbím]
kidnapper	rrëmbyes (m)	[rəmbýɛs]

| ransom | shpërblesë (f) | [ʃpərblésə] |
| to demand ransom | kërkoj shpërblesë | [kərkój ʃpərblésə] |

to rob (vt)	grabis	[grabís]
robbery	grabitje (f)	[grabítjɛ]
robber	grabitës (m)	[grabítəs]

to extort (vt)	zhvat	[ʒvat]
extortionist	zhvatës (m)	[ʒvátəs]
extortion	zhvatje (f)	[ʒvátjɛ]

to murder, to kill	vras	[vras]
murder	vrasje (f)	[vrásjɛ]
murderer	vrasës (m)	[vrásəs]

gunshot	e shtënë (f)	[ɛ ʃténə]
to fire (~ a shot)	qëlloj	[cəɫój]
to shoot to death	qëlloj për vdekje	[cəɫój pər vdékjɛ]
to shoot (vi)	qëlloj	[cəɫój]
shooting	të shtëna (pl)	[tə ʃténa]
incident (fight, etc.)	incident (m)	[intsidént]

Тоpe

fight, brawl	përleshje (f)	[pərléʃɛ]
Help!	Ndihmë!	[ndíhmə!]
victim	viktimë (f)	[viktímə]

to damage (vt)	dëmtoj	[dəmtój]
damage	dëm (m)	[dəm]
dead body, corpse	kufomë (f)	[kufómə]
grave (~ crime)	i rëndë	[i rə́ndə]

to attack (vt)	sulmoj	[sulmój]
to beat (to hit)	rrah	[rah]
to beat up	sakatoj	[sakatój]
to take (rob of sth)	rrëmbej	[rəmbéj]
to stab to death	ther për vdekje	[θɛr pər vdékjɛ]
to maim (vt)	gjymtoj	[ɟymtój]
to wound (vt)	plagos	[plagós]

blackmail	shantazh (m)	[ʃantáʒ]
to blackmail (vt)	bëj shantazh	[bəj ʃantáʒ]
blackmailer	shantazhist (m)	[ʃantaʒíst]

protection racket	rrjet mashtrimi (m)	[rjét maʃtrími]
racketeer	mashtrues (m)	[maʃtrúɛs]
gangster	gangster (m)	[gaŋstér]
mafia, Mob	mafia (f)	[máfia]

pickpocket	vjedhës xhepash (m)	[vjéðəs dʒépaʃ]
burglar	hajdut (m)	[hajdút]
smuggling	trafikim (m)	[trafikím]
smuggler	trafikues (m)	[trafikúɛs]

forgery	falsifikim (m)	[falsifikím]
to forge (counterfeit)	falsifikoj	[falsifikój]
fake (forged)	fals	[fáls]

161. Breaking the law. Criminals. Part 2

rape	përdhunim (m)	[pərðuním]
to rape (vt)	përdhunoj	[pərðunój]
rapist	përdhunues (m)	[pərðunúɛs]
maniac	maniak (m)	[maniák]

prostitute (fem.)	prostitutë (f)	[prostitútə]
prostitution	prostitucion (m)	[prostitutsión]
pimp	tutor (m)	[tutór]

drug addict	narkoman (m)	[narkomán]
drug dealer	trafikant droge (m)	[trafikánt drógɛ]
to blow up (bomb)	shpërthej	[ʃpərθéj]
explosion	shpërthim (m)	[ʃpərθím]

to set fire	**vë flakën**	[və flákən]
arsonist	**zjarrvënës** (m)	[zjarvénəs]
terrorism	**terrorizëm** (m)	[tɛrorízəm]
terrorist	**terrorist** (m)	[tɛroríst]
hostage	**peng** (m)	[pɛŋ]
to swindle (deceive)	**mashtroj**	[maʃtrój]
swindle, deception	**mashtrim** (m)	[maʃtrím]
swindler	**mashtrues** (m)	[maʃtrúɛs]
to bribe (vt)	**jap ryshfet**	[jap ryʃfét]
bribery	**ryshfet** (m)	[ryʃfét]
bribe	**ryshfet** (m)	[ryʃfét]
poison	**helm** (m)	[hɛlm]
to poison (vt)	**helmoj**	[hɛlmój]
to poison oneself	**helmohem**	[hɛlmóhɛm]
suicide (act)	**vetëvrasje** (f)	[vɛtəvrásjɛ]
suicide (person)	**vetëvrasës** (m)	[vɛtəvrásəs]
to threaten (vt)	**kërcënoj**	[kərtsənój]
threat	**kërcënim** (m)	[kərtsəním]
to make an attempt	**tentoj**	[tɛntój]
attempt (attack)	**atentat** (m)	[atɛntát]
to steal (a car)	**vjedh**	[vjɛð]
to hijack (a plane)	**rrëmbej**	[rəmbéj]
revenge	**hakmarrje** (f)	[hakmárjɛ]
to avenge (get revenge)	**hakmerrem**	[hakmérɛm]
to torture (vt)	**torturoj**	[torturój]
torture	**torturë** (f)	[tortúrə]
to torment (vt)	**torturoj**	[torturój]
pirate	**pirat** (m)	[pirát]
hooligan	**huligan** (m)	[huligán]
armed (adj)	**i armatosur**	[i armatósur]
violence	**dhunë** (f)	[ðúnə]
illegal (unlawful)	**ilegal**	[ilɛgál]
spying (espionage)	**spiunazh** (m)	[spiunáʒ]
to spy (vi)	**spiunoj**	[spiunój]

162. Police. Law. Part 1

justice	**drejtësi** (f)	[drɛjtəsí]
court (see you in ~)	**gjykatë** (f)	[ɟykátə]

judge	gjykatës (m)	[ɟykátəs]
jurors	anëtar jurie (m)	[anətár juríɛ]
jury trial	gjyq me juri (m)	[ɟyc mɛ jurí]
to judge, to try (vt)	gjykoj	[ɟykój]
lawyer, attorney	avokat (m)	[avokát]
defendant	pandehur (m)	[pandéhur]
dock	bankë e të pandehurit (f)	[bánkə ɛ tə pandéhurit]
charge	akuzë (f)	[akúzə]
accused	i akuzuar (m)	[i akuzúar]
sentence	vendim (m)	[vɛndím]
to sentence (vt)	dënoj	[dənój]
guilty (culprit)	fajtor (m)	[fajtór]
to punish (vt)	ndëshkoj	[ndəʃkój]
punishment	ndëshkim (m)	[ndəʃkím]
fine (penalty)	gjobë (f)	[ɟóbə]
life imprisonment	burgim i përjetshëm (m)	[burgím i pərjétʃəm]
death penalty	dënim me vdekje (m)	[dəním mɛ vdékjɛ]
electric chair	karrige elektrike (f)	[karígɛ ɛlɛktríkɛ]
gallows	varje (f)	[várjɛ]
to execute (vt)	ekzekutoj	[ɛkzɛkutój]
execution	ekzekutim (m)	[ɛkzɛkutím]
prison, jail	burg (m)	[búrg]
cell	qeli (f)	[cɛlí]
escort (convoy)	eskortë (f)	[ɛskórtə]
prison guard	gardian burgu (m)	[gardián búrgu]
prisoner	i burgosur (m)	[i burgósur]
handcuffs	pranga (f)	[práŋa]
to handcuff (vt)	vë prangat	[və práŋat]
prison break	arratisje nga burgu (f)	[aratísjɛ ŋa búrgu]
to break out (vi)	arratisem	[aratísɛm]
to disappear (vi)	zhduk	[ʒduk]
to release (from prison)	dal nga burgu	[dál ŋa búrgu]
amnesty	amnisti (f)	[amnistí]
police	polici (f)	[politsí]
police officer	polic (m)	[políts]
police station	komisariat (m)	[komisariát]
billy club	shkop gome (m)	[ʃkop gómɛ]
bullhorn	altoparlant (m)	[altoparlánt]
patrol car	makinë patrullimi (f)	[makínə patruɫími]
siren	alarm (m)	[alárm]

to turn on the siren	**ndez sirenën**	[ndɛz sirénən]
siren call	**zhurmë alarmi** (f)	[ʒúrmə alármi]

crime scene	**skenë krimi** (f)	[skénə krími]
witness	**dëshmitar** (m)	[dəʃmitár]
freedom	**liri** (f)	[lirí]
accomplice	**bashkëpunëtor** (m)	[baʃkəpunətór]
to flee (vi)	**zhdukem**	[ʒdúkɛm]
trace (to leave a ~)	**gjurmë** (f)	[ɟúrmə]

163. Police. Law. Part 2

search (investigation)	**kërkim** (m)	[kərkím]
to look for ...	**kërkoj ...**	[kərkój ...]
suspicion	**dyshim** (m)	[dyʃím]
suspicious (e.g., ~ vehicle)	**i dyshuar**	[i dyʃúar]
to stop (cause to halt)	**ndaloj**	[ndalój]
to detain (keep in custody)	**mbaj të ndaluar**	[mbáj tə ndalúar]

case (lawsuit)	**padi** (f)	[padí]
investigation	**hetim** (m)	[hɛtím]
detective	**detektiv** (m)	[dɛtɛktív]
investigator	**hetues** (m)	[hɛtúɛs]
hypothesis	**hipotezë** (f)	[hipotézə]

motive	**motiv** (m)	[motív]
interrogation	**marrje në pyetje** (f)	[márjɛ nə pýɛtjɛ]
to interrogate (vt)	**marr në pyetje**	[mar nə pýɛtjɛ]
to question (~ neighbors, etc.)	**pyes**	[pýɛs]
check (identity ~)	**verifikim** (m)	[vɛrifikím]

round-up (raid)	**kontroll në grup** (m)	[kontróɫ nə grúp]
search (~ warrant)	**bastisje** (f)	[bastísjɛ]
chase (pursuit)	**ndjekje** (f)	[ndjékjɛ]
to pursue, to chase	**ndjek**	[ndjék]
to track (a criminal)	**ndjek**	[ndjék]

arrest	**arrestim** (m)	[arɛstím]
to arrest (sb)	**arrestoj**	[arɛstój]
to catch (thief, etc.)	**kap**	[kap]
capture	**kapje** (f)	[kápjɛ]

document	**dokument** (m)	[dokumént]
proof (evidence)	**provë** (f)	[próvə]
to prove (vt)	**dëshmoj**	[dəʃmój]
footprint	**gjurmë** (f)	[ɟúrmə]
fingerprints	**shenja gishtash** (pl)	[ʃéɲa gíʃtaʃ]
piece of evidence	**provë** (f)	[próvə]
alibi	**alibi** (f)	[alibí]

innocent (not guilty)	i pafajshëm	[i pafájʃəm]
injustice	padrejtësi (f)	[padrɛjtəsí]
unjust, unfair (adj)	i padrejtë	[i padréjtə]

criminal (adj)	kriminale	[kriminálɛ]
to confiscate (vt)	konfiskoj	[konfiskój]
drug (illegal substance)	drogë (f)	[drógə]
weapon, gun	armë (f)	[ármə]
to disarm (vt)	çarmatos	[tʃarmatós]
to order (command)	urdhëroj	[urðərój]
to disappear (vi)	zhduk	[ʒduk]

law	ligj (m)	[liɟ]
legal, lawful (adj)	ligjor	[liɟór]
illegal, illicit (adj)	i paligjshëm	[i palíɟʃəm]

| responsibility (blame) | përgjegjësi (f) | [pərɟɛɟəsí] |
| responsible (adj) | përgjegjës | [pərɟéɟəs] |

NATURE

The Earth. Part 1

164. Outer space

space	hapësirë (f)	[hapəsírə]
space (as adj)	hapësinor	[hapəsinór]
outer space	kozmos (m)	[kozmós]
world	botë (f)	[bótə]
universe	univers	[univérs]
galaxy	galaksi (f)	[galaksí]
star	yll (m)	[yɬ]
constellation	yllësi (f)	[yɬəsí]
planet	planet (m)	[planét]
satellite	satelit (m)	[satɛlít]
meteorite	meteor (m)	[mɛtɛór]
comet	kometë (f)	[kométə]
asteroid	asteroid (m)	[astɛroíd]
orbit	orbitë (f)	[orbítə]
to revolve (~ around the Earth)	rrotullohet	[rotuɬóhɛt]
atmosphere	atmosferë (f)	[atmosférə]
the Sun	Dielli (m)	[diéti]
solar system	sistemi diellor (m)	[sistémi diɛɬór]
solar eclipse	eklips diellor (m)	[ɛklíps diɛɬór]
the Earth	Toka (f)	[tóka]
the Moon	Hëna (f)	[héna]
Mars	Marsi (m)	[mársi]
Venus	Venera (f)	[vɛnéra]
Jupiter	Jupiteri (m)	[jupitéri]
Saturn	Saturni (m)	[satúrni]
Mercury	Merkuri (m)	[mɛrkúri]
Uranus	Urani (m)	[uráni]
Neptune	Neptuni (m)	[nɛptúni]
Pluto	Pluto (f)	[plúto]
Milky Way	Rruga e Qumështit (f)	[rúga ɛ cúməʃtit]

| Great Bear (Ursa Major) | Arusha e Madhe (f) | [arúʃa ɛ máðɛ] |
| North Star | ylli i Veriut (m) | [ýłi i vériut] |

Martian	Marsian (m)	[marsián]
extraterrestrial (n)	jashtëtokësor (m)	[jaʃtətokəsór]
alien	alien (m)	[alién]
flying saucer	disk fluturues (m)	[dísk fluturúɛs]

spaceship	anije kozmike (f)	[aníjɛ kozmíkɛ]
space station	stacion kozmik (m)	[statsión kozmík]
blast-off	ngritje (f)	[ŋrítjɛ]

engine	motor (m)	[motór]
nozzle	dizë (f)	[dízə]
fuel	karburant (m)	[karburánt]

cockpit, flight deck	kabinë pilotimi (f)	[kabínə pilotími]
antenna	antenë (f)	[anténə]
porthole	dritare anësore (f)	[dritárɛ anəsórɛ]
solar panel	panel solar (m)	[panél solár]
spacesuit	veshje astronauti (f)	[véʃjɛ astronáuti]

| weightlessness | mungesë graviteti (f) | [muŋésə gravitéti] |
| oxygen | oksigjen (m) | [oksiɟén] |

| docking (in space) | ndërlidhje në hapësirë (f) | [ndərlíðjɛ nə hapəsírə] |
| to dock (vi, vt) | stacionohem | [statsionóhɛm] |

observatory	observator (m)	[obsɛrvatór]
telescope	teleskop (m)	[tɛlɛskóp]
to observe (vt)	vëzhgoj	[vəʒgój]
to explore (vt)	eksploroj	[ɛksplorój]

165. The Earth

the Earth	Toka (f)	[tóka]
the globe (the Earth)	globi (f)	[glóbi]
planet	planet (m)	[planét]

atmosphere	atmosferë (f)	[atmosférə]
geography	gjeografi (f)	[ɟɛografí]
nature	natyrë (f)	[natýrə]

globe (table ~)	glob (m)	[glob]
map	hartë (f)	[hártə]
atlas	atlas (m)	[atlás]

Europe	Evropa (f)	[ɛvrópa]
Asia	Azia (f)	[azía]
Africa	Afrika (f)	[afríka]

Australia	Australia (f)	[australía]
America	Amerika (f)	[amɛríka]
North America	Amerika Veriore (f)	[amɛríka vɛrióɾɛ]
South America	Amerika Jugore (f)	[amɛríka jugóɾɛ]

Antarctica	Antarktika (f)	[antarktíka]
the Arctic	Arktiku (m)	[arktíku]

166. Cardinal directions

north	veri (m)	[vɛrí]
to the north	drejt veriut	[dréjt vériut]
in the north	në veri	[nə vɛrí]
northern (adj)	verior	[vɛrióɾ]

south	jug (m)	[jug]
to the south	drejt jugut	[dréjt júgut]
in the south	në jug	[nə jug]
southern (adj)	jugor	[jugóɾ]

west	perëndim (m)	[pɛɾəndím]
to the west	drejt perëndimit	[dréjt pɛɾəndímit]
in the west	në perëndim	[nə pɛɾəndím]
western (adj)	perëndimor	[pɛɾəndimóɾ]

east	lindje (f)	[líndjɛ]
to the east	drejt lindjes	[dréjt líndjɛs]
in the east	në lindje	[nə líndjɛ]
eastern (adj)	lindor	[lindóɾ]

167. Sea. Ocean

sea	det (m)	[dét]
ocean	oqean (m)	[ocɛán]
gulf (bay)	gji (m)	[ɟi]
straits	ngushticë (f)	[ŋuʃtítsə]

land (solid ground)	tokë (f)	[tókə]
continent (mainland)	kontinent (m)	[kontinént]

island	ishull (m)	[íʃuɫ]
peninsula	gadishull (m)	[gadíʃuɫ]
archipelago	arkipelag (m)	[arkipɛlág]

bay, cove	gji (m)	[ɟi]
harbor	port (m)	[port]
lagoon	lagunë (f)	[lagúnə]
cape	kep (m)	[kɛp]

atoll	atol (m)	[atól]
reef	shkëmb nënujor (m)	[ʃkəmb nənujór]
coral	koral (m)	[korál]
coral reef	korale nënujorë (f)	[korálɛ nənujórə]

deep (adj)	i thellë	[i θétə]
depth (deep water)	thellësi (f)	[θɛtəsí]
abyss	humnerë (f)	[humnérə]
trench (e.g., Mariana ~)	hendek (m)	[hɛndék]
current (Ocean ~)	rrymë (f)	[rýmə]
to surround (bathe)	rrethohet	[rɛθóhɛt]

| shore | breg (m) | [brɛg] |
| coast | bregdet (m) | [brɛgdét] |

flow (flood tide)	batica (f)	[batítsa]
ebb (ebb tide)	zbaticë (f)	[zbatítsə]
shoal	cekëtinë (f)	[tsɛkətínə]
bottom (~ of the sea)	fund i detit (m)	[fúnd i détit]

wave	dallgë (f)	[dátgə]
crest (~ of a wave)	kreshtë (f)	[kréʃtə]
spume (sea foam)	shkumë (f)	[ʃkúmə]
storm (sea storm)	stuhi (f)	[stuhí]
hurricane	uragan (m)	[uragán]
tsunami	cunam (m)	[tsunám]
calm (dead ~)	qetësi (f)	[cɛtəsí]
quiet, calm (adj)	i qetë	[i cétə]

| pole | pol (m) | [pol] |
| polar (adj) | polar | [polár] |

latitude	gjerësi (f)	[ɟɛrəsí]
longitude	gjatësi (f)	[ɟatəsí]
parallel	paralele (f)	[paralélɛ]
equator	ekuator (m)	[ɛkuatór]

sky	qiell (m)	[cíɛt]
horizon	horizont (m)	[horizónt]
air	ajër (m)	[ájər]

lighthouse	fanar (m)	[fanár]
to dive (vi)	zhytem	[ʒýtɛm]
to sink (ab. boat)	fundosje	[fundósjɛ]
treasures	thesare (pl)	[θɛsárɛ]

168. Mountains

| mountain | mal (m) | [mal] |
| mountain range | vargmal (m) | [vargmál] |

mountain ridge	kresht malor (m)	[kréʃt malór]
summit, top	majë (f)	[májə]
peak	maja më e lartë (f)	[mája mə ɛ lártə]
foot (~ of the mountain)	rrëza e malit (f)	[rəza ɛ málit]
slope (mountainside)	shpat (m)	[ʃpat]

volcano	vullkan (m)	[vuɫkán]
active volcano	vullkan aktiv (m)	[vuɫkán aktív]
dormant volcano	vullkan i fjetur (m)	[vuɫkán i fjétur]

eruption	shpërthim (m)	[ʃpərθím]
crater	krater (m)	[kratér]
magma	magmë (f)	[mágmə]
lava	llavë (f)	[ɫávə]
molten (~ lava)	i shkrirë	[i ʃkrírə]

canyon	kanion (m)	[kanión]
gorge	grykë (f)	[grýkə]
crevice	çarje (f)	[tʃárjɛ]
abyss (chasm)	humnerë (f)	[humnérə]

pass, col	kalim (m)	[kalím]
plateau	pllajë (f)	[pɫájə]
cliff	shkëmb (m)	[ʃkəmb]
hill	kodër (f)	[kódər]

glacier	akullnajë (f)	[akuɫnájə]
waterfall	ujëvarë (f)	[ujəvárə]
geyser	gejzer (m)	[gɛjzér]
lake	liqen (m)	[licén]

plain	fushë (f)	[fúʃə]
landscape	peizazh (m)	[pɛizáʒ]
echo	jehonë (f)	[jɛhónə]

alpinist	alpinist (m)	[alpiníst]
rock climber	alpinist shkëmbßinjsh (m)	[alpiníst ʃkəmbiɲʃ]
to conquer (in climbing)	pushtoj majën	[puʃtój májən]
climb (an easy ~)	ngjitje (f)	[ɲítjɛ]

169. Rivers

river	lum (m)	[lum]
spring (natural source)	burim (m)	[burím]
riverbed (river channel)	shtrat lumi (m)	[ʃtrat lúmi]
basin (river valley)	basen (m)	[basén]
to flow into ...	rrjedh ...	[rjéð ...]

| tributary | derdhje (f) | [dérðjɛ] |
| bank (of river) | breg (m) | [brɛg] |

current (stream)	rrymë (f)	[rýmə]
downstream (adv)	rrjedhje e poshtme	[rjéðjɛ ɛ póʃtmɛ]
upstream (adv)	rrjedhje e sipërme	[rjéðjɛ ɛ sípərmɛ]

inundation	vërshim (m)	[vərʃím]
flooding	përmbytje (f)	[pərmbýtjɛ]
to overflow (vi)	vërshon	[vərʃón]
to flood (vt)	përmbytet	[pərmbýtɛt]

| shallow (shoal) | cekëtinë (f) | [tsɛkətínə] |
| rapids | rrjedhë (f) | [rjéðə] |

dam	digë (f)	[dígə]
canal	kanal (m)	[kanál]
reservoir (artificial lake)	rezervuar (m)	[rɛzɛrvuár]
sluice, lock	pendë ujore (f)	[péndə ujórɛ]

water body (pond, etc.)	plan hidrik (m)	[plan hidrík]
swamp (marshland)	kënetë (f)	[kənétə]
bog, marsh	moçal (m)	[motʃ ál]
whirlpool	vorbull (f)	[vórbuɫ]

stream (brook)	përrua (f)	[pərúa]
drinking (ab. water)	i pijshëm	[i píjʃəm]
fresh (~ water)	i freskët	[i fréskət]

ice	akull (m)	[ákuɫ]
to freeze over	ngrihet	[ŋríhɛt]
(ab. river, etc.)		

170. Forest

| forest, wood | pyll (m) | [pyɫ] |
| forest (as adj) | pyjor | [pyjór] |

thick forest	pyll i ngjeshur (m)	[pyɫ i ɲɟéʃur]
grove	zabel (m)	[zabél]
forest clearing	lëndinë (f)	[ləndínə]

| thicket | pyllëz (m) | [pýɫəz] |
| scrubland | shkurre (f) | [ʃkúrɛ] |

| footpath (troddenpath) | shteg (m) | [ʃtɛg] |
| gully | hon (m) | [hon] |

tree	pemë (f)	[pémə]
leaf	gjeth (m)	[ɟɛθ]
leaves (foliage)	gjethe (pl)	[ɟéθɛ]
fall of leaves	rënie e gjetheve (f)	[rəníɛ ɛ ɟéθɛvɛ]
to fall (ab. leaves)	bien	[bíɛn]

top (of the tree)	maje (f)	[májɛ]
branch	degë (f)	[dégə]
bough	degë (f)	[dégə]
bud (on shrub, tree)	syth (m)	[syθ]
needle (of pine tree)	shtiza pishe (f)	[ʃtíza píʃɛ]
pine cone	lule pishe (f)	[lúlɛ píʃɛ]
tree hollow	zgavër (f)	[zgávər]
nest	fole (f)	[folé]
burrow (animal hole)	strofull (f)	[strófuɫ]
trunk	trung (m)	[truŋ]
root	rrënjë (f)	[réɲə]
bark	lëvore (f)	[ləvórɛ]
moss	myshk (m)	[myʃk]
to uproot (remove trees or tree stumps)	shkul	[ʃkul]
to chop down	pres	[prɛs]
to deforest (vt)	shpyllëzoj	[ʃpyɫəzój]
tree stump	cung (m)	[tsúŋ]
campfire	zjarr kampingu (m)	[zjar kampíŋu]
forest fire	zjarr në pyll (m)	[zjar nə pyɫ]
to extinguish (vt)	shuaj	[ʃúaj]
forest ranger	roje pyjore (f)	[rójɛ pyjórɛ]
protection	mbrojtje (f)	[mbrójtjɛ]
to protect (~ nature)	mbroj	[mbrój]
poacher	gjahtar i jashtëligjshëm (m)	[ɟahtár i jaʃtəlíʃʃəm]
steel trap	grackë (f)	[grátskə]
to gather, to pick (vt)	mbledh	[mbléð]
to lose one's way	humb rrugën	[húmb rúgən]

171. Natural resources

natural resources	burime natyrore (pl)	[burímɛ natyrórɛ]
minerals	minerale (pl)	[minɛrálɛ]
deposits	depozita (pl)	[dɛpozíta]
field (e.g., oilfield)	fushë (f)	[fúʃə]
to mine (extract)	nxjerr	[ndzjér]
mining (extraction)	nxjerrje mineralesh (f)	[ndzjérjɛ minɛrálɛʃ]
ore	xehe (f)	[dzéhɛ]
mine (e.g., for coal)	minierë (f)	[miniérə]
shaft (mine ~)	nivel (m)	[nivél]
miner	minator (m)	[minatór]
gas (natural ~)	gaz (m)	[gaz]

gas pipeline	gazsjellës (m)	[gazsjéłəs]
oil (petroleum)	naftë (f)	[náftə]
oil pipeline	naftësjellës (f)	[naftəsjéłəs]
oil well	pus nafte (m)	[pus náftɛ]
derrick (tower)	burim nafte (m)	[burím náftɛ]
tanker	anije-cisternë (f)	[aníjɛ-tsistérnə]

sand	rërë (f)	[rérə]
limestone	gur gëlqeror (m)	[gur gəlcɛrór]
gravel	zhavorr (m)	[ʒavór]
peat	torfë (f)	[tórfə]
clay	argjilë (f)	[arɟílə]
coal	qymyr (m)	[cymýr]

iron (ore)	hekur (m)	[hékur]
gold	ar (m)	[ár]
silver	argjend (m)	[arɟénd]
nickel	nikel (m)	[nikél]
copper	bakër (m)	[bákər]

zinc	zink (m)	[zink]
manganese	mangan (m)	[maŋán]
mercury	merkur (m)	[mɛrkúr]
lead	plumb (m)	[plúmb]

mineral	mineral (m)	[minɛrál]
crystal	kristal (m)	[kristál]
marble	mermer (m)	[mɛrmér]
uranium	uranium (m)	[uraniúm]

The Earth. Part 2

172. Weather

weather	**moti** (m)	[móti]
weather forecast	**parashikimi i motit** (m)	[paraʃikími i mótit]
temperature	**temperaturë** (f)	[tɛmpɛratúrə]
thermometer	**termometër** (m)	[tɛrmométər]
barometer	**barometër** (m)	[barométər]
humid (adj)	**i lagësht**	[i lágəʃt]
humidity	**lagështi** (f)	[lagəʃtí]
heat (extreme ~)	**vapë** (f)	[vápə]
hot (torrid)	**shumë nxehtë**	[ʃúmə ndzéhtə]
it's hot	**është nxehtë**	[əʃtə ndzéhtə]
it's warm	**është ngrohtë**	[əʃtə ŋróhtə]
warm (moderately hot)	**ngrohtë**	[ŋróhtə]
it's cold	**bën ftohtë**	[bən ftóhtə]
cold (adj)	**i ftohtë**	[i ftóhtə]
sun	**diell** (m)	[díɛɬ]
to shine (vi)	**ndriçon**	[ndritʃón]
sunny (day)	**me diell**	[mɛ díɛɬ]
to come up (vi)	**agon**	[agón]
to set (vi)	**perëndon**	[pɛrəndón]
cloud	**re** (f)	[rɛ]
cloudy (adj)	**vranët**	[vránət]
rain cloud	**re shiu** (f)	[rɛ ʃíu]
somber (gloomy)	**vranët**	[vránət]
rain	**shi** (m)	[ʃi]
it's raining	**bie shi**	[bíɛ ʃi]
rainy (~ day, weather)	**me shi**	[mɛ ʃi]
to drizzle (vi)	**shi i imët**	[ʃi i ímət]
pouring rain	**shi litar** (m)	[ʃi litár]
downpour	**stuhi shiu** (f)	[stuhí ʃíu]
heavy (e.g., ~ rain)	**i fortë**	[i fórtə]
puddle	**brakë** (f)	[brákə]
to get wet (in rain)	**lagem**	[lágɛm]
fog (mist)	**mjegull** (f)	[mjéguɬ]
foggy	**e mjegullt**	[ɛ mjéguɬt]

| snow | borë (f) | [bórə] |
| it's snowing | bie borë | [bíɛ bórə] |

173. Severe weather. Natural disasters

thunderstorm	stuhi (f)	[stuhí]
lightning (~ strike)	vetëtimë (f)	[vɛtətímə]
to flash (vi)	vetëton	[vɛtətón]

thunder	bubullimë (f)	[bubuɫímə]
to thunder (vi)	bubullon	[bubuɫón]
it's thundering	bubullon	[bubuɫón]

| hail | breshër (m) | [bréʃər] |
| it's hailing | po bie breshër | [po biɛ bréʃər] |

| to flood (vt) | përmbytet | [pərmbýtɛt] |
| flood, inundation | përmbytje (f) | [pərmbýtjɛ] |

earthquake	tërmet (m)	[tərmét]
tremor, shoke	lëkundje (f)	[ləkúndjɛ]
epicenter	epiqendër (f)	[ɛpicéndər]

| eruption | shpërthim (m) | [ʃpərθím] |
| lava | llavë (f) | [ɫávə] |

twister	vorbull (f)	[vórbuɫ]
tornado	tornado (f)	[tornádo]
typhoon	tajfun (m)	[tajfún]

hurricane	uragan (m)	[uragán]
storm	stuhi (f)	[stuhí]
tsunami	cunam (m)	[tsunám]

cyclone	ciklon (m)	[tsiklón]
bad weather	mot i keq (m)	[mot i kɛc]
fire (accident)	zjarr (m)	[zjar]
disaster	fatkeqësi (f)	[fatkɛcəsí]
meteorite	meteor (m)	[mɛtɛór]

avalanche	ortek (m)	[orték]
snowslide	rrëshqitje bore (f)	[rəʃcítjɛ bórɛ]
blizzard	stuhi bore (f)	[stuhí bórɛ]
snowstorm	stuhi bore (f)	[stuhí bórɛ]

Fauna

174. Mammals. Predators

predator	grabitqar (m)	[grabitcár]
tiger	tigër (m)	[tígər]
lion	luan (m)	[luán]
wolf	ujk (m)	[ujk]
fox	dhelpër (f)	[ðélpər]
jaguar	jaguar (m)	[jaguár]
leopard	leopard (m)	[lɛopárd]
cheetah	gepard (m)	[gɛpárd]
black panther	panterë e zezë (f)	[pantérə ɛ zézə]
puma	puma (f)	[púma]
snow leopard	leopard i borës (m)	[lɛopárd i bórəs]
lynx	rrëqebull (m)	[rəcébuɫ]
coyote	kojotë (f)	[kojótə]
jackal	çakall (m)	[tʃakáɫ]
hyena	hienë (f)	[hiénə]

175. Wild animals

animal	kafshë (f)	[káfʃə]
beast (animal)	bishë (f)	[bíʃə]
squirrel	ketër (m)	[kétər]
hedgehog	iriq (m)	[iríc]
hare	lepur i egër (m)	[lépur i égər]
rabbit	lepur (m)	[lépur]
badger	vjedull (f)	[vjéduɫ]
raccoon	rakun (m)	[rakún]
hamster	hamster (m)	[hamstér]
marmot	marmot (m)	[marmót]
mole	urith (m)	[uríθ]
mouse	mi (m)	[mi]
rat	mi (m)	[mi]
bat	lakuriq (m)	[lakuríc]
ermine	herminë (f)	[hɛrmínə]
sable	kunadhe (f)	[kunáðɛ]

marten	shqarth (m)	[ʃcarθ]
weasel	nuselalë (f)	[nusɛlálə]
mink	vizon (m)	[vizón]

| beaver | kastor (m) | [kastór] |
| otter | vidër (f) | [vídər] |

horse	kali (m)	[káli]
moose	dre brilopatë (m)	[drɛ brilopátə]
deer	dre (f)	[drɛ]
camel	deve (f)	[dévɛ]

bison	bizon (m)	[bizón]
wisent	bizon evropian (m)	[bizón ɛvropián]
buffalo	buall (m)	[búaɫ]

zebra	zebër (f)	[zébər]
antelope	antilopë (f)	[antilópə]
roe deer	dre (f)	[drɛ]
fallow deer	dre ugar (m)	[drɛ ugár]
chamois	kamosh (m)	[kamóʃ]
wild boar	derr i egër (m)	[dér i égər]

whale	balenë (f)	[balénə]
seal	fokë (f)	[fókə]
walrus	lopë deti (f)	[lópə déti]
fur seal	fokë (f)	[fókə]
dolphin	delfin (m)	[dɛlfín]

bear	ari (m)	[arí]
polar bear	ari polar (m)	[arí polár]
panda	panda (f)	[pánda]

monkey	majmun (m)	[majmún]
chimpanzee	shimpanze (f)	[ʃimpánzɛ]
orangutan	orangutan (m)	[oraŋután]
gorilla	gorillë (f)	[gorítə]
macaque	majmun makao (m)	[majmún makáo]
gibbon	gibon (m)	[gibón]

elephant	elefant (m)	[ɛlɛfánt]
rhinoceros	rinoqeront (m)	[rinocɛrónt]
giraffe	gjirafë (f)	[ɟiráfə]
hippopotamus	hipopotam (m)	[hipopotám]

| kangaroo | kangur (m) | [kaŋúr] |
| koala (bear) | koala (f) | [koála] |

mongoose	mangustë (f)	[maŋústə]
chinchilla	çinçila (f)	[tʃintʃíla]
skunk	qelbës (m)	[célbəs]
porcupine	ferrëgjatë (m)	[fɛrəɟátə]

176. Domestic animals

cat	mace (f)	[mátsɛ]
tomcat	maçok (m)	[matʃók]
dog	qen (m)	[cɛn]

horse	kali (m)	[káli]
stallion (male horse)	hamshor (m)	[hamʃór]
mare	pelë (f)	[pélə]

cow	lopë (f)	[lópə]
bull	dem (m)	[dém]
ox	ka (m)	[ka]

sheep (ewe)	dele (f)	[délɛ]
ram	dash (m)	[daʃ]
goat	dhi (f)	[ði]
billy goat, he-goat	cjap (m)	[tsjáp]

| donkey | gomar (m) | [gomár] |
| mule | mushkë (f) | [múʃkə] |

pig, hog	derr (m)	[dɛr]
piglet	derrkuc (m)	[dɛrkúts]
rabbit	lepur (m)	[lépuɾ]

| hen (chicken) | pulë (f) | [púlə] |
| rooster | gjel (m) | [ʝél] |

duck	rosë (f)	[rósə]
drake	rosak (m)	[rosák]
goose	patë (f)	[pátə]

| tom turkey, gobbler | gjel deti i egër (m) | [ʝél déti i égər] |
| turkey (hen) | gjel deti (m) | [ʝél déti] |

domestic animals	kafshë shtëpiake (f)	[káfʃə ʃtəpiákɛ]
tame (e.g., ~ hamster)	i zbutur	[i zbútur]
to tame (vt)	zbus	[zbus]
to breed (vt)	rrit	[rit]

farm	fermë (f)	[férmə]
poultry	pulari (f)	[pularí]
cattle	bagëti (f)	[bagətí]
herd (cattle)	kope (f)	[kopé]

stable	stallë (f)	[stáłə]
pigpen	stallë e derrave (f)	[stáłə ɛ déravɛ]
cowshed	stallë e lopëve (f)	[stáłə ɛ lópəvɛ]
rabbit hutch	kolibe lepujsh (f)	[kolíbɛ lépujʃ]
hen house	kotec (m)	[kotéts]

177. Dogs. Dog breeds

dog	qen (m)	[cɛn]
sheepdog	qen dhensh (m)	[cɛn ðɛnʃ]
German shepherd	pastor gjerman (m)	[pastór ɟɛrmán]
poodle	pudël (f)	[púdəl]
dachshund	dakshund (m)	[dákshund]
bulldog	bulldog (m)	[buɫdóg]
boxer	bokser (m)	[boksér]
mastiff	mastif (m)	[mastíf]
Rottweiler	rotvailer (m)	[rotvailér]
Doberman	doberman (m)	[dobɛrmán]
basset	baset (m)	[basét]
bobtail	bishtshkurtër (m)	[biʃtʃkúrtər]
Dalmatian	dalmat (m)	[dalmát]
cocker spaniel	koker spaniel (m)	[kokér spaniél]
Newfoundland	terranova (f)	[tɛranóva]
Saint Bernard	Seint-Bernard (m)	[séint-bɛrnárd]
husky	haski (m)	[háski]
Chow Chow	çau çau (m)	[tʃáu tʃáu]
spitz	dhelpërush (m)	[ðɛlpərúʃ]
pug	karlino (m)	[karlíno]

178. Sounds made by animals

barking (n)	lehje (f)	[léhjɛ]
to bark (vi)	leh	[lɛh]
to meow (vi)	mjaullin	[mjauɫín]
to purr (vi)	gërhimë	[gərhímə]
to moo (vi)	bën mu	[bən mú]
to bellow (bull)	pëllet	[pəɫét]
to growl (vi)	hungërin	[huŋərín]
howl (n)	hungërimë (f)	[huŋərímə]
to howl (vi)	hungëroj	[huŋərój]
to whine (vi)	angullin	[aɲuɫín]
to bleat (sheep)	blegërin	[blɛgərín]
to oink, to grunt (pig)	hungërin	[huŋərín]
to squeal (vi)	klith	[kliθ]
to croak (vi)	bën kuak	[bən kuák]
to buzz (insect)	zukat	[zukát]
to chirp	gumëzhin	[gumeʒín]
(crickets, grasshopper)		

179. Birds

bird	zog (m)	[zog]
pigeon	pëllumb (m)	[pəɫúmb]
sparrow	harabel (m)	[harabél]
tit (great tit)	xhixhimës (m)	[dʒidʒimə́s]
magpie	laraskë (f)	[laráskə]
raven	korb (m)	[korb]
crow	sorrë (f)	[sórə]
jackdaw	galë (f)	[gálə]
rook	sorrë (f)	[sórə]
duck	rosë (f)	[rósə]
goose	patë (f)	[pátə]
pheasant	fazan (m)	[fazán]
eagle	shqiponjë (f)	[ʃcipóɲə]
hawk	gjeraqinë (f)	[ɟɛracínə]
falcon	fajkua (f)	[fajkúa]
vulture	hutë (f)	[hútə]
condor (Andean ~)	kondor (m)	[kondór]
swan	mjellmë (f)	[mjéɫmə]
crane	lejlek (m)	[lɛjlék]
stork	lejlek (m)	[lɛjlék]
parrot	papagall (m)	[papagáɫ]
hummingbird	kolibri (m)	[kolíbri]
peacock	pallua (m)	[paɫúa]
ostrich	struc (m)	[struts]
heron	çafkë (f)	[tʃáfkə]
flamingo	flamingo (m)	[flamíŋo]
pelican	pelikan (m)	[pɛlikán]
nightingale	bilbil (m)	[bilbíl]
swallow	dallëndyshe (f)	[daɫəndýʃɛ]
thrush	mëllenjë (f)	[məɫéɲə]
song thrush	grifsha (f)	[grífʃa]
blackbird	mëllenjë (f)	[məɫéɲə]
swift	dallëndyshe (f)	[daɫəndýʃɛ]
lark	thëllëzë (f)	[θəɫə́zə]
quail	trumcak (m)	[trumtsák]
woodpecker	qukapik (m)	[cukapík]
cuckoo	kukuvajkë (f)	[kukuvájkə]
owl	buf (m)	[buf]
eagle owl	buf mbretëror (m)	[buf mbrɛtərór]

wood grouse	fazan i pyllit (m)	[fazán i pýłit]
black grouse	fazan i zi (m)	[fazán i zí]
partridge	thëllëzë (f)	[θəłéːzə]

starling	gargull (m)	[gárguł]
canary	kanarinë (f)	[kanarínə]
hazel grouse	fazan mali (m)	[fazán máli]
chaffinch	trishtil (m)	[triʃtíl]
bullfinch	trishtil dimri (m)	[triʃtíl dímri]

seagull	pulëbardhë (f)	[puləbárðə]
albatross	albatros (m)	[albatrós]
penguin	penguin (m)	[pɛŋuín]

180. Birds. Singing and sounds

to sing (vi)	këndoj	[kəndój]
to call (animal, bird)	thërras	[θərás]
to crow (rooster)	kakaris	[kakarís]
cock-a-doodle-doo	kikiriku	[kikiríku]

to cluck (hen)	kakaris	[kakarís]
to caw (crow call)	krokas	[krokás]
to quack (duck call)	bën kuak kuak	[bən kuák kuák]
to cheep (vi)	pisket	[piskét]
to chirp, to twitter	cicëroj	[tsitsərój]

181. Fish. Marine animals

| bream | krapuliq (m) | [krapulíc] |
| carp | krap (m) | [krap] |

perch	perç (m)	[pɛrtʃ]
catfish	mustak (m)	[musták]
pike	mlysh (m)	[mlýʃ]

| salmon | salmon (m) | [salmón] |
| sturgeon | bli (m) | [blí] |

herring	harengë (f)	[haréŋə]
Atlantic salmon	salmon Atlantiku (m)	[salmón atlantíku]
mackerel	skumbri (m)	[skúmbri]
flatfish	shojzë (f)	[ʃójzə]

zander, pike perch	troftë (f)	[tróftə]
cod	merluc (m)	[mɛrlúts]
tuna	tunë (f)	[túnə]
trout	troftë (f)	[tróftə]

eel	ngjalë (f)	[ɲʝálə]
electric ray	peshk elektrik (m)	[pɛʃk ɛlɛktrík]
moray eel	ngjalë morel (f)	[ɲʝálə morél]
piranha	piranja (f)	[piráɲa]

shark	peshkaqen (m)	[pɛʃkacén]
dolphin	delfin (m)	[dɛlfín]
whale	balenë (f)	[balénə]

crab	gaforre (f)	[gafórɛ]
jellyfish	kandil deti (m)	[kandíl déti]
octopus	oktapod (m)	[oktapód]

starfish	yll deti (m)	[yɫ déti]
sea urchin	iriq deti (m)	[iríc déti]
seahorse	kalë deti (m)	[kálə déti]

oyster	midhje (f)	[míðjɛ]
shrimp	karkalec (m)	[karkaléts]
lobster	karavidhe (f)	[karavíðɛ]
spiny lobster	karavidhe (f)	[karavíðɛ]

182. Amphibians. Reptiles

| snake | gjarpër (m) | [ʝárpər] |
| venomous (snake) | helmues | [hɛlmúɛs] |

| viper | nepërka (f) | [nɛpérka] |
| cobra | kobra (f) | [kóbra] |

| python | piton (m) | [pitón] |
| boa | boa (f) | [bóa] |

grass snake	kular (m)	[kulár]
rattle snake	gjarpër me zile (m)	[ʝárpər mɛ zílɛ]
anaconda	anakonda (f)	[anakónda]

lizard	hardhucë (f)	[harðútsə]
iguana	iguana (f)	[iguána]
monitor lizard	varan (m)	[varán]
salamander	salamandër (f)	[salamándər]

| chameleon | kameleon (m) | [kamɛlɛón] |
| scorpion | akrep (m) | [akrép] |

| turtle | breshkë (f) | [bréʃkə] |
| frog | bretkosë (f) | [brɛtkósə] |

| toad | zhabë (f) | [ʒábə] |
| crocodile | krokodil (m) | [krokodíl] |

183. Insects

insect, bug	insekt (m)	[insékt]
butterfly	flutur (f)	[flútur]
ant	milingonë (f)	[miliŋónə]
fly	mizë (f)	[mízə]
mosquito	mushkonjë (f)	[muʃkóɲə]
beetle	brumbull (m)	[brúmbuɫ]

wasp	grerëz (f)	[grérəz]
bee	bletë (f)	[blétə]
bumblebee	greth (m)	[grɛθ]
gadfly (botfly)	zekth (m)	[zɛkθ]

| spider | merimangë (f) | [mɛrimáŋə] |
| spiderweb | rrjetë merimange (f) | [rjétə mɛrimáŋɛ] |

dragonfly	pilivesë (f)	[pilivésə]
grasshopper	karkalec (m)	[karkaléts]
moth (night butterfly)	molë (f)	[mólə]

cockroach	kacabu (f)	[katsabú]
tick	rriqër (m)	[ríčər]
flea	plesht (m)	[plɛʃt]
midge	mushicë (f)	[muʃítsə]

locust	gjinkallë (f)	[ɟinkáɫə]
snail	kërmill (m)	[kərmíɫ]
cricket	bulkth (m)	[búlkθ]
lightning bug	xixëllonjë (f)	[dzidzəɫóɲə]
ladybug	mollëkuqe (f)	[moɫəkúcɛ]
cockchafer	vizhë (f)	[víʒə]

leech	shushunjë (f)	[ʃuʃúɲə]
caterpillar	vemje (f)	[vémjɛ]
earthworm	krimb toke (m)	[krímb tókɛ]
larva	larvë (f)	[lárvə]

184. Animals. Body parts

beak	sqep (m)	[scɛp]
wings	flatra (pl)	[flátra]
foot (of bird)	këmbë (f)	[kémbə]
feathers (plumage)	pupla (pl)	[púpla]
feather	pupël (f)	[púpəl]
crest	kreshtë (f)	[kréʃtə]

| gills | velëz (f) | [véləz] |
| spawn | vezë peshku (f) | [vézə péʃku] |

larva	larvë (f)	[lárvə]
fin	krah (m)	[krah]
scales (of fish, reptile)	luspë (f)	[lúspə]

fang (canine)	dhëmb prerës (m)	[ðəmb prérəs]
paw (e.g., cat's ~)	shputë (f)	[ʃpútə]
muzzle (snout)	turi (m)	[turí]
maw (mouth)	gojë (f)	[gójə]
tail	bisht (m)	[biʃt]
whiskers	mustaqe (f)	[mustácɛ]

| hoof | thundër (f) | [θúndər] |
| horn | bri (m) | [brí] |

carapace	karapaks (m)	[karapáks]
shell (of mollusk)	guaskë (f)	[guáskə]
eggshell	lëvozhgë veze (f)	[ləvóʒgə vézɛ]

| animal's hair (pelage) | qime (f) | [címɛ] |
| pelt (hide) | lëkurë kafshe (f) | [ləkúrə káfʃɛ] |

185. Animals. Habitats

| habitat | banesë (f) | [banésə] |
| migration | migrim (m) | [migrím] |

mountain	mal (m)	[mal]
reef	shkëmb nënujor (m)	[ʃkəmb nənujór]
cliff	shkëmb (m)	[ʃkəmb]

forest	pyll (m)	[pyɫ]
jungle	xhungël (f)	[dʒúŋəl]
savanna	savana (f)	[savána]
tundra	tundra (f)	[túndra]

steppe	stepa (f)	[stépa]
desert	shkretëtirë (f)	[ʃkrɛtətírə]
oasis	oazë (f)	[oázə]

sea	det (m)	[dét]
lake	liqen (m)	[licén]
ocean	oqean (m)	[ocɛán]

swamp (marshland)	kënetë (f)	[kənétə]
freshwater (adj)	ujëra të ëmbla	[újəra tə əmbla]
pond	pellg (m)	[pɛɫg]
river	lum (m)	[lum]

| den (bear's ~) | strofull (f) | [strófuɫ] |
| nest | fole (f) | [folé] |

tree hollow	zgavër (f)	[zgávər]
burrow (animal hole)	strofull (f)	[strófuł]
anthill	mal milingonash (m)	[mal miliŋónaʃ]

Flora

186. Trees

tree	pemë (f)	[pémə]
deciduous (adj)	gjethor	[ɟɛθór]
coniferous (adj)	halor	[halór]
evergreen (adj)	përherë të gjelbra	[pərhérə tə ɟélbra]
apple tree	pemë molle (f)	[pémə mótɛ]
pear tree	pemë dardhe (f)	[pémə dárðɛ]
sweet cherry tree	pemë qershie (f)	[pémə cɛrʃíɛ]
sour cherry tree	pemë qershi vishnje (f)	[pémə cɛrʃí víʃɲɛ]
plum tree	pemë kumbulle (f)	[pémə kúmbutɛ]
birch	mështekna (f)	[məʃtékna]
oak	lis (m)	[lis]
linden tree	bli (m)	[blí]
aspen	plep i egër (m)	[plɛp i égər]
maple	panjë (f)	[páɲə]
spruce	bredh (m)	[brɛð]
pine	pishë (f)	[píʃə]
larch	larsh (m)	[lárʃ]
fir tree	bredh i bardhë (m)	[brɛð i bárðə]
cedar	kedër (m)	[kédər]
poplar	plep (m)	[plɛp]
rowan	vadhë (f)	[váðə]
willow	shelg (m)	[ʃɛlg]
alder	verr (m)	[vɛr]
beech	ah (m)	[ah]
elm	elm (m)	[élm]
ash (tree)	shelg (m)	[ʃɛlg]
chestnut	gështenjë (f)	[gəʃtéɲə]
magnolia	manjolia (f)	[maɲólia]
palm tree	palma (f)	[pálma]
cypress	qiparis (m)	[ciparís]
mangrove	rizoforë (f)	[rizofórə]
baobab	baobab (m)	[baobáb]
eucalyptus	eukalipt (m)	[ɛukalípt]
sequoia	sekuojë (f)	[sɛkuójə]

187. Shrubs

bush	shkurre (f)	[ʃkúrɛ]
shrub	kaçube (f)	[katʃúbɛ]

grapevine	hardhi (f)	[harðí]
vineyard	vreshtë (f)	[vréʃtə]

raspberry bush	mjedër (f)	[mjédər]
blackcurrant bush	kaliboba e zezë (f)	[kalibóba ɛ zézə]
redcurrant bush	kaliboba e kuqe (f)	[kalibóba ɛ kúcɛ]
gooseberry bush	shkurre kulumbrie (f)	[ʃkúrɛ kulumbríɛ]

acacia	akacie (f)	[akátsiɛ]
barberry	krespinë (f)	[krɛspínə]
jasmine	jasemin (m)	[jasɛmín]

juniper	dëllinjë (f)	[dəlíɲə]
rosebush	trëndafil (m)	[trəndafíl]
dog rose	trëndafil i egër (m)	[trəndafíl i égər]

188. Mushrooms

mushroom	kërpudhë (f)	[kərpúðə]
edible mushroom	kërpudhë ushqyese (f)	[kərpúðə uʃcýɛsɛ]
poisonous mushroom	kërpudhë helmuese (f)	[kərpúðə hɛlmúɛsɛ]
cap (of mushroom)	koka e kërpudhës (f)	[kóka ɛ kərpúðəs]
stipe (of mushroom)	bishti i kërpudhës (m)	[bíʃti i kərpúðəs]

cep (Boletus edulis)	porcini (m)	[portsíni]
orange-cap boletus	kërpudhë kapuç-verdhë (f)	[kərpúðə kapútʃ-vérðə]
birch bolete	porcinela (f)	[portsinéla]
chanterelle	shanterele (f)	[ʃantɛrélɛ]
russula	rusula (f)	[rúsula]

morel	morele (f)	[morélɛ]
fly agaric	kësulkuqe (f)	[kəsulkúcɛ]
death cap	kërpudha e vdekjes (f)	[kərpúða ɛ vdékjɛs]

189. Fruits. Berries

fruit	frut (m)	[frut]
fruits	fruta (pl)	[frúta]

apple	mollë (f)	[móʈə]
pear	dardhë (f)	[dárðə]

plum	kumbull (f)	[kúmbuɫ]
strawberry (garden ~)	luleshtrydhe (f)	[luleʃtrýðɛ]
sour cherry	qershi vishnje (f)	[cɛrʃí víʃɲɛ]
sweet cherry	qershi (f)	[cɛrʃí]
grape	rrush (m)	[ruʃ]

raspberry	mjedër (f)	[mjédər]
blackcurrant	kaliboba e zezë (f)	[kalibóba ɛ zézə]
redcurrant	kaliboba e kuqe (f)	[kalibóba ɛ kúcɛ]
gooseberry	kulumbri (f)	[kulumbrí]
cranberry	boronica (f)	[boronítsa]

orange	portokall (m)	[portokáɫ]
mandarin	mandarinë (f)	[mandarínə]
pineapple	ananas (m)	[ananás]
banana	banane (f)	[banánɛ]
date	hurmë (f)	[húrmə]

lemon	limon (m)	[limón]
apricot	kajsi (f)	[kajsí]
peach	pjeshkë (f)	[pjéʃkə]
kiwi	kivi (m)	[kívi]
grapefruit	grejpfrut (m)	[grɛjpfrút]

berry	manë (f)	[mánə]
berries	mana (f)	[mána]
cowberry	boronicë mirtile (f)	[boronítsə mirtílɛ]
wild strawberry	luleshtrydhe e egër (f)	[luleʃtrýðɛ ɛ égər]
bilberry	boronicë (f)	[boronítsə]

190. Flowers. Plants

flower	lule (f)	[lúlɛ]
bouquet (of flowers)	buqetë (f)	[bucétə]

rose (flower)	trëndafil (m)	[trəndafíl]
tulip	tulipan (m)	[tulipán]
carnation	karafil (m)	[karafíl]
gladiolus	gladiolë (f)	[gladiólə]

cornflower	lule misri (f)	[lúlɛ mísri]
harebell	lule këmborë (f)	[lúlɛ kəmbórə]
dandelion	luleradhiqe (f)	[lulɛraðícɛ]
camomile	kamomil (m)	[kamomíl]

aloe	aloe (f)	[alóɛ]
cactus	kaktus (m)	[kaktús]
rubber plant, ficus	fikus (m)	[fíkus]
lily	zambak (m)	[zambák]
geranium	barbarozë (f)	[barbarózə]

hyacinth	zymbyl (m)	[zymbýl]
mimosa	mimoza (f)	[mimóza]
narcissus	narcis (m)	[nartsís]
nasturtium	lule këmbore (f)	[lúlɛ kəmbórɛ]

orchid	orkide (f)	[orkidé]
peony	bozhure (f)	[boʒúrɛ]
violet	vjollcë (f)	[vjóɬtsə]
pansy	lule vjollca (f)	[lúlɛ vjóɬtsa]
forget-me-not	mosmëharro (f)	[mosməharó]
daisy	margaritë (f)	[margarítə]

poppy	lulëkuqe (f)	[luləkúcɛ]
hemp	kërp (m)	[kə́rp]
mint	mendër (f)	[méndər]

lily of the valley	zambak i fushës (m)	[zambák i fúʃəs]
snowdrop	luleborë (f)	[lulɛbórə]

nettle	hithra (f)	[híθra]
sorrel	lëpjeta (f)	[ləpjéta]
water lily	zambak uji (m)	[zambák úji]
fern	fier (m)	[fíɛr]
lichen	likene (f)	[likénɛ]
conservatory (greenhouse)	serrë (f)	[sérə]
lawn	lëndinë (f)	[ləndínə]
flowerbed	kënd lulishteje (m)	[kənd lulíʃtɛjɛ]

plant	bimë (f)	[bímə]
grass	bar (m)	[bar]
blade of grass	fije bari (f)	[fíjɛ bári]

leaf	gjeth (m)	[ɟɛθ]
petal	petale (f)	[pɛtálɛ]
stem	bisht (m)	[biʃt]
tuber	zhardhok (m)	[ʒarðók]

young plant (shoot)	filiz (m)	[filíz]
thorn	gjemb (m)	[ɟémb]

to blossom (vi)	lulëzoj	[luləzój]
to fade, to wither	vyshket	[výʃkɛt]
smell (odor)	aromë (f)	[arómə]
to cut (flowers)	pres lulet	[prɛs lúlɛt]
to pick (a flower)	mbledh lule	[mbléð lúlɛ]

191. Cereals, grains

grain	drithë (m)	[dríθə]
cereal crops	drithëra (pl)	[dríθəra]

ear (of barley, etc.)	kaush (m)	[kaúʃ]
wheat	grurë (f)	[grúrə]
rye	thekër (f)	[θékər]
oats	tërshërë (f)	[tərʃérə]
millet	mel (m)	[mɛl]
barley	elb (m)	[ɛlb]
corn	misër (m)	[mísər]
rice	oriz (m)	[oríz]
buckwheat	hikërr (m)	[híkər]
pea plant	bizele (f)	[bizélɛ]
kidney bean	groshë (f)	[gróʃə]
soy	sojë (f)	[sójə]
lentil	thjerrëz (f)	[θjérəz]
beans (pulse crops)	fasule (f)	[fasúlɛ]

REGIONAL GEOGRAPHY

Countries. Nationalities

192. Politics. Government. Part 1

politics	politikë (f)	[politíkə]
political (adj)	politike	[politíkɛ]
politician	politikan (m)	[politikán]
state (country)	shtet (m)	[ʃtɛt]
citizen	nënshtetas (m)	[nənʃtétas]
citizenship	nënshtetësi (f)	[nənʃtɛtəsí]
national emblem	simbol kombëtar (m)	[simból kombətár]
national anthem	himni kombëtar (m)	[hímni kombətár]
government	qeveri (f)	[cɛvɛrí]
head of state	kreu i shtetit (m)	[kréu i ʃtétit]
parliament	parlament (m)	[parlamént]
party	parti (f)	[partí]
capitalism	kapitalizëm (m)	[kapitalízəm]
capitalist (adj)	kapitalist	[kapitalíst]
socialism	socializëm (m)	[sotsialízəm]
socialist (adj)	socialist	[sotsialíst]
communism	komunizëm (m)	[komunízəm]
communist (adj)	komunist	[komuníst]
communist (n)	komunist (m)	[komuníst]
democracy	demokraci (f)	[dɛmokratsí]
democrat	demokrat (m)	[dɛmokrát]
democratic (adj)	demokratik	[dɛmokratík]
Democratic party	parti demokratike (f)	[partí dɛmokratíkɛ]
liberal (n)	liberal (m)	[libɛrál]
liberal (adj)	liberal	[libɛrál]
conservative (n)	konservativ (m)	[konsɛrvatív]
conservative (adj)	konservativ	[konsɛrvatív]
republic (n)	republikë (f)	[rɛpublíkə]
republican (n)	republikan (m)	[rɛpublikán]

Republican party	parti republikane (f)	[partí rɛpublikánɛ]
elections	zgjedhje (f)	[zɟéðjɛ]
to elect (vt)	zgjedh	[zɟɛð]
elector, voter	zgjedhës (m)	[zɟéðəs]
election campaign	fushatë zgjedhore (f)	[fuʃátə zɟɛðórɛ]

voting (n)	votim (m)	[votím]
to vote (vi)	votoj	[votój]
suffrage, right to vote	e drejta e votës (f)	[ɛ dréjta ɛ vótəs]

candidate	kandidat (m)	[kandidát]
to be a candidate	jam kandidat	[jam kandidát]
campaign	fushatë (f)	[fuʃátə]

| opposition (as adj) | opozitar | [opozitár] |
| opposition (n) | opozitë (f) | [opozítə] |

visit	vizitë (f)	[vizítə]
official visit	vizitë zyrtare (f)	[vizítə zyrtárɛ]
international (adj)	ndërkombëtar	[ndərkombətár]

| negotiations | negociata (f) | [nɛgotsiáta] |
| to negotiate (vi) | negocioj | [nɛgotsiój] |

193. Politics. Government. Part 2

society	shoqëri (f)	[ʃocərí]
constitution	kushtetutë (f)	[kuʃtɛtútə]
power (political control)	pushtet (m)	[puʃtét]
corruption	korrupsion (m)	[korupsión]

| law (justice) | ligj (m) | [liɟ] |
| legal (legitimate) | ligjor | [liɟór] |

| justice (fairness) | drejtësi (f) | [drɛjtəsí] |
| just (fair) | e drejtë | [ɛ dréjtə] |

committee	komitet (m)	[komitét]
bill (draft law)	projektligj (m)	[projɛktlíɟ]
budget	buxhet (m)	[budʒét]
policy	politikë (f)	[politíkə]
reform	reformë (f)	[rɛfórmə]
radical (adj)	radikal	[radikál]

power (strength, force)	fuqi (f)	[fucí]
powerful (adj)	i fuqishëm	[i fucíʃəm]
supporter	mbështetës (m)	[mbəʃtétəs]
influence	ndikim (m)	[ndikím]
regime (e.g., military ~)	regjim (m)	[rɛɟím]
conflict	konflikt (m)	[konflíkt]

| conspiracy (plot) | komplot (m) | [komplót] |
| provocation | provokim (m) | [provokím] |

to overthrow (regime, etc.)	rrëzoj	[rəzój]
overthrow (of government)	rrëzim (m)	[rəzím]
revolution	revolucion (m)	[rɛvolutsión]

| coup d'état | grusht shteti (m) | [grúʃt ʃtéti] |
| military coup | puç ushtarak (m) | [putʃ uʃtarák] |

crisis	krizë (f)	[krízə]
economic recession	recesion ekonomik (m)	[rɛtsɛsión ɛkonomík]
demonstrator (protester)	protestues (m)	[protɛstúɛs]
demonstration	protestë (f)	[protéstə]
martial law	ligj ushtarak (m)	[liʝ uʃtarák]
military base	bazë ushtarake (f)	[bázə uʃtarákɛ]

| stability | stabilitet (m) | [stabilitét] |
| stable (adj) | stabil | [stabíl] |

| exploitation | shfrytëzim (m) | [ʃfrytəzím] |
| to exploit (workers) | shfrytëzoj | [ʃfrytəzój] |

racism	racizëm (m)	[ratsízəm]
racist	racist (m)	[ratsíst]
fascism	fashizëm (m)	[faʃízəm]
fascist	fashist (m)	[faʃíst]

194. Countries. Miscellaneous

foreigner	i huaj (m)	[i húaj]
foreign (adj)	huaj	[húaj]
abroad (in a foreign country)	jashtë shteti	[jáʃtə ʃtéti]

emigrant	emigrant (m)	[ɛmigránt]
emigration	emigracion (m)	[ɛmigratsión]
to emigrate (vi)	emigroj	[ɛmigrój]

the West	Perëndimi (m)	[pɛrəndími]
the East	Lindja (f)	[líndja]
the Far East	Lindja e Largët (f)	[líndja ɛ lárgət]

civilization	civilizim (m)	[tsivilizím]
humanity (mankind)	njerëzia (f)	[ɲɛrəzía]
the world (earth)	bota (f)	[bóta]
peace	paqe (f)	[pácɛ]
worldwide (adj)	botëror	[botərór]
homeland	atdhe (f)	[atðé]
people (population)	njerëz (m)	[ɲérəz]

population	**popullsi** (f)	[poputsí]
people (a lot of ~)	**njerëz** (m)	[ɲérəz]
nation (people)	**komb** (m)	[komb]
generation	**brez** (m)	[brɛz]

territory (area)	**zonë** (f)	[zónə]
region	**rajon** (m)	[rajón]
state (part of a country)	**shtet** (m)	[ʃtɛt]

tradition	**traditë** (f)	[tradítə]
custom (tradition)	**zakon** (m)	[zakón]
ecology	**ekologjia** (f)	[ɛkoloɟía]

Indian (Native American)	**Indian të Amerikës** (m)	[indián tə amɛríkəs]
Gypsy (masc.)	**jevg** (m)	[jɛvg]
Gypsy (fem.)	**jevge** (f)	[jévgɛ]
Gypsy (adj)	**jevg**	[jɛvg]

empire	**perandori** (f)	[pɛrandorí]
colony	**koloni** (f)	[kolоní]
slavery	**skllevëri** (m)	[sktɛvərí]
invasion	**pushtim** (m)	[puʃtím]
famine	**uria** (f)	[uría]

195. Major religious groups. Confessions

religion	**religjion** (m)	[rɛliɟión]
religious (adj)	**religjioz**	[rɛliɟióz]

faith, belief	**fe, besim** (m)	[fé], [bɛsím]
to believe (in God)	**besoj**	[bɛsój]
believer	**besimtar** (m)	[bɛsimtár]

atheism	**ateizëm** (m)	[atɛízəm]
atheist	**ateist** (m)	[atɛíst]

Christianity	**Krishterimi** (m)	[kriʃtɛrími]
Christian (n)	**i krishterë** (m)	[i kriʃtérə]
Christian (adj)	**krishterë**	[kriʃtérə]

Catholicism	**Katolicizëm** (m)	[katolitsízəm]
Catholic (n)	**Katolik** (m)	[katolík]
Catholic (adj)	**katolik**	[katolík]

Protestantism	**Protestantizëm** (m)	[protɛstantízəm]
Protestant Church	**Kishë Protestante** (f)	[kíʃə protɛstántɛ]
Protestant (n)	**Protestant** (m)	[protɛstánt]

Orthodoxy	**Ortodoksia** (f)	[ortodoksía]
Orthodox Church	**Kishë Ortodokse** (f)	[kíʃə ortodóksɛ]

Orthodox (n)	**Ortodoks** (m)	[ortodóks]
Presbyterianism	**Presbiterian** (m)	[prɛsbitɛrián]
Presbyterian Church	**Kishë Presbiteriane** (f)	[kíʃə prɛsbitɛriánɛ]
Presbyterian (n)	**Presbiterian** (m)	[prɛsbitɛrián]
Lutheranism	**Luterianizëm** (m)	[lutɛrianízəm]
Lutheran (n)	**Luterian** (m)	[lutɛrián]
Baptist Church	**Kishë Baptiste** (f)	[kíʃə baptístɛ]
Baptist (n)	**Baptist** (m)	[baptíst]
Anglican Church	**Kishë Anglikane** (f)	[kíʃə aŋlikánɛ]
Anglican (n)	**Anglikan** (m)	[aŋlikán]
Mormonism	**Mormonizëm** (m)	[mormonízəm]
Mormon (n)	**Mormon** (m)	[mormón]
Judaism	**Judaizëm** (m)	[judaízəm]
Jew (n)	**çifut** (m)	[tʃifút]
Buddhism	**Budizëm** (m)	[budízəm]
Buddhist (n)	**Budist** (m)	[budíst]
Hinduism	**Hinduizëm** (m)	[hinduízəm]
Hindu (n)	**Hindu** (m)	[híndu]
Islam	**Islam** (m)	[islám]
Muslim (n)	**Mysliman** (m)	[myslimán]
Muslim (adj)	**Mysliman**	[myslimán]
Shiah Islam	**Islami Shia** (m)	[islámi ʃía]
Shiite (n)	**Shiitë** (f)	[ʃíitə]
Sunni Islam	**Islami Suni** (m)	[islámi súni]
Sunnite (n)	**Sunit** (m)	[sunít]

196. Religions. Priests

priest	**prift** (m)	[prift]
the Pope	**Papa** (f)	[pápa]
monk, friar	**murg, frat** (m)	[murg], [frat]
nun	**murgeshë** (f)	[murgéʃə]
pastor	**pastor** (m)	[pastór]
abbot	**abat** (m)	[abát]
vicar (parish priest)	**famullitar** (m)	[famuɬitár]
bishop	**peshkop** (m)	[pɛʃkóp]
cardinal	**kardinal** (m)	[kardinál]
preacher	**predikues** (m)	[prɛdikúɛs]

preaching	predikim (m)	[prɛdikím]
parishioners	faullistë (f)	[fauɫístə]
believer	besimtar (m)	[bɛsimtár]
atheist	ateist (m)	[atɛíst]

197. Faith. Christianity. Islam

Adam	Adam (m)	[adám]
Eve	eva (f)	[éva]
God	Zot (m)	[zot]
the Lord	Zoti (m)	[zóti]
the Almighty	i Plotfuqishmi (m)	[i plotfucíʃmi]
sin	mëkat (m)	[məkát]
to sin (vi)	mëkatoj	[məkatój]
sinner (masc.)	mëkatar (m)	[məkatár]
sinner (fem.)	mëkatare (f)	[məkatárɛ]
hell	ferr (m)	[fɛr]
paradise	parajsë (f)	[parájsə]
Jesus	Jezus (m)	[jézus]
Jesus Christ	Jezu Krishti (m)	[jézu kríʃti]
the Holy Spirit	Shpirti i Shenjtë (m)	[ʃpírti i ʃéɲtə]
the Savior	Shpëtimtar (m)	[ʃpətimtár]
the Virgin Mary	e Virgjëra Meri (f)	[ɛ vírɟəra méri]
the Devil	Djalli (m)	[djáɫi]
devil's (adj)	i djallit	[i djáɫit]
Satan	Satani (m)	[satáni]
satanic (adj)	satanik	[sataník]
angel	engjëll (m)	[éɲɟəɫ]
guardian angel	engjëlli mbrojtës (m)	[éɲɟəɫi mbrójtəs]
angelic (adj)	engjëllor	[ɛɲɟəɫór]
apostle	apostull (m)	[apóstuɫ]
archangel	kryeengjëll (m)	[kryɛéɲɟəɫ]
the Antichrist	Antikrishti (m)	[antikríʃti]
Church	Kishë (f)	[kíʃə]
Bible	Bibla (f)	[bíbla]
biblical (adj)	biblik	[biblík]
Old Testament	Dhiata e Vjetër (f)	[ðiáta ɛ vjétər]
New Testament	Dhiata e Re (f)	[ðiáta ɛ ré]
Gospel	ungjill (m)	[uɲɟíɫ]

Holy Scripture	**Libri i Shenjtë** (m)	[líbri i ʃéɲtə]
Heaven	**parajsa** (f)	[parájsa]
Commandment	**urdhëresë** (f)	[urðərésə]
prophet	**profet** (m)	[profét]
prophecy	**profeci** (f)	[profɛtsí]
Allah	**Allah** (m)	[aɫáh]
Mohammed	**Muhamed** (m)	[muhaméd]
the Koran	**Kurani** (m)	[kuráni]
mosque	**xhami** (f)	[dʒamí]
mullah	**hoxhë** (m)	[hódʒə]
prayer	**lutje** (f)	[lútjɛ]
to pray (vi, vt)	**lutem**	[lútɛm]
pilgrimage	**pelegrinazh** (m)	[pɛlɛgrináʒ]
pilgrim	**pelegrin** (m)	[pɛlɛgrín]
Mecca	**Mekë** (f)	[mékə]
church	**kishë** (f)	[kíʃə]
temple	**tempull** (m)	[témpuɫ]
cathedral	**katedrale** (f)	[katɛdrálɛ]
Gothic (adj)	**Gotik**	[gotík]
synagogue	**sinagogë** (f)	[sinagógə]
mosque	**xhami** (f)	[dʒamí]
chapel	**kishëz** (m)	[kíʃəz]
abbey	**abaci** (f)	[ábatsi]
monastery	**manastir** (m)	[manastír]
bell (church ~s)	**kambanë** (f)	[kambánə]
bell tower	**kulla e kambanës** (f)	[kúɫa ɛ kambánəs]
to ring (ab. bells)	**bien**	[bíɛn]
cross	**kryq** (m)	[kryc]
cupola (roof)	**kupola** (f)	[kupóla]
icon	**ikona** (f)	[ikóna]
soul	**shpirt** (m)	[ʃpirt]
fate (destiny)	**fat** (m)	[fat]
evil (n)	**e keqe** (f)	[ɛ kécɛ]
good (n)	**e mirë** (f)	[ɛ mírə]
vampire	**vampir** (m)	[vampír]
witch (evil ~)	**shtrigë** (f)	[ʃtrígə]
demon	**djall** (m)	[djáɫ]
spirit	**shpirt** (m)	[ʃpirt]
redemption (giving us ~)	**shëlbim** (m)	[ʃəlbím]
to redeem (vt)	**shëlbej**	[ʃəlbéj]
church service, mass	**meshë** (f)	[méʃə]

to say mass	lus meshë	[lús méʃə]
confession	rrëfim (m)	[rəfím]
to confess (vi)	rrëfej	[rəféj]
saint (n)	shenjt (m)	[ʃɛɲt]
sacred (holy)	i shenjtë	[i ʃéɲtə]
holy water	ujë i bekuar (m)	[újə i bɛkúar]
ritual (n)	ritual (m)	[rituál]
ritual (adj)	ritual	[rituál]
sacrifice	sakrificë (f)	[sakrifítsə]
superstition	besëtytni (f)	[bɛsətytní]
superstitious (adj)	supersticioz	[supɛrstitsióz]
afterlife	jeta e përtejme (f)	[jéta ɛ pərtéjmɛ]
eternal life	përjetësia (f)	[pərjɛtəsía]

MISCELLANEOUS

198. Various useful words

background (green ~)	sfond (m)	[sfónd]
balance (of situation)	ekuilibër (m)	[ɛkuilíbər]
barrier (obstacle)	pengesë (f)	[pɛŋésə]
base (basis)	bazë (f)	[bázə]
beginning	fillim (m)	[fiɫím]
category	kategori (f)	[katɛgorí]
cause (reason)	shkak (m)	[ʃkak]
choice	zgjedhje (f)	[zɟéðjɛ]
coincidence	rastësi (f)	[rastəsí]
comfortable (~ chair)	i rehatshëm	[i rɛhátʃəm]
comparison	krahasim (m)	[krahasím]
compensation	shpërblim (m)	[ʃpərblím]
degree (extent, amount)	nivel (m)	[nivél]
development	zhvillim (m)	[ʒviɫím]
difference	ndryshim (m)	[ndryʃím]
effect (e.g., of drugs)	efekt (m)	[ɛfékt]
effort (exertion)	përpjekje (f)	[pərpjékjɛ]
element	element (m)	[ɛlɛmént]
end (finish)	fund (m)	[fund]
example (illustration)	shembull (m)	[ʃémbuɫ]
fact	fakt (m)	[fakt]
frequent (adj)	i shpeshtë	[i ʃpéʃtə]
growth (development)	rritje (f)	[rítjɛ]
help	ndihmë (f)	[ndíhmə]
ideal	ideal (m)	[idɛál]
kind (sort, type)	lloj (m)	[ɫoj]
labyrinth	labirint (m)	[labirínt]
mistake, error	gabim (m)	[gabím]
moment	moment (m)	[momént]
object (thing)	objekt (m)	[objékt]
obstacle	pengesë (f)	[pɛŋésə]
original (original copy)	origjinal (m)	[oriɟinál]
part (~ of sth)	pjesë (f)	[pjésə]
particle, small part	grimcë (f)	[grímtsə]
pause (break)	pushim (m)	[puʃím]

position	pozicion (m)	[pozitsión]
principle	parim (m)	[parím]
problem	problem (m)	[problém]

process	proces (m)	[protsés]
progress	ecje përpara (f)	[étsjɛ pərpára]
property (quality)	cilësi (f)	[tsiləsí]
reaction	reagim (m)	[rɛagím]
risk	rrezik (m)	[rɛzík]

secret	sekret (m)	[sɛkrét]
series	seri (f)	[sɛrí]
shape (outer form)	formë (f)	[fórmə]
situation	situatë (f)	[situátə]
solution	zgjidhje (f)	[zɟíðjɛ]

standard (adj)	standard	[standárd]
standard (level of quality)	standard (m)	[standárd]
stop (pause)	pauzë (f)	[paúzə]
style	stil (m)	[stil]

system	sistem (m)	[sistém]
table (chart)	tabelë (f)	[tabélə]
tempo, rate	ritëm (m)	[rítəm]
term (word, expression)	term (m)	[tɛrm]

thing (object, item)	gjë (f)	[ɟə]
truth (e.g., moment of ~)	e vërtetë (f)	[ɛ vərtétə]
turn (please wait your ~)	kthesë (f)	[kθésə]
type (sort, kind)	tip (m)	[tip]
urgent (adj)	urgjent	[urɟént]

urgently (adv)	urgjentisht	[urɟɛntíʃt]
utility (usefulness)	vegël (f)	[végəl]
variant (alternative)	variant (m)	[variánt]
way (means, method)	rrugëzgjidhje (f)	[rugəzɟíðjɛ]
zone	zonë (f)	[zónə]

www.ingramcontent.com/pod-product-compliance
Lightning Source LLC
LaVergne TN
LVHW051302080426
835509LV00020B/3111